Witnessing the
Change

A participant observer's story of the Nigerian 2015 presidential election

By

Olalekan W. Adigun

Acknowledgements

I owe gratitude to God for the successful completion of this work. With Him with me all through the perilous times and daunting challenges throughout the coursework and the research for this work.

I must appreciate my teachers at the University of Lagos, Akoka starting with my MSc Thesis Supervisor Dr. Felix O. Awosika, always making me realize the need to do better and improve on whatever I have done. I must also salute the scholarly depths of my Professors in the Department of Political Science, University of Lagos: Browne Onuoha, HOD, Solomon O. Akinboye, and Tunde Babawale out of which I tapped in doing this work.

I must also not forget the intellectual dexterity of Drs: Rasheed Akinyemi, M.M Fadakinte, G.S.M Okeke, Emmanuel I. Onah, Dele Ashiru, Laja Soniran, and others in the Department who I have at some point tapped from their knowledge.

I owe much appreciation to Mr. Philip Amiola a former colleague who originally suggested the idea of writing this book to me.

To my former colleagues at TRW Consult Ltd Messers: Babatunde Oladele, Sam Adeyemi, Benneth Njoku, Patrick Abadom, Kayode Ariyibi, Remi Otuneye, Dolapo Adelana. Mrs Omatseye Oti, Miss Iyabo Fahm, Miss Morenike Adams, and Miss Simbiat Bakare, I must thank you for your support all through this work.

I will also not forget members of my family who got less of my attention during my time studying and preparing for this work. I must not forget my mother, *Alhaja* Lateefat Adigun to whom I chose to dedicate this work.

At the Gandhi Research Library, University of Lagos, Akoka, (where I completed this work) I am grateful to them for the support of their incredible staff.

I am also grateful to ABU Global Research, UNILAG for their invaluable support during this project.

All the credits for this work goes to the above named persons and institutions, but I absorb them and those cited as References in this work of all errors in interpretation and judgment that may arise from the work.

Olalekan W. Adigun,

Akoka, Lagos.

Dedication

This book is dedicated to General Muhammadu Buhari and all those who lost their lives *Witnessing the Change*!

This page intentionally left blank

Contents

SECTION ONE
The Build Up

How History Was Made

I never set out to write this book. Some events prompted me to do so. I was employed as a research intern in a public relations firm in Lagos, in early 2015. I soon discovered that many in the office were politically conscious. As politically conscious as many of my colleagues were, it appeared I was the only person supporting the All Progressives Congress (APC) presidential candidate, General Muhammadu Buhari. We debated on whether Nigerians would vote for Buhari in the February (later March 2015) election or not.

Despite being outnumbered, out fired and out voiced, I stood my ground. The election came; the rest is history.

An in-house editor in my workplace, Mr. Philip Amiola, himself a strong supporter of President Goodluck Jonathan, urged me to put these developments into writing. I hesitated for some personal reasons but when the urge became too strong for me to bear; I started compiling materials for this book. Lo, my pen began dancing.

How did I get involved in that historic election? This is one of the stories my colleagues probably never knew.

In 2010 the state of President Umaru Musa Yar'Adua's health had become an issue of public discourse. Things were not made easier by the administration's attempts to play down the matter. No one had heard from the President for months. Nigerians were told on several occasions that the President was alive and well by the administration's officials and the president's family.

The call for his Vice, Dr. Goodluck Jonathan, became frequent and disquieting for the administration.

This was a looming constitutional crisis which brought about the so-called "doctrine of necessity."

Like many Nigerians, I joined the popular call "for reason to prevail." I remember joining the Save Nigeria Group rally in Abuja, as an undergraduate then. Were we truly trying to "save" Nigeria?

Although, some who called for Vice President Jonathan to be sworn in had other reasons known to them that were of little interest to me at the time. All that mattered to me then was for "Nigeria to move forward."

During a symposium to mark Nigeria's 50th Independence Anniversary, organized by the Obafemi Awolowo University Students' Union, Ile-Ife, in 2010, I said: "We should start appreciating the need to adhere strictly to the spirit of the Constitution. If there are things we should do as future political leaders, they should be: to set the pace for the political order; to provide fresh political perspectives by defining and redefining political realities and shaping the trends in the political order, not to act as mere observers which profit no one in particular."

This statement, made over 5 years ago, still shapes my perspectives on major political issues.

That same year, President Yar'Adua died and Goodluck Jonathan was sworn in as President. Many soon forgot about the titanic battle that helped bring in President Jonathan with 2011 presidential election in sight.

The 2011 presidential election soon became a "Goodluck" election. Since most citizens wanted good luck, one didn't need the genius to predict that Jonathan would win the election. Whether *good luck* would continue with Jonathan throughout his administration was to be tested soon.

On New Year Day, 2012, the Federal Government announced the withdrawal of subsidy on Premium Motor Spirit (PMS) also known as fuel or petrol. This meant that Nigerians, henceforth, would pay N141 per litre on gasoline. This led to a spontaneous public outcry, expectedly, and the emergence of the action group Occupy Nigeria.

I participated in the one-week long, Occupy Nigeria, fuel subsidy protests in Ojota, Lagos. For most of us present at the Gani Fawehinmi Freedom Park (the main venue of the protests), it was a fight to finish. Slogans like "*N65 or nothing*", "*We Need Change*" and the likes united us.

A number of protesters on that same ground had campaigned vociferously, a year earlier, for Goodluck Jonathan to be sworn-in, first, as acting President and later during the election. The fact that old enemies soon become friends and old friends turn enemies sometimes defines the game of politics, should not worry any impartial observer of political events.

Things went well days into the protests. The movement was gaining serious momentum. In Lagos and Kano (two of Nigeria's biggest cities), the crowds were swelling like bees. Jonathan's administration fearing the Egyptian-like "revolution" brought in soldiers a week after to disperse protesters at Ojota. The fierce-looking men in green had just one instruction – to quell any gathering.

In parenthesis, a year earlier, the revolution in Egypt had consumed Hosni Mubarak. The *Arab Spring* started just like that.

Realizing this, Jonathan's advisors probably advised him to take decisive action or things would get out of hand. This turned out, in my opinion, one of the few of bad decisions the administration made.

Some of us have not forgiven them for that act of betrayal.

How fast things changed. Jonathan was not different from others before him after all. He wasn't the *humble man* that *had no shoes*.

In my opinion, the administration was not strategic in handling the matter at all. Since it is difficult to prove one's good intentions, it is for posterity to decide whether the decision was made in the interest of the masses or not.

This propelled me and many others to take decisive actions *for a change of regime in 2015.*

To make good on my decisions, I first resorted to the use of my pen. I started writing dissecting articles on Jonathan's administration for some online news platforms, including *Premium Times*.

Things got really bad for Jonathan's administration with the kidnap and subsequent handling of over 200 Chibok girls. Many of the administration's supporters resorted to playing ethnic cards and there was no deliberate attempt to stop the dangerous trend.

To counter the argument that Jonathan could not lose the 2015 presidential election, I did a research on the possibility of incumbents losing in Africa. I soon discovered about four cases of incumbent presidents losing their seats, including the celebrated case in Malawi where sitting president and gender activist, Joyce Banda, lost. In my estimation, if a peaceful transition is possible in any part of Africa, then Nigeria is no exception!

In 2015, I volunteered for #iHaveDecided (then led by Dupe Killa), an effective grassroots movement galvanizing support for Buhari's Campaign effort. Apart from engaging in street campaigns, the group was very active on social media.

I wrote and granted interviews on the need to vote for the Buhari/Osinbajo ticket. When the battle on Twitter became intense, group members responded to every charge brought up by PDP supporters.

As far as I was concerned, financial gratifications were secondary. The need to save our dear country from avoidable collapse was the motivation. Whether I regret my actions at that period is another matter.

Many of the articles I wrote at that time form part of this book. If you read them when they were published, this will be a memory refresher.

While writing this book, I realized how fast things have changed and how much we have forgotten about the historic election.

Chapter One
Background to the Historic Election

In March 2015, Nigerian politics underwent a historic change. A change that will be remembered as the year an opposition party's candidate defeated an incumbent in Nigeria's electoral history. In a country where few incumbents have accepted defeat or in some cases, opposition hardly tolerated.

In Africa where: Prime Minister Leabua Jonathan of Lesotho voided the 1970 election he and his Party lost; Dr. Hastings Kamusu Banda declared himself President for Life in Malawi; Robert Mugabe of Zimbabwe who in his 80s is still waxing strong in power, etc., the arrival of General Muhammadu Buhari, the All Progressives Congress (APC) presidential candidate, signalled a change in not only Nigerian politics but also in Nigerian voting patterns. The campaign that Buhari ran in 2015, powered by Change, in the build up to the election is to be considered as nothing less than spectacular. His victory signalled a political shift similar to MKO Abiola's landslide victory in 1993, which had been near inconceivable four years earlier.

In 2003, few Nigerians had believed Buhari, himself a former Military Head of State, would ever have a second stint in the Presidency largely due to his seeming negative public perception, while he signalled his first intention of return to power as a democratically elected president, let alone considered voting for him.

Never before 2015 have Nigerians voted an (aged 72-year-old) man against a much younger, incumbent, Goodluck Jonathan, 54, as President. There was a prevalent belief that some of his financially viable APC rivals, like former Vice President Atiku Abubakar and Kano State Governor Rabiu Musa Kwankwaso, would head the party's bid for the presidency after Buhari publicly gave up contesting further elections after 2011. This further emphasizes the unforeseen nature of Buhari's victory and makes the question of what happened in those four years that transformed Buhari from an "impossible president" to become the President even more salient.

The 2015 election will remain for a long time a reference point for elections in Nigeria. As a result of this, a detailed explanation of the root causes of decision making as it pertains to the outcome of the election will be necessary. The election saw a "serial loser" win an incumbent in a keenly contested ballot which many people thought was impossible.

This book provides a fresh participant observer's perspective on the root cause(s) into the inner thinking of decision making as to why the main political parties- the All Progressives Congress (APC) and People's Democratic Party (PDP)- in arriving at their choices of presidential candidates.

Did the PDP just decide to field Jonathan simply because of the so-called "incumbency factor"? If yes, could that have been the only factor the party considered in selecting its candidate? Why did the party decide to close its doors to a competitive presidential primary?

We can equally ask: Did the APC decide to field Buhari for the election because of his charisma? Why did Buhari decide to take a shot again in 2015 after he had previously said in 2011 that he would not contest for the office again? Did APC ever think it would win the election?

Can we argue that PDP lost the 2015 presidential election because of: its long years in Aso Rock? Can we say it was due to poor handling or choices of campaign themes or was it due to effective APC propaganda? The following pages provide the answers to these questions and more!

This book will explore the twelve years to Buhari's election as President in the following sections. The sections will appear in non-chronological order and will offer a focused analysis of the twelve-year period.

The first chapter explores events from July 2003 to February 2014 including the formidable roadblocks before General Buhari's emergence as democratically-elected president. An understanding of these years is vital to understanding how Buhari developed into a serious contender for the APC nomination. In particular, it will focus on the formation of the CPC and the merger of opposition parties to form the APC in 2013. It will lay a strong foundation for the analysis of how Buhari defeated his party rivals and ultimately, President Goodluck Jonathan, in later chapters.

The second chapter will look at some theoretical framework guiding the author's perspective. This will look at the critical decisions (using the decision-making theories) that shaped the outcome of the 2015 presidential elections commencing from the merger of political parties to form the APC.

The third chapter will progress from October 2014, after Buhari's announcement that he had entered the presidential race. This chapter ends following Buhari's victory at the party primaries in December 2014.

This period was pivotal to Buhari's campaign, for it was during this time that he faced his toughest opponents, Atiku Abubakar and Rabiu Musa Kwankwaso.

Considering the first ever successful political merger in the country, the convergence of four political parties (ACN, ANPP, CPC and APGA); its successful inaugural convention; and the general unpopularity of President Jonathan, Buhari's victory in March 2015 can be seen as equally, if not more important than the Presidential elections. For some, the question was not whether the next President would be an APC or PDP candidate, but whether Nigeria would inaugurate its first opposition president or elect a "former dictator" as its democratically-elected leader.

It further analyses the pre-election months and touches Buhari's selection of Professor Yemi Osinbajo as a running mate upon the campaign trail, and its implications for the campaign. The chapter also looks at the changing perceptions of the Nigerian voters between 2011 and 2015 elections.

The section ends with a conclusion that summarizes and gives the book of the previous chapters and globally contextualizes the election to bring out its importance.

The second part of the book deals with the author's interventions and essays written during the period of intense campaigns and other issues shaping the election.

This book is structured around an intrinsic case study of Muhammadu Buhari. It is centred on his rise in popularity that not only led to him winning the presidential nomination of the APC but also the presidential election in 2015.

An intrinsic case study is a study of a case (e.g., person, specific group, occupation, department, organisation) where the case itself is of primary interest in the exploration. The exploration is driven by a desire to know more about the uniqueness of the case rather than to build theory, or to know how the case represents other cases.

Why Buhari?

This section offers a contextual explanation of Buhari, documenting his career path from his re-entry into politics in 2003 and his previous attempts at the Presidency before his victory in 2015. The analysis of this period will elucidate why he chose to run for the Presidency for four consecutive times.

The later focus of this section is an analysis of two landmark moments during this period, the formation of the Congress for Progressive Change (CPC), the merger of opposition parties to form the All Progressives Congress (APC) in 2013, and the formidable barriers against Buhari's candidacy since 2003 within and outside his party before his victory in 2015.

A military coup brought Buhari to power in late 1983 – successfully ending the Second Republic headed by President Shehu Shagari – and another military (bloodless) coup will later oust him from power in August 1985. It appears much of an irony that the same General who effectively ended Nigeria's second experiment with democracy, by toppling a democratically elected government will be the same man who sought the people's vote for the exalted office of the president.

After many years out of power, including his detention in Benin till 1988, he chose to return to politics after his retirement from the military. Buhari contested the presidential election as the candidate of the All Nigeria People's Party (ANPP) in April 2003 and lost to incumbent President, Chief Olusegun Obasanjo. Buhari approached the courts to seek redress for what he called a "flawed election".

At the appeals court hearing of the case against the election results, Buhari's attorneys continued to make points with the judges and with the public by presenting evidence of fraud, intimidation, and rigging. Obasanjo's attorneys admitted their defense in this suit would not refute the allegations of rigging but would rely on the fact that removing Obasanjo and holding another election could be "disruptive."

The 2011election created a paradigm shift in Nigeria's political landscape. In the eve of the year's presidential election, Buhari, in a rare display of emotions, said he will not seek election to the office of the president afterward. What made him swallow his words in 2015 having lost three consecutive elections.

Buhari: A Brief Biography

Buhari was born on December 17, 1942, in the ancient city of Daura, Katsina state, in northwestern Nigeria. He is reported to be the twenty-third child of his father. Buhari was raised by his mother after his father died when he was about four years old. He attended primary school in Daura and Mai'adua before proceeding to Katsina Model School in 1953, and to Katsina Provincial Secondary School (now Government College, Katsina) from 1956 to 1961.

Buhari enrolled in the Nigerian Military Training College (NMTC) in 1961. In February 1964, the College was upgraded to an officer commissioning unit of the Nigerian Army and renamed the Nigerian Defence Academy (NDA) (prior to 1964, the Nigerian government sent cadets who had completed their NMTC preliminary training to mostly Commonwealth military academies for officer cadet training). From 1962 to 1963, Buhari underwent officer cadet training at Mons Officer Cadet School in Aldershot in England.

Buhari was one of the leaders of the military coup of December 1983 that overthrew the democratically elected government of President Shehu Shagari. At the time of the coup plot, Buhari was the General Officer Commanding (GOC), Third Armored Division in Jos. With the successful execution of the coup by General Buhari, Tunde Idiagbon was appointed Chief of General Staff.

The coup ended Nigeria's short-lived Second Republic and a period of multi-party democracy started in 1979. Buhari justified the military's seizure of power by castigating the civilian government as hopelessly corrupt and promptly suspended Nigeria's Second Republic (1979-83).

Buhari was overthrown by General Ibrahim B. Babangida in August 1985 and detained in Benin till 1988.

Buhari's Political Adventure

It will be fair to look at Buhari's political adventures for us to understand why his victory is unique.

After a long time out of public life (since 1988), save for a brief stint as chairman of the Petroleum Tax Fund (PTF) under late Head of State, General Sani Abacha, Buhari appeared again to seek the presidency in 2002.

Buhari declared for the All People's Party (APP) later known as the All Nigerian People's Party (ANPP). The party was formed in late 1998 during a transition from military to civilian rule by a coalition of associations that received considerable support under the regime of Sani Abacha.

It did not take him long to realize the forces against his presidential ambition were within his own party and were bent on scuttling his return to power. He won the party nominations for the presidency and picked former Senate President, late Chuba Okadigbo, from Anambra State as his running mate.

Both polled a total of 12,710,022 votes representing about 32 percent of the votes.

Not much could Senator Okadigbo, from Igbo-speaking South-East add to the electoral fortune he enjoyed in the Hausa-dominated North-East even though Buhari made a strong case for fraud after the election.

A former Minister of Petroleum Resources, Professor Tam David-West, said that Buhari never lost the 2003 election but was rigged out.

Buhari's decision to appoint Chuba Okadigbo is a vote-catching strategy in a country where politics President ethnic and religious factors.

The 2007 presidential election may have convinced Buhari on the need to examine those he calls allies. In the buildup to the election, he selected his party chairman, Chief Edwin Umezeoke, an Igbo man and devout Catholic, as his running mate.

The ANPP ticket came up against Alhaji Musa Yar'Adua, another candidate from the same state with Buhari, running on the platform of the People's Democratic Party (PDP). He polled 6,605,299 votes against Mr. Yar'Adua's 26,638,063.

Like the 2003 election, Buhari protested the result going all the way to the Supreme Court.

The prevailing mood in Nigeria at the time seem to congratulate the president-elect which means Buhari's suit at the Election Petition Tribunal had first lost it in the Court of Public Opinion even before its final outcome. Nonetheless, on May 29, 2007, Yar'Adua was inaugurated amidst protests from Buhari's supporters.

Many saw the victory of PDP as a first for Nigeria. It was the first election of intellectuals to the top seats – a university graduate and a former lecturer, Musa Yar'Adua paired with a Ph.D. degree holder, Dr. Goodluck Ebele Jonathan.

On resumption of office, Yar'Adua, admitting his election was largely flawed, offered to form a Government of National Unity (GNU).

Against Buhari's case in the election tribunal, ANPP's national chairman, Ume-Ezeoke, who doubled as his running mate, accepted to serve in the GNU.

Buhari saw this as a major act of betrayal. He said, through his spokesman, Osita Okechukwu, in an interview with The Nation, on the decision to join the GNU: "He (Ume-Ezeoke) is coming to terms with the fact that the PDP only wants to use the idea of the GNU to legitimise an illegality."

Buhari, himself, said in an interview with The Nation: "I have discovered that the people who drafted me into politics were not sincere after all; they only wanted to use me to get appointments or for their aggrandizement and not to serve the nation or the masses.

"My position was that there should be no discussion between the ANPP and the PDP until after the completion of all the court cases, both at the national and state levels. I made my position known to them in writing.

"I don't really see any rationale behind their participation in the GNU. Therefore, I regard their acceptance to participate in the GNU as betrayal of the nation and the masses.

"Initially, I and the party had cogent reasons that the elections, particularly the presidential elections, were not conducted properly; therefore, there was no presidential election at all." This time, the General need not be told that he was no longer relevant to the ANPP after he told newsmen that he would review his membership of the party.

As the preparations for 2011 election thickened, it became obvious that any realistic hope for the opposition to take over from the ruling PDP was for opposition parties to form a strong alliance.

As a result of the schism in the ANPP, Buhari's supporters under the name, The Buhari Organization (TBO), formed in 2006, which often clashed with the ANPP leadership, saw the need to form a new party for the next election. When the ANPP decided to join the GNU, TBO saw the need to review their relationship with the party. Buhari formally left the ANPP and joined the CPC in March 2010. He said that he had supported the founding of the CPC "as a solution to the debilitating, ethical and ideological conflicts in my former party the ANPP".

Although the CPC had rapidly gained support in the North of Nigeria, fielding many candidates in the National elections in April 2011, there were concerns that it did not have the same financial resources as the incumbent People's Democratic Party (PDP) which boasted of several state governors, government ministers who were in control of important oil blocs.

How the CPC would pull the stunt against a party like the PDP and an emerging political force, the Action Congress of Nigeria (ACN), which controlled the South West was to be seen after the election. With this picture in mind, the CPC leadership then needed to get the support of ACN's leadership.

When the first round of elections held on 9 April, the CPC came third in both Senate and House of Representatives seats gained. In the Senate, the PDP won 53 seats, followed by the ACN with 13 seats, CPC 6 seats, ANPP 4 seats, and other parties took 4 seats. In the House, the PDP gained 123 seats, ACN 45, CPC 21, ANPP 11 and other parties 18 seats.

Buhari ran as CPC candidate in the presidential election held on 16 April 2011. After discussions between the party and the ACN proved abortive, he won 12,214,853 votes, coming second to the incumbent President Goodluck Jonathan of the PDP, who polled 22,495,187 votes and was declared the winner.

This time Buhari decided not to seek redress in court but said he would not prevent his party from doing so partly because of his experiences in previous elections.

The Formation of APC

In anticipation of the 2015 elections, opposition parties became more determined to unseat the ruling People's Democratic Party (PDP).

To do so, Congress for Progressives Change (CPC), Action Congress of Nigeria (ACN), the All Nigerian People's Party (ANPP) and a faction of the All Progressives Grand Alliance (APGA) merged to form the All Progressives Congress (APC) in February 2013.

The resolution announcing the party's formation was signed by Tom Ikimi; two ACN representatives; Senator Annie Okonkwo on behalf of the APGA; former governor of Kano State, Mallam Ibrahim Shekarau; the chairman of ANPP's merger committee; and Garba Shehu, the chairman of CPC's merger committee.

Apart from this being a landmark in Nigerian politics, many doubted the possibility of APC going into the election as a united front. Dr. Doyin Okupe, Senior Special Assistant to President Goodluck Jonathan on Public Affairs, described the merger of opposition political parties on the platform of the All Progressives Congress (APC) as a weak association that would crumble and disappear by 2014, a year before the next general election.

Okupe's statement can be taken from the fact that merger of opposition parties was known to have failed in Nigeria's electoral history especially the unfortunate case of the Progressives People's Alliance (PPA) in 1982.

The fact that not only did the APC survived several scares of implosions, but also won the presidential election with Buhari as its candidate makes it more remarkable.

Chapter Two

Decision Making and 2015 Presidential Election

Politicians make decisions on the minute basis. At their best, politicians can make decisions that preserve peace, protect human rights and advance economic well-being. At their worst, however, they – particularly those on the losing side struggle for power. They turn to tyranny, economic ruin, looting, and barbarism. Good or bad, decision making is a fulcrum in politics.

A large part of what politicians do is decision making. The range of issues confronting political parties or organisations involves making strategic choices.

Decision makers during political campaigns are often faced with a great complexity of big and small challenges requiring decisive action in line with laid down principles and policies governing behaviour and choices. A candidate running for office or his campaign director, in the process of trying to satisfy the various corporate interests within and without his institutional framework, is the decision maker who must often have to choose between various competing policies options that will bring about the expected end- winning the election. This is not as simple as it sounds, especially in an often complicated sphere as electoral contests.

Political decision-making, for instance, deals with the effective optimization of resources. The essence of responsible political decision is very often the need for just, equitable and deliberate or conscious optimization of resources that are held in trust for the society or institutions, by political actors. This "effective allocation", however, involves the notion of trade-offs. This implies that the more the main actors direct its resources towards the attainment of particular ends (in this case, of elections), the less it has the ability to deploy the same resources to meet other pressing needs. Invariably, decision makers make decisions based on existing or available resources.

Decision making is, therefore, that thinking that results in the choice among alternative courses of action. The degree of acceptability a political campaign enjoys among the people can, in a sense, be measured in terms of the extent to which its choices reflect the uninfluenced decision of its leadership, rather than to what extent its actions or choices are predetermined by the events in its immediate and extended environment.

In October 1962 the Kennedy administration discovered there were Soviet missiles in Cuba. The administration responded by imposing a blockade (or quarantine) of Cuba which forced the Soviets to remove the missiles from Cuba. This one single event, many believed, could have led to a nuclear war. This became a major reference point for future US-Soviet relations during the Cold War. This led a political scientist, Graham Allison to write the classic, *The Essence of Decision: Explaining the Cuban Missile Crisis.*

In that book, Allison explains, using decision-making models, the motives of both United States (US) and Soviet leaders in handling the Soviets installation of medium range nuclear facilities in Cuba[i]. Though the book was first published in 1971, nine years after the Cuban missile crisis happened, the theoretical explanations offered in the book on such an important political phenomenon is great addition to the literature. A landmark phenomenon like the Cuban Missile Crisis required a thorough analysis devoid of pedestrian or ideological bias.

Similarly, a theoretical explanation on the historic 2015 presidential election is necessary for the expansion of discussions and addition to the literature on Nigerian elections. The fact that not many of such explanations have been done after such landmark political events shows the state of political discourse in the country.

The 2015 presidential election would not have been won without important decisions being made. We will look at some of these decisions; how they apply to the election; and the political actors who made these *critical decisions*.

One of such decisions is the APC's choice of Professor Yemi Osinbajo as the running mate to General Muhammadu Buhari in the 2015 presidential election. This is one decision that, in my opinion, proved the critical difference between the two leading parties in the election.

For the position, there were candidates like Rivers State Governor, Rt Hon. Rotimi Amaechi and former Ekiti state Governor, Dr. Kayode Fayemi. The former is reported to be one of the main financiers of the party's presidential bid. The fact that he hails from the same region with the PDP's presidential candidate made some people flirt with the idea of his possible nomination as the party's Vice Presidential candidate. According to Amaechi's camp, if he was chosen, he would break the hegemony of the PDP in the South-South. They said that with his charisma, he would lead the APC's forces in the region.

These arguments look enticing on the surface for Amaechi but political decisions rarely run on sentiments. I say this because, if we agree that Amaechi should have been selected as running mate to Buhari purely on the basis of financing the party's presidential ambition, there might have been some complications.

The first is that the party may have faced the needless possibility of fielding two candidates it may keep defending. The APC might defend Buhari against the tag of "Islamic fundamentalist" while also defending Amaechi for corruption. This would also strengthen PDP's argument that the APC is a "corrupt" party. The PDP already painted a picture of Amaechi as a corrupt man in the media. The PDP supporters appear to have been trained to say "Both parties are the same."

Again, there were many persons who equally financed the party's ambitions, including former Governor Fayemi. It would never have been a wise decision if Amaechi was selected for the position. There would have been serious reactions in several parts of the country and the PDP would have been the major beneficiary.

In other to maintain party unity, the party made Amaechi Director-General of APC's Presidential Campaign Organisation, after the disappointment of not making the Vice Presidency slot. There were fears that the Rivers State Governor would stand aloof after the disappointment of not being selected as Buhari's running mate. The fact that it took him more than a week to resume his duties added impetus to this rumour. Nerves were calmed after the politician spoke through his media office that he was set to resume duties as Director-General of the campaign.

Political scientists speak of prospect theory. By this, they mean a psychological theory of political decision making under risk. In fact, as will later be demonstrated, although the use of prospect theory in politics is still quite rare, this theory is particularly apt for accounting for the situations in which political actors typically find themselves: the situations in which decisions have to be made under conditions of uncertainty and serious risks. This theory is so useful for understanding personality traits since some individuals would prefer not to take risks at all.

Looking at decision making in Buhari's 2015 presidential campaign, we will focus on the following:

(i) The decision maker

(ii) The alternative course of actions

(iii) Events

(iv) Payoffs, and

(v) Uncertainty.

The *decision maker* is the agent charged with the responsibility for making the decision and may be an entity or individual, a corporation or government agency, etc. In the context of Buhari's 2015campaign, the decision maker was/were General Buhari himself, his strategists, his party (APC) or campaign organisation, TBO and the voters ultimately.

We may recall that Buhari made the decision not to run again for the presidency in 2011. Why did he choose to run again in 2015? Could he be surer of winning this time? At 72, why couldn't Buhari support a younger candidate for the office?

After three previous attempts, would losing a fourth one make him a serial loser? Why were Buhari's strategists urging him on? If he lost, what would happen? These questions at that time bothered me and many others.

There were those who argued that Buhari would step down for younger candidates like the Speaker of the House of Representatives, Aminu Tambuwal or former EFCC Chairman, Mallam Nuhu Ribadu. Rumour was rife at some points that political big wigs including Bola Tinubu were in favour of the Speaker of the House of Representatives, Aminu Tambuwal for the position. It was then reported that Tinubu seriously considered adopting the embattled Speaker Tambuwal, as the party's presidential candidate. It was believed that Tambuwal had more national acceptance than Buhari, and could deploy a huge war chest to floor President Goodluck Jonathan in a presidential election. Some sources cited Tinubu's stance in 2011 against Buhari after the proposed alliance between the ACN and CPC collapsed.

I also flirted with the idea of APC picking the younger Tambuwal if Buhari will not have a "national acceptance" especially in the South-Eastern part of the country. This, I recall, was some period before the General will signal his intention officially for the position. As I will later find out, it was a clever disinformation and diversion from some professional agents of disinformation. It later turned out that Mr. Tambuwal was only interested in contesting to become the governor of Sokoto state. The rest, as they say, is history.

The *alternative course of action* is the pool of choices jostling for adoption by the decision maker. It is actually the adoption of any or more of these lines of action that is the decision itself.

The issue is how to discern among these options which are the most appropriate in the light of the prevailing circumstances.

In 2014, there were rumours that Buhari's strategists may flirt with the idea of fielding a political heavyweight, like Bola Tinubu, a Muslim, as running mate to General Buhari, another Muslim as a vote-winning tactic in the South West. This was later confirmed by no less a person than Chief Femi Fani-Kayode who at the time was a member of the APC. In several of his articles, he cited unconfirmed sources as his "source" of this information. The fact that he would join the PDP later confirmed the views of some of us that FFK, as he is called by his admirers, is an unserious politician employed to destabilize the APC.

In parenthesis, I wrote an article at the time, *Fani-Kayode: Saying "Yes" When You Mean to Say "No"* to portray FFK to Nigerians for whom he really is, an agent of disinformation. We will deal more with FFK and other PDP's agents of influence in the second part of this book.

While it might be true that some of Buhari's strategists must have flirted with the idea of a Muslim-Muslim ticket, one is left to wonder how it would have been discussed at the level of the APC which has a Christian, no-nonsense Chairman, Chief John Odigie-Oyegun. Let us even assume that it was discussed during the Chairmanship of Chief Bisi Akande who is a Muslim. Akande is not known to be a fanatical or fundamentalist Muslim that will play politics with such sensitive issue like religion. The risks involved in the APC being tagged an "Islamic party" by the opposition for fielding a "Muslim-Muslim ticket" in a secular state like Nigeria appeared too much for the party at the time.

On the other hand, the PDP may have risked appointing APC turncoat, Fani-Kayode (FFK) as its presidential campaign spokesman. The party might have viewed his experience working with the APC as an advantage. It may also have considered the fact that FFK is from the South West, a region with huge voting population, as an electoral advantage. Whether FFK was qualified for the job at the time of the election is another matter. We will look at this later.

There are *events and occurrences that affect the achievement of the objectives of the decision maker and are outside his control.* They are imposed on the decision maker by virtue of the fact that we live in a complex and interdependent society. The events constitute a mutually exclusive and complete set of outcomes; hence, one and only one of them can occur.

Even before he signaled his intention to once again contest for the presidential seat, Buhari was to face some landmines. There were those who would fight back. There were those who feared him more than death.

His reputation as a no-nonsense anti-corruption crusader was not going down well in some parts of the country.

Some declared that *"over my dead body"* would Buhari become president. Some PDP chieftains reportedly said they would leave the country should Buhari win the election.

Few weeks to February 14, 2015, the Independent National Electoral Commission (INEC) decided to postpone the presidential election by six weeks. They based their reason on the military's onslaught against Boko Haram in the North East. There were also speculations as to whether or not the election would hold at all.

Another thing was whether or not to sack the INEC chair, Professor Attahiru Jega. Though PDP continually denied it, there was a serious effort to sack the electoral boss. I said this because of two incidents that happened during the campaign. First, on my way to work one morning, in towards the end of January 2015 I ran into an unusual traffic from Fadeyi to Obanikoro, Lagos. I often leave home around 8:10 am to resume in my office at Ilupeju at 8:30 am since office hours start by 9:00 am. This particular day was not to be. We were held in traffic for close to an hour. What was the cause of the traffic? A group, known as the

Oodua People's Congress (OPC) was having a protest. "What are they protesting for?" a fellow commuter asked loudly.

As I later got to know from the fliers they distributed, their first demand was the sacking of Jega. Their other demand was the cancellation of the use of Permanent Voter Cards (PVCs) which they see as an attempt by Jega to "rig" the election.

In parenthesis, the OPC is one of the groups that have endorsed President Jonathan for re-election. As dramatic as their rally turned, defacing all campaign posters of the APC along the Ikorodu road, extortions and intimidations of pedestrians soon became the order of the day.

In the week before the OPC rally, another group loyal to President Jonathan, Movement for the Actualization of the Sovereign State of Biafra (MASSOB) had held a rally in several parts of the South East to press for the same demand- to sack Jega.

In sacking Jega, it was alleged that the younger brother of a PDP governor in the South West had been penciled down to replace the INEC boss just weeks to the election. I was so convinced that the protests by these front groups were just clever attempts to scuttle the election of which the PDP will be the main beneficiary.

The second thing that got me convinced that there was a serious attempt to sack Jega was my second visit to Apapa for another maritime conference. This one was attended by the "who's who" in the industry. This was sometimes before the six weeks' postponement of the election. It was at this conference that I knew how viable the industry is. To cut the story short, I met a man (I will not like to mention his name in print), from Akwa Ibom state. I was trying to discuss business with him after I was introduced to him by one of my sponsors to the conference. Somehow, we digressed from business and we started discussing politics. "You Yoruba people are not supporting GEJ. Why now?" I smiled and pretended like I did not like politics. I was there for business, not to discuss politics. At least, that was what my sponsors to the conference wanted. "Don't worry, when Jonathan wins, I will give you a job in NIMASA."

I wondered how he knew I was looking for a job. The idea of getting a job in the Nigerian Maritime Safety Agency (NIMASA) got me really excited. I started discussing politics with this man. He became so sure that Jonathan will win the election but that "APC people will only make noise. We will first sack Jega. After that, we will win the election." I was too shocked to speak. What does he mean "we" sacking Jega? I never argued with him that Jonathan or PDP will not win the election. Nothing could convince this man otherwise. Since then, I watched out for news on the "sacking of Jega" which never came. I have only called him once since the election to discuss business. The idea of Jonathan losing election never came up and I made no attempt to raise it.

All these were decisions beyond Buhari or APC's control as at the time of the campaign.

Payoff refers to the net benefit the decision maker receives for his choice from the alternative course of actions in making his decision. More often than not, the core goal of any political campaign is to win the election. The extent to which this is safeguarded could be considered the rationale for the acceptance of Buhari to enter into an "unholy alliance" with persons considered to be politicians with *tainted images* to form the APC. This went a long way in Buhari's victory in the 2015 presidential election.

Uncertainty refers to not being sure about the reactions or events that a decision will trigger off. It requires making predictions or assigning probabilities to events.

Karl E. Weick and Kathleen M. Sutcliffe in their book, *Managing the Unexpected,* argued that the uncertainties happen as a result of our unpreparedness for the unexpected. The maintained that uncertainty "...often audit our resilience. They affect how much we stretch without breaking and how well we recover. Some of these...are mild. But others are brutal." In political decision-making, this appears to be the brutal fact. As the command goes: "Expect the unexpected."

On Buhari's 2015 campaign, the decision to concentrate the campaign on four of Nigeria's six geo-political zones, leaving the rest for his opponent may have been a serious risk. This might also have increased the "bloc voting" against him in the two geo-political zones he lost. Looking at the decisions made during the elections, one can come to the following conclusions:

First, let us look at the decision on media management. While the APC appointed media professionals to handle its core media issues, the PDP appointed more politically-inclined persons for the role. Insults do not win arguments; just as propaganda hardly wins wars. The fact that FFK speaks Queen's English so well does not make him a better spokesman that Garba Shehu who spent several years as Newspaper Editor.

The APC spokesman, Lai Muhammed is, in the opinion of many, better in handling sensitive media issues than his PDP counterpart, Olisa Metuh. While the APC spokesman was always on the pages of newspapers in the run-up to the election bringing up issues, the PDP relied on its financial war chest to do the job.

Second, APC did a better job of conflict management than PDP. When it became obvious that party unity was essential to win the election, all factions in the party were pacified. Amaechi was appointed the Director-General of the party's campaign. Atiku's media adviser, Garba Shehu was appointed APC campaign spokesman, to pacify the former Vice President. Kayode Fayemi was appointed the head of policy and strategy. There are more politically-conscious decisions made by the party in the run-up to the election. All these boxes were not ticked in the PDP.

A review of PDP's political campaigns since 2011 yields several explanations regarding its political techniques. Since no scientific study have been carried on this matter on both parties (PDP and APC) on their use of political techniques for election purposes, a review of newspapers during the 2015 election by the author reveal some interesting details.

While contents of some themes may have changed to reflect the reality of Nigeria's changing political landscape, the principal goal of the PDP's effort have remained to weaken, and if possible, cripple the APC's growing relevance in polity thereby creating a favourable environment for the advancement of PDP's objectives. The following are specific objectives of PDP's 2015 campaign objectives.

1. To influence Northern, South Western and Nigerian public opinion in believing that the APC leaders are selfish, power hungry and bloodthirsty cannibals who are the major cause of insecurity in Nigeria because of their inordinate ambition to rule by making the country "ungovernable for President Jonathan".

2. To demonstrate that APC is an aggressive, violent, reactionary tribalistic party pursuing "Islamic agenda" (and similar sinister agendas) in Nigeria that is unfit to govern a pluralistic society.

3. To isolate the APC from its core Northern supporters and other key allies and as much as possible, discredit groups or zones which seek to support APC and its candidate.

4. To demonstrate that APC is an unreliable, disorganized and unprepared for governance at the Federal level by laying emphasis on any cracks within the party;
5. To distort public opinion with the view to distracting Nigerians on the reality of PDP's ambition to rule the nation for many more years.
6. To portray its candidate, Goodluck Jonathan, as a faultless, humble and perfect gentleman to be trusted by Nigerians.

A review of activities of the APC from 2013 reveals that why the party's themes and issues might have changed during the election, it's the party's political techniques have largely remained the same- to weaken the PDP and its allies; to project positively its achievements in other to create a favourable opinion for it to win the 2015 presidential election. Unlike its rival, the PDP, its objectives are more direct. The APC intends to:

1. Influence southern (especially South-East and South-South) to believe that President Jonathan and the PDP will not serve their interests and that the party is the major cause(s) of the underdevelopment in the regions.
2. Dismiss the rumour that APC is a party pursuing "Islamic" agenda and that it was actually PDP that created insurgent groups like Boko Haram.
3. Portray PDP as a violent, corrupt, power hungry and desperate party that cannot be further trusted with political power at the federal level.
4. Sponsor and create situations that magnify crisis in the PDP in other to portray it as an unreliable, undemocratic party.
5. Divert attention away from all accusations the PDP might raise against the APC and its presidential candidate, General Muhammadu Buhari.

In looking at the decisions made during the campaigns, from a purely observer's point of view, the result of the election shows who made better decisions.

Chapter Three

The Road to 2014 APC Convention

This chapter looks at how Buhari, a "former dictator", was to secure victory over his rivals in APC including former Vice President, Atiku Abubakar; Kano state Governor, Rabiu Musa Kwankwaso; and Imo state Governor, Rochas Okorocha. It will explore the Buhari Phenomenon and how he was able to turn around his hitherto poor electoral fortunes and his personal lifestyle to hit the campaign for the party nomination. Later, it will look at what looks like an early pitfall during the December 10, 2014, primaries. It examines Buhari's selection of a running mate in Professor Yemi Osinbajo upon the campaign trail and its implications for the campaign. It also looks at the changing perceptions of Nigerian voters between 2011 and 2015 elections.

The Buhari Phenomenon
One of the main areas that would seemingly separate the candidates, and arguably one of the most important over the course of the APC primaries was the branding of Buhari. The success of the Buhari brand can be identified as one of the reasons he won the party primaries and ultimately the main election. It has been established that there is a link between appearance and impression formation. The difference and contrast between Buhari and other candidates became apparent almost immediately to the voters. Buhari, in his 70s, was made to appear more youthful, in an attempt to appeal to the young voters, a demography that all candidates would heavily target. He was photographed wearing bow ties, suits (to dispel the widely-held belief that he is an Islamic fundamentalist), displaying many youthful gestures like giving "high five" to his grandchildren and shaking of women in public (something he almost never did in his three previous outings, which irked some of his "fundamentalist" supporters). The main messages Buhari's media team did their best to push out was his simple lifestyle and his anti-corruption stance.

Buhari was the *"Change"*, Buhari was *"not one of them"*, he was *"different"*, which made it seem effortless to build a powerful brand around him. At 72, he was considered too old by his opponents, but his supporters christened him *"Sai Baba"* or *"Baba mai Gaskiya ne"*, which literarily means in Hausa, *"The man that is honest or truthful"*. The use of the internet played a large role in this. As at 2011, Buhari was not active on any social media platform, leaving the space largely for President Jonathan and his supporters. In 2015, Buhari's supporters had more visibility than his rivals. Therefore, by Buhari's application of a grassroots brand interlinked with social media he was able to become very much the candidate of the people, with skilled use of social media tools such as Facebook, Twitter, YouTube, ThisisBuhari.com and hashtags like #iHaveDecided, to connect with the young voters.

Buhari's strategists also positioned him as a pro-poor politician under attack from "corrupt" remiges. He was pictured to have watched a live soccer match at the National Stadium in Abuja which only a few high-profile politicians would dare to do. His near-assassination in

2014 in Kaduna was portrayed as a direct reaction from those who fear his winning the election. He could not pay N27 million for the purchase of APC Nomination form since he had just N4 million in his bank account from his pension as against what his peers had in their accounts. His supporters had to do "crowd funding" for him to raise money to purchase the form and to run the election. It was reported that some of his supporters vowed to purchase the nomination form for him rather than him collecting a loan.

From the start Buhari's campaign had to move fast to catch up with those of his rivals through a strong branding campaign. By the end of the first quarter of 2014, the impact of the online campaigns was beginning to show in the comments of people on Facebook, Twitter and other social media platforms in political discussions. It was reported that Buhari rarely had a day go by without a fresh update on his Facebook page. As at the time he won the nomination, he had a following of over 149,000 people who subscribed to his online posts. This online presence made Buhari win virtually all online opinion polls conducted before the party primaries. A poll conducted by online new media, *Nigerian Eye,* on the eve of the Party Convention in Lagos showed Buhari leading with over 70 percent of the votes.

APC Convention and Beyond
Lagos is generally considered the primary "home" of the APC so few were surprised it was the venue of December 10, 2014, Convention. The city apart from being considered a "safe ground" for the party, boasts of the second largest registered voters in the federation, after Kano (another APC state). The choice of Lagos for the party Convention could just be for strategic and security reasons given the fact that the PDP had its own Convention in Abuja on the same day. Not surprisingly, four other aspirants – former Vice President, Atiku Abubakar; Kano State Governor, Rabiu Kwankwaso; Imo State Governor, Rochas Okorocha; and *Leadership* Newspaper publisher, Sam Nda-Isaiah – had jointly asked for a venue outside Lagos, which they considered "home" to an APC national leader and former Lagos State governor, Bola Tinubu; hence will unfairly favour Buhari against "more centrally located Abuja". The party's Convention Committee chair, Dr. Kayode Fayemi, in his response to the aspirants' protests argued about the issue of venue, that the initial plan of the committee and the party was to hold the event in Abuja but that the APC changed gear because the ruling PDP was also holding its convention almost at the same time. He said it would be difficult for the two dominant parties to be holding events of such magnitude at the same time and in the same location.

The influence of money in the contest was vividly captured by the chairman of the Plateau State chapter of the party, Hon Latep Dabang, who promised that all the state's delegates will vote for Atiku Abubakar because of the financial support he had always rendered to the party. Atiku, a former Vice President was reported to have booked over 4,000 hotel rooms to be provided gratis to the party's delegates coming for the convention in Lagos. As a result of this clear change of dynamics due to the power of money, there were good reasons for Buhari's camp to fear. It was reported that days to the convention, Atiku, *Vanguard* reported: "...has visited 35 states of the country was in a dead heat with Buhari in the pursuit of the ticket." There was an earlier disclosure by the Director-General of Atiku Campaign Organisation, Professor Babalola Aborishade that the *Turaki Adamawa* had secured and sealed 4,000 out of possible 8,000 delegates, was said to have thrown Buhari's camp into a frenzy, leading to certain master-stroke decisions that eventually delivered the day to him, leading to strong speculations that the odds may not favour him in the primaries. With money playing a decisive role in politics, Buhari appeared to need important support from party members with financial muscles, like Bola Tinubu and Rivers State Governor, Rotimi

Amaechi, to help him at such crucial time. This only proves that Buhari had a formidable political establishment to confront money.

Amaechi will later be appointed Director-General of the party's presidential campaign organisation, as against his preferred Vice Presidency slot, a move the Rivers state chapter of PDP calls "a ploy by the opposition party to further drain the resources of the state to finance a failing Presidential project."

Ultimately, money was to also play a role in Buhari winning the presidential primaries. One gets the impression that Nigeria was far more ready for a strong, incorruptible and disciplined General than just "money bag" politicians as president. This explains why all opinion polls leading to the primaries were all in favour of Buhari to face President Jonathan in the general election. At the end of the "horse trading" Convention night at Teslim Balogun Stadium in Surulere, Buhari polled 3430 votes against those of Kano State governor, Dr. Rabiu Kwankwanso; former Vice President, Atiku Abubakar; *Owelle* Rochas Okorocha and Sam Nda-Isaiah who got 974, 954, 624 and 10 votes respectively.

Chapter Four

The Long Race to Aso Rock

The focus of this chapter is to explore the months leading to the 2015 Nigerian presidential election. This section seeks to evaluate the dynamics of external factors that were to affect Buhari's campaign, affirming whether they were to affect Buhari's candidacy in a negative or a positive way, in particular, Buhari's appointment of Professor Yemi Osinbajo (SAN) as his running mate. These require analysis as they were both to affect the outcome of the election.

The Choice of Buhari's Running Mate
After the APC Convention, one decision that may have threatened the party's chances, not minding the successful completion of the primaries, was the choice of Buhari's running mate. As important as this decision was, Buhari knew it was not his making if he wanted to win the election. Choosing a running mate is not often as easy as making the announcement of the running mate; it often requires some technical considerations like regional balance, party unity, religious considerations, team spirit and other factors.

The choice of Professor Yemi Osinbajo (SAN) as Buhari's running mate came as a surprise to many people considering the fact that most people were thinking of the APC *compensating* the more *politically formidable* Rotimi Amaechi who had gone through a lot since joining the party from PDP. The choice was even made more surprising because it was speculated largely in the media that the party, in desperation to win the presidency, may settle for a "Muslim-Muslim" ticket for the 2015 presidential election. This speculation was further fueled by the fact that Buhari, in an interview with *The Cable,* said he was not opposed to having a Muslim as a running mate.

The PDP spokesman, Olisa Metuh, was reported on*Naij* to have said about the APC vice presidential candidate: "Who is Osinbajo? He was an ordinary commissioner and we have hundreds of commissioners in the country. The APC vice presidential candidate is an unknown individual in politics. He is not a threat to PDP."

It will again be observed that the choice of the legal luminary may not have done much to challenge President Jonathan's firewall in the South-East and South-South, but apparently was effective in chipping away his popularity among Christian fundamentalists. Whether Pentecostal Christians turned out to vote for Buhari because of the choice of Osinbajo is another matter altogether.

The Redeemed Christian Church of God (RCCG), where Professor Osinbajo is held in high esteem, is one of the most ubiquitous brands in Nigeria, with its General Overseer, Pastor Adeboye, enjoying wide-reaching influence well beyond the membership of the church. The PDP and President Jonathan enjoyed the "implied" support of Pastor Adeboye in 2011 when a picture of him being prayed for by the popular man of God went viral. This was not to be the case in 2015, as it is the opposition that had the Adeboye-optics in its favour. There was a tape recording of Pastor Adeboye "endorsing" Osinbajo in the presence of President Jonathan as someone that can be trusted "with any task" sometimes in 2011 in one of the President's visits to the Church. The APC used this audio largely as an "endorsement" by Pastor Adeboye for the Senior Advocate of Nigeria (SAN).

In addition to what looked like a tacit support of the largest Pentecostal Christian denomination, Osinbajo also represents a credible and competent fresh face in politics around whom youth movements can crystalize. The Buhari campaign was able to garner the support of an impressive host of major and minor power brokers from influential religious leaders and social media warlords in different parts of the country, many of whom, stayed neutral in 2011.

These new breed of supporters, in addition to securing the youth vote, were able to help build citizen-driven movements such as the #iHaveDecided movement which had the ability to tap into latent non-pecuniary motivations of young people to not only vote but more importantly canvass, donate and get-out-the-vote *(GOTV)* on the election day. The availability of such volunteer hands also reduced the financial burden on the campaign which became onerous in a final lap against an incumbent with a seemingly bottomless pocket.

The Certificate "saga"

It will be difficult to have any discussion about the 2015 presidential election without the mention of Buhari's West African School Certificate (WASC) saga that nearly threatened his election. In January, 2015 there was a clamor over the inability of Buhari to produce his Secondary School Leaving Certificate. The certificate issue later became a saga after the Nigerian army which earlier claimed it had the certificate later retracted its statement saying the certificate was not in its possession.

Trouble started, when, after Buhari explained in an affidavit submitted to the Independent National Electoral Commission (INEC) that all his academic credentials were with the Secretary, Military Board. The Army rejoined that they did not keep the certificates of any serving or retired officer or soldier.

In response to this, the PDP Presidential Campaign Organisation through its spokesman, Chief Femi Fani-Kayode, accused INEC of encouraging illegality by accepting the APC presidential candidate, General Muhammadu Buhari's claim of possessing the minimum educational qualification, to contest the exalted office of the presidency without attaching copies of his educational certificates.

Even when Government College, Katsina (previously Katsina Provincial School) released Buhari's results on his request, it led to an accusation of forgery against him.

Fani-Kayode said: "Yesterday, General Muhammadu Buhari made a shocking and belated disclosure that the Independent National Electoral Commission (INEC) has his documents. He has not been specific about the documents he is referring to but it is very clear that this is yet another squalid attempt to give the Nigerian people the impression that INEC has his certificate. If this is true, it represents a somersault from his original position which was that INEC has his affidavit and it once again reveals General Buhari for what he is."

The Will captured the situation perfectly when it reported: "With this latest antic, General Buhari is obviously trying to smuggle a newly-acquired certificate into INEC through the backdoor. If this is true and if INEC allows such a thing to happen, it would put a serious question mark on its impartiality and credibility. It would mean that it has collected his newly-acquired certificate, 40 days outside the stipulation of the Law."

Buhari's certificate became an issue only during the 2015 presidential election. Since he started contesting in 2003, his certificate had never been an issue.

How will Buhari, a retired military general, not have the basic educational qualifications to be Nigerian president? This was the question I asked one of his critics during the election.

I equally remembered then that Namadi Sambo, then Vice President, swore an affidavit that his original certificates were burnt. PDP supporters were willing to take Sambo's explanations but would not spare Buhari for being "careless". It was clear thereupon that they had something to hold on to in order to stall his presidential ambition.

Several letters were written to several foreign bodies, including the West African Examinations Council (WAEC). Many people soon became "authorities" on educational history.

A Gospel artiste Sammy Okposo, and a known supporter of President Goodluck Jonathan asked that Buhari should be "flogged" for forgery. He wrote on his Instagram page: *"From perjury to forgery: Buhari or whoever forged that certificate needs to be flogged. Prior to the formation of a central govt by Gowon, all regions had separate curriculums. Only the western region offered a local language in both their curriculum and WASC! It was after a central govt was formed and a universal educational curriculum was developed and adopted which included other local languages in 1974! So which WASC did Buhari write in 1961 that included Hausa?"*

Though he later apologized for the unfortunate statement, his point was taken seriously in many quarters. *Premium Times* investigators quickly went to work. They discovered contrary to what Sammy Okposo said, that the University of Cambridge Local Examinations Syndicate, UCLES, now Cambridge Assessment, offered local languages as at 1961. The University also confirmed that its grades during that year were issued in numbers, not letters. At that point, a lot of minds were already made up –even if an original certificate miraculously surfaced, it would still be *forged*.

Buhari's supporters also responded well. To them, even if Buhari presented a National Electric Power Authority (NEPA) bill as "certificate", they would vote for him.

Reflecting on all these later, I saw how easy it is for the human mind to be manipulated, in some cases, willingly. I also came to the conclusion that propaganda only works when there are people ready to believe them. Humans believe only what they want to believe. Once they hold their beliefs, there is little or nothing anyone could do.

To buttress this point, I attended a maritime lecture in the heat of a debate on Buhari's certificate saga in Apapa, Lagos. The presenter was a young maritime consultant. The organizers had done a good job of publicizing him as one of the finest minds in the maritime industry.

At the recess during the program, I found myself sitting with this man during launch. We started discussing the policies in the maritime industry including the recently established Maritime University in Delta state. He spoke of Jonathan as being the best thing to happen to the industry and I told him my view about Jonathan. He knew I was in support of Buhari but he made one profound statement. He said: "Buhari cannot be *my* president." When I asked for his reasons he said: "He did not go to school. He is an illiterate."

At this point, there wasn't any need arguing with him since his mind was already made up. Even the educated are not insulated from ignorance!

A Governor's Wish for Buhari

The history of the 2015 presidential election will be incomplete without the mention of the contributions of some characters. One of those actors whose decisions contributed to Buhari's victory is the Governor of Ekiti State. A year earlier, he had unseated Dr. Kayode Fayemi. Wanting to be seen working hard, he became so visible during the campaign. Buhari got an unusual support from this governor who would prefer he lost the election.

In what started as a big joke suddenly became a reality. In a desperate bid to stop the emergence of General Muhammadu Buhari, in the heat of the 2015 presidential election, Fayose did the unthinkable. He single-handedly placed an "obituary" of a living person, General Buhari, on the front pages of *The Punch* and *The Sun* (January 19, 2015).

Did he have a reason for this? In the unfortunate advertorial, Fayose wrote: "Will you allow history to repeat itself? Enough of State burials." This, he told Nigerians who listened to him eagerly.

Suffice to say that many political analysts described the advert as one of the lowest moments of the PDP campaign in the run-up to the election. Even his party distanced itself later, I understand, from the unfortunate pronouncement.

Not showing any sign of being embarrassed, *prophet* Fayose would later do his utmost to make his prophecies come to pass. This prophecy had to come to pass. He told the world that Buhari had advanced stage cancer, even coming up with a *medical report* from "Ahmadu Bello Teaching Hospital".

It was later made public that there is no hospital by that name. We are only familiar with the Ahmadu Bello University Teaching Hospital (ABUTH).

On February 21, 2015, General Buhari went to London. Fayose got to work once more. He said Buhari traveled to London to be treated at a hospital located at Cavendish Street, Cavendish Square, W2 London West End. The governor didn't end his drama there. He denied that Buhari was in London to deliver a keynote address at Chatham House (or the Royal Institute for International Affairs) as he was not slated to speak on the said day.

"Buhari has gone on medical checkup," he said. He claimed he had it on "good authority" that the General was ill, hence unfit to lead. He insisted that Buhari must produce his medical report. Many people believed the gospel according to Fayose.

On February 27, 2015 Buhari delivered a well-received lecture at Chatham House, London. The rest, as they say, is history!

Within this whole drama of accusations and counter accusations, many Nigerians chose to believe whatever their *lords* made them believe. Many of us literally fought on social media on the state of Buhari's health. I recall a post by someone, obviously a PDP supporter, who responded to a post on Facebook saying: "He will soon die." I was shocked. I wondered why any sane person will wish a living person dead. Is this what politics is all about? Didn't local folktales teach us to wish each other well?

Even in war, generals don't wish their opponents dead. When the opposing generals are captured, they are treated with respect. Why will anyone, for political reasons, pray for the death of their opponent? This bothered me and many people a lot during the campaign.

My sister, Modinat, asked (watching the drama on television): "What is it about Chatham House?" She wasn't a Buhari supporter like me, but I know she doesn't like President Jonathan. As far as I knew, she wasn't prepared to vote. She did her voter's registration while she was a Corps member in Kano, in 2014 and did not bother to renew before the election.

"Is Buhari just campaigning now that they remembered he is going London?" She wondered. I didn't bother replying and she wasn't expecting me to either.

The Real Buhari

It is important at this point to say that according to a German philosopher even truth sometimes needs its own propaganda. In a political game as intense as the 2015 presidential campaign, it will be extremely difficult avoiding the use of overt and covert propaganda. Also in the game of politics where everyone can claim "God is on my side", the use of overt and covert political techniques by parties is understandable. In this section, we shall be taking a look at the techniques adopted by both parties.

Both the APC and PDP appeared to deploy similar propaganda techniques. The techniques include the use of Specialized Media stations, Social Media platforms, Pseudo Organizations, Agents of Influence and Forgeries.

For the PDP, Specialized Media stations include "objective" messages from platforms like *The Vanguard, The Union, The Trent*, Hope for Nigeria, African Independent Television (AIT). The AIT freely broadcast messages deliberately created to discredit the APC presidential candidate, General Muhammadu Buhari and those considered positive for the PDP and its candidate, President Goodluck Jonathan.

Newspapers like *The Vanguard* and *The Union* (especially the later) are responsible for coming up with specially created disinformation and insinuate crisis in the opposition. Messages like, "APC to trade-off presidential ambitions for some states" are just to show the public that the APC is really not interested in the presidency. The online versions of these media platforms and their main allies, *The Trent* and Hope for Nigeria, post news favourable only to the PDP.

As part of campaign techniques in 2015, the PDP sponsored some organizations to act as "fronts" in certain sectors. For instance, in other to counter the influence of APC in the North, the party sponsored the Northern Elders Council (NEC) against the more well-known Northern Elders Forum (NEF) which had a hostile attitude to the PDP candidate. The NEC was promoted by the PDP hierarchy as the "true and popular representatives of the Hausas". The group's leader, Tanko Yankassai, is a well-known PDP chieftain. There were several other groups funded or supported by the party as part of its campaign techniques.

Apart from front organizations, there were also agents of influence either paid or co-opted by the PDP machinery to work for it. These agents are either political specialists working for newspapers, journalists, columnists, religious leaders, academics, musicians. The principal objective of the use of agents of influence is to explore the agent's position in his or field to promote political positions favourable to the PDP. This was used during the agitation for postponement of the presidential election. On one of its political programmes, AIT invited well-known agents of influence like the *Afenifere* scribe, Yinka Odunmakin and former governor of old Kaduna state, Balarabe Musa to argue for the postponement of the election.

It is difficult to prove the case of forgery against either of the parties, but it was largely insinuated that there was a clear case of forgery in the "medical certificate" presented to prove that General Buhari had advanced cancer from Ahmadu Bello Teaching Hospital. There was also the case of forgery when it was alleged that a letter from Cambridge

University denying that Hausa was offered in 1961 in its examinations which were a major contention during the election.

On the part of the APC, there are *Sahara Reporters, The Nation*, and Television Continental (TVC) as specialized media stations. These stations provided effective counters to charges raised against APC and its candidates.

The APC also, like the PDP, created organizations to act as fronts. There were series of allegations that the #BringBackOurGirls group was largely a front organization for the presidential ambition of the APC. This was strongly denied by the party when the Chairman, Technical Committee of the APC, Chief Audu Ogbe, in 2014 said the campaign was led by "members of our party."

Forgeries might have been used by the APC also during the campaign, but this been difficult to prove. The release of results of the APC candidate leaves a lot still shrouded in secrecy and leaving rooms for speculations. Let us now look at a specific instance, *The Real Buhari*.

On January 7, 2015, just days after he took office as Director of Media and Publicity of the PDP Presidential Campaign Organisation, Femi Fani-Kayode gave an important clue on how he would run his office. His team would have to expose Mr. Buhari, *for who he really is*. He would expose the real Buhari for Nigerians to know.

Speaking at a press conference, Fani-Kayode said: "It is our full intention to expose General Muhammadu Buhari for what he really is, what he stands for and the great danger that his candidacy portends for the unity of the Nigerian state and the peace and well-being of the Nigerian people.

"We believe that General Buhari represents the darkness and that President Jonathan represents the light. We believe that General Buhari represents a return to an ugly past, which is best forgotten while President Jonathan represents our hope for a greater and better future.

"We believe that the APC, on which platform General Buhari is contesting the presidential election, represents everything that is unholy and unwholesome in our society and that the PDP represents all that is decent and good."

In the said press conference, he mentioned Buhari's name more than the number of times he did his boss. This made a lot of us believe that Buhari had become a thorn in PDP's flesh. They worried about him more than they thought about winning the election.

At this point, the APC campaign was yet to be clear how the PDP intended to handle its campaign. In any case, this was how the concept of *The Real Buhari* was conceived.

Before we proceed, let us admit at this point that both parties used Overt and Covert political techniques or propaganda during the campaigns in varying degrees. The only caveat is that one must watch one's back well in using it hence it backfires!

The media understandably played pivotal roles during the campaign. As the presidential election drew nearer, tensions arose in both camps. Vitriol pours into the air from partisan political actors became common and even greater quantities of propaganda were released every day.

A local television station, Africa Independent Television (AIT) owned by a PDP chieftain, Dr. Raymond Dokpesi, began a series known as *The Real Buhari*. The series was one of the attempts at reminding Nigerians of Buhari's *crimes* especially in his first stint in office as Head of State.

It was on *The Real Buhari* that Nigerians heard that Buhari's military regime was the first to sentence a woman to death by firing squad. He hates women, they said. The social media was awash with information from the documentary.

I ordinarily do not have issues with the use of propaganda in elections but in using it, one must be clever. It has no neutral effect as it can sometimes do the opposite of what one intended. The case of *The Real Buhari* proved so fatal for the PDP for several reasons:

First, it made no attempt at sinking issues with facts. How does one explain the obvious error that Buhari killed Mrs Funmilayo Ransome-Kuti, who died in 1978 when Buhari's military regime started in 1984? How does one explain the fact that a *well-researched documentary* did not know that Maitatsine operated largely under Shehu Shagari's administration but had little to do with Buhari's military regime? A simple *Google* search could have saved the writers of the documentary that embarrassment. It appears facts and details did not matter to those behind the documentary other than "just get it out."

Second, it is only filled with insults and deliberate lies. What has Buhari's daughter and wife's death got to do with presidential capacity? Trivialities like this only make a mockery of the whole affair.

I must confess, the documentary made me scared. Apart from my support for Buhari, I know a lie when I see one.

Many Nigerians believe that the information provided in the documentary should be proved, while others believe every word said in the documentary.

If the PDP has employed the services of good political specialists, they would have realized that they failed to complicate the simple and simplify the complicated in their message on *The Real Buhari*. The contents were not only wrong but contain obvious lies that can easily be disproved.

To show how effective *The Real Buhari* documentary was, AIT put up an online poll on its website. The figures were more than what the television station's management had bargained for. Needless to say, the poll was pulled down few hours after it showed that Buhari was leading with about 76 per cent of the vote cast. The management cited hacking as the reason for pulling down the poll, but this was never proven.

The PDP, in trying to achieve its objective of demonstrating that APC is an "aggressive, violent, reactionary tribalist party pursuing Islamic agenda" in Nigeria probably didn't do a good job appealing to Northern voters by providing a better alternative. The party acted as though coming being a Northerner or a Muslim is satanic by the scaremongering using "Islamization agenda" a core message of *The Real Buhari!*

The Election
On March 28, 2015, the Nigerian electorate chose the first opposition candidate as president for the first time in history. The polls had predicted that Buhari would win the election but few predicted the extent of the victory. Having fought such a hard primary contest against candidates like Atiku, Kwankwaso, Rochas Okorocha and the likes in the primaries, defeating incumbent president Jonathan, who contested the PDP primaries alone appeared much easier!

Over fifteen million people voted for Buhari, making him the first opposition candidate to win a presidential election in the annals of Nigeria history. Buhari's victory in 2015 simply symbolized the change that Nigerians were ready for.

It can be argued that Buhari defeated Jonathan because he was a stronger candidate. Buhari's single campaign message of *Change* had more appeal at a time when nearly two out of every three Nigerian felt the country was headed in the wrong direction according to a poll by a Europe-based political research firm, Eurasia Group. The result of the poll coming just a few days before the presidential election and from a firm which had earlier predicted a win for PDP, created a major problem for Jonathan as there was a general consensus against the administration. This general perception stemmed from the seeming lack of political will to fight corruption, insurgency and the poor information management system of the Jonathan campaign.

Upon analyzing the results of the 2015 Presidential election it is clear that ethnicity and religion proved to be no obstacles for Buhari as he won the Muslim-dominated North West and Christian dominated South West, North Central, and North East. The biggest victories for Buhari in previous elections were recorded in North Central and South West Nigeria. This only shows that much ground was covered in 2015 election than in previous ones. The General had suffered heavy losses in these two regions largely because of his perceived religious fanaticism and his role in the 1983 Coup which left many Yoruba leaders from the South West (including Chiefs Obafemi Awolowo, Olabisi Onabanjo and Michael Ajasin) with bitter experiences during the Junta.

The appointment of Professor Yemi Osinbajo must have upturned Buhari's electoral misfortunes among Yoruba voters considering the fact that the eminent lawyer was connected to the powerful Awolowo political dynasty by marriage – he is married to the late Obafemi Awolowo's granddaughter. This made the decision to pick the Senior Advocate of Nigeria a tactical move.

As confirmed results of the election trooped in, Buhari polled a total of 15,424,921 votes, winning in four of Nigeria's six geopolitical zones, against President Jonathan's 12,853,162 votes from a decisive victory in two zones. A cursory look at these results shows that Buhari gained an additional 3 million votes over what he polled in 2011, and covered two additional geo-political zones (North Central and South West) while President Jonathan lost over 10 million votes against what he polled four years earlier.

The difference between the two elections can be seen in several factors which include: the general perceptions among Nigerians of Jonathan as a weak leader; the escalation of Boko Haram insurgency; massive corruption rocking the administration; poor conflict resolution mechanism in PDP; the new improved image of Buhari, the APC and others – these contributed to a victory for the General.

Chapter Five
The Buhari's Victory

Against all admonitions from family members to stay back, as the result declaration drew to the final stage, I went to work that day. There were genuine fears that there would be possible post-election violence as the results were not going in favour of the President.

I received a call that day from a friend, David, who told me Buhari could not win the election even if the results said so. I asked him why and he said I should watch how events would unfold. I did not want to take this guy seriously because he had a history of supplying me false information. He was a fan of Jonathan and his passionate support was well appreciated.

When I say he has a history of supplying me with false information, I mean it. This guy, it was, who told me in the heat of the campaigns that Buhari was stoned in Lagos when he came for a campaign rally at Teslim Balogun Stadium. It turned out a blatant lie. He earlier told me that General Buhari had collapsed in a rally in Uyo. He said he was even considering withdrawing from the race. "APC is in shambles," he told me in excitement. Again, it was this same guy that told me he had information that PDP would defeat Buhari even in Kano.

Even though I knew him to be a PDP disinformation agent, something in me wanted to believe him. That morning, I got a strange email titled: *Why Buhari Lost,* forwarded to me by a former classmate at the Obafemi Awolowo University, Ile-Ife. To say this while ballot counting was ongoing added to my worries.

As I read the mail, I suspected there must have been some attempts to cause confusion. The mail contained an article ready for publication *as soon as Jonathan was declared the winner*. Would they rig this election again? I became unsettled from then on. I thought of the worst. I remember sighting a full-page advertorial *congratulating* Jonathan on his *victory* in some newspapers on my way to work that morning. The threat of rigging the election looked real.

At work that day, I wasn't myself. I recall accompanying my boss to meet a client that same day. Apart from that, I doubt if I did any other thing in the office. I stayed close to the television at the reception of my office to get detailed results. I should never be told of this historic moment. First-hand information is more trustworthy than third party hearsay.

Before I go on, it will be historically unfair to neglect the drama that played out during the declaration of results in Abuja. When it had become clear that President Goodluck Jonathan was bound to lose the election with the results in all the states ready, his supporters wouldn't just give up without a fight. One of them was Godsday Orubebe.

Elder Godsday Orubebe is Nigeria's former Minister of State for Niger Delta Affairs. Mr Orubebe acted as a polling agent for the PDP at the presidential election collation centre. In a breath-taking moment – 20 minutes – that nearly threatened the security of the nation, Nigerians and the world watched his rare display of drama (if it can be called that). He alleged that INEC Chairman, Professor Attahiru Jega, had taken side with the APC while state results were being declared.

If it were not for Jega's calm disposition, maybe Nigeria's democracy would have been truncated at that point. I remember the Cuban Missile crisis of 1962. If the US had anyone with an inflammable temperament instead of John F. Kennedy as her president, that incident could have sparked World War III.

Barely minutes after the INEC chairman settled in to commence collation, apologizing for commencing late, which was due to logistics issues, the politician, accused Jega of being "very partisan" and compromising.

He said, "We [the PDP] have lost confidence in you because you are partisan." He used words like "tribalistic" and others to describe the electoral commission boss.

In parenthesis, the PDP had clandestinely designed a ploy to sack Jega in the run-up to the election. Some groups had publicly demonstrated for Jega to be sacked. The Oodua People's Congress (OPC) held some massive rallies in Lagos to press for the sacking of Jega. The Movement for the Actualisation of the Sovereign State of Biafra (MASSOB) held some well-attended rallies in some South-Eastern states to press for same. There were other groups pressing too. All these groups had something in common – they had all endorsed the PDP candidate, Dr. Goodluck Jonathan, for re-election.

Given this background, for Orubebe to have publicly admitted his party had "lost confidence" in Jega meant the party only went into the election as a matter of *fait accompli.*

On the surface, the fact that over the course of four years earlier, General Muhammadu Buhari's victory was inconceivable to many Nigerians makes his 2015 victory a tremendous achievement. Yet, in an intriguing event after few days of the announcement of election results, at 11:00 pm on March 31, 2015, Buhari was declared Nigeria's president-elect.

Over the course of this analysis, the case in how Buhari was able to accomplish this tremendous achievement has been addressed. By using Buhari's decision to allow his CPC to form an alliance with other parties to produce the APC as the starting point of "giving up" contesting future election after the 2011 elections, one was able to gain an understanding of how the Buhari phenomenon emerged onto the political scene. However, it is through the analysis of how Buhari was able to overcome his rivals in the APC that we are able to gain an understanding of the strength of Buhari.

Throughout the APC primaries, Buhari went from strength to strength. There were other favourites but the charismatic Buhari employed strong campaign techniques which saw a heavy reliance on social media and grassroots mobilization to project his message to a younger and more diverse voting publics.

Instead of letting his low financial war chest to deter his effort, he made it his strength. Buhari, through his message of *"Change"* and a strong drive for social change, was able to brand himself as the candidate to back. Just as he hadn't been part of the corrupt system in Nigerian politics, his position as an *outsider* gave him a credible edge as the man needed to put Nigeria on track. Buhari was the clean-break candidate. The efficiency with which he ran his campaign, the handling of the "certificate saga", the appointment of Professor Yemi Osinbajo as his running-mate and the general unpopularity of the Jonathan administration among Nigerians, pushed Buhari to victory.

Why did Jonathan accept defeat without a fight?

During my interactions with President Jonathan's supporters during the campaigns, I discovered that many did not believe that he will lose the election. This also applies to Buhari's supporters, many of whom have been with him since he started contesting in 2003.

Why Jonathan Conceded Defeat

On Saturday, March 14, 2015 I was at Freedom Park, Victoria Island, Lagos to grant an interview to #Youth4Change[ii]. During the interview (which has since been published on YouTube), I spoke about the need for the youths to turn out in their large numbers to vote. Though it was supposed to be a non-Partisan affair, I used the opportunity to canvass for votes for the APC presidential candidate. As I was leaving the Park to journey back home, around 11.00am, I decided to make a stop over to purchase of a copy of *The Sun*. No sooner had I paid the newspaper vendor than a man- who should be in his late 40s or early 50s accosted me. "Can I read your paper?" he said. I told him I was in a hurry as I had an urgent appointment to keep. He smiled and said: "No problem." After this, he asked who I would be voting for in the election. I expected this man to have understood because I was putting on a T-shirt with the bold inscription, #iHaveDecided with the pictures of General Muhammadu Buhari and Professor Yemi Osinbajo on it. His question looked more like a rhetorical question to me. After coming out of the confusion as to whether I should give this man a stern or friendly look, I told him I will be voting Buhari.

At this point, the man asked why. I told him it will take Buhari to solve the problem of insurgency and corruption in the country. He wasn't pleased. But he said: 'It is because of Osinbajo that you want to vote APC. APC is a devilish party, my brother. You are too decent for that kind of party." He went on, ranting, cajoling and in some case with frustration he said, "Anyway, God has prevailed. Jonathan has won already." The vendor and some other people standing to read newspapers at the vendor's stand thundered (in what looked like the tone of someone from Akwa Ibom or Cross Rivers state), "Help me tell am. Goodluck don win." I laughed and said no additional word.

As I was on my way back to my house, I thought about what will happen should Buhari win the election. With the tension in the country especially as some members of the president's "kitchen cabinet" has threatened violence if "our son" does not win.

The question has always been why Jonathan accepted defeat in the midst of the background to the tension-filled election. At that point, ex-militant leader, Asari Dokubo, has threatened (on the 2015 presidential election) that there will be blood. The militant leader reportedly said: "We will fight, because in this battle, there is no retreat, no surrender. We will not take any prisoner of war. It will be a total battle."

With the understanding that the peace of the nation rested on the shoulders of the two leading presidential candidates, some prominent Nigerians led by a former Military Head of State, Abdusalami Abubakar, under the name, National Peace Committee, decided to meet both leaders with the view to make them commit to post-election peace by signing a pact on the 14th of January, 2015.

Though many, especially Jonathan's supporters have argued that he conceded defeat as a result of this, but events after the election reveal that it wasn't as a result of solely the actions of the peace committee.

I did an analysis of similar situations in Africa in countries where incumbent presidents have lost and conceded defeat, the result was revealing. I found out that no African president (or no president for that matter) wants to give up power just easily. As I write, (January 16, 2017), the political situation in The Gambia is deteriorating fast with President Yahya Jammeh insisting he will not relinquish his position even though he lost in December 2016 to his rival, Adama Barrow. There appears to be only a military solution to the problem in that country.

Also, Lesotho, in 1970, for instance, when early results indicated that the Prime Minister, Chief Leabua Jonathan, and his party, the Bathoso National Party (BNP) might lose to its rival, Bathosoland Congress Party (BCP), he voided the results citing "irregularities". After nullifying the election, he declared a state of emergency, suspended the constitution, dissolved the parliament and assumed absolute power in the tiny nation surrounded by apartheid South Africa. To cut short the long story, things became so difficult as a result of political turbulence, from both internal and external sources until a military takeover in the country in 1986.

In the early 1990s, the great Zambian politician, Dr. Kenneth Kaunda lost the country's presidential election. Like many of his peers at the time, he faced the temptation to annul the election. In his sensational book, *Wars, Guns, and Votes,* Paul Collier writes about democracy and political violence in Africa. He argued that the political elites in Africa are the major beneficiaries of political violence. Collier (on why Kaunda couldn't annul the election and set the country on fire) argues: "(former US President) Jimmy Carter was in the country leading a team of election observers. As the results started to come in, Carter sensed what to do. Rushing to the presidential palace, he felt Kaunda's pain and stayed there until it was too late to annul the election. After all, he had lived through a similar experience. With Carter there in the palace, Kaunda had little choice but to accept the defeat." (p. 17). To show how uneasy Kaunda's decision was, Collier wrote: "...reputedly, he then went around the capitals of Africa advising presidents not to make his mistake."

While it may be debatable that the timely intervention of Carter in Zambian 1991 election was responsible for Kaunda's decision, it must be acknowledged that the former US president's role (himself losing the 1980 presidential election), kept Kaunda's reputation abroad as an African statesman.

As recently as 2012, it took the French army to help remove Laurent Gbagbo who stayed put after losing to Alassane Quattaraa year earlier. He was made to face the International Criminal Court (ICC) for crimes against humanity. With Quattara's case been the most recent, I guess that influenced Jonathan's decision in no small way after the United States and United Kingdom will not back him if he dared stay longer.

Talking of timing, on March 30, 2015, while the collations and counting of the votes were still in process, the United States and the United Kingdom issued a stern warning against the rigging of the election. In a joint statement credited to UK foreign secretary, Philip Hammond and US secretary of state, John Kerry, they warned against the "disturbing indications" of the possibility of rigging the election due to some "deliberate political interference."

The statement went further to add that: "The Governments of the United States and the United Kingdom would be *very concerned* by any attempt to undermine the independence of the Electoral Commission (INEC), or its Chairman, Prof. Jega; or in any way distort the expressed will of the Nigerian people."

With frank statements like these coming from two of the most powerful countries in the world, there appeared to be little or nothing Jonathan or his "kitchen cabinet" could to than to accept defeat in good faith.

SECTION TWO

Part 1

Leadership Perspectives

A Perspective on Leadership

An adage says, "Show me your friend and I will tell you who you are." This should be re-framed "Show me your leader and I will tell you the follower you are." This shows that leaders and followers co-create each other. There can be no leadership without followership and the reverse is also true. In his wonderful book, *The Wretched of the Earth*, French-born Algerian statesman, Frantz Fanon argued that ultimately the people get the kind of leaders they deserve; and the leaders deserve the kind of followers they get. After all, a leader is anyone called to guide, teach, command, motivate, inspire or plan. By this, we all are leaders.

The National Association of Nigerian Students (NANS) had a glorious past in the 70s and the 80s due to its strong stance in defense of interests of students and the downtrodden in the society. But what went wrong suddenly? Today it is difficult to distinguish NANS activities from motor park touts. The Nigerian Union of Journalists (NUJ) made this point early 2014 when Delta State NANS Joint Campus Committee executives paid the Union a courtesy visit. So where are the leaders of tomorrow? Like NANS, a University Campus branch of the Non-Academic Staff Union of Universities and Other Educational Institutions (NASU) did something quite amusing. Its members' monetized benefits were allegedly cornered by the Vice Chancellor thus provoking the Union to embark on an indefinite strike.

It is instructive to know that the union leader, on being summarily promoted by the university management from level 4 to 7 suddenly abandoned the poor workers and mortgaged their future for personal gratification. Do we still have the moral authority to question our leaders when they collect huge World Bank/IMF loans and these never get home?

The Academic Staff Union of Universities (ASUU) embarked on industrial action in 2009. The Union accused the Minister of Education, Dr. Sam Egwu, of not heeding to the plights of the union because of the fact that he like other high-ranking public officials in government had his children in foreign universities.

Suffice to say that ASUU threatened to publish the names of public officers' children in foreign universities. The Minister also claimed he had the names of children of ASUU members studying abroad and threatened to publish their names. We are yet to see any list from both sides until this day!

These instances were cited to justify the assertion that leaders and followers are co-creators.

Dynamism is one of the hallmarks of leadership. If we continue to use the same old responses, worn-out theories, old failed approaches instead of creating new ones we honestly aren't expecting things to change. I am sure no one recalls experiencing bomb blasts being a daily practice two decades ago. These are the realities we live by in Nigeria today. But to respond with overtly short-staffed, ill-equipped security agencies to a fire-emitting Boko Haram squad is, to say the least, crooked thinking.

The Americans were told in clear language that they were in the 21st Century and no longer the Civil War, Cold War, Vietnam, or Gulf War Years of the 20th Century during the 9/11 attacks.

Robert Greene in his book, *The 33 Strategies of War* noted that there is nothing good that comes out of fighting the last war. Just as a confused leader cannot lead effectively, a divided, unfocused, disorganized and disoriented people cannot follow. The latter will be taken advantage of by unscrupulous politicians for cheap political gains. So, leaders and followers are not independent of each other.

Only clear-headed persons can effectively lead. But clear-headedness without visions is like tea without sugar. Since the needs of today are not necessarily those of tomorrow, good leaders try to phantom them in advance to avoid creating a vacuum. It is this lack of vision that made countries like Ghana to do better than we are presently doing. Great visionaries like Kwame Nkrumah who have visions presently elude us.

Also, a leader must know which role to play per time. He must be able to discern the role he plays in every situation. At war time, he is the Commander-in-Chief or Chief Security Officer; at peace time he is the Father of the Nation, shunning partisanship in every form; during the period of a division, he is the uniting figure and so on.

In Nigeria, it appears our leaders don't know what role is expected of them per time; therefore, they get poor advice from their advisors who are only bent on flattering their master's ego.

Great leaders spend their time understanding the needs of their people. When others are bothered about winning the next election, or their party, or tribal origin, they do their best to satisfy their people. They are like marketers who are told to satisfy the needs of their customers, to guarantee their loyalty. It is this great truth that Franklin D. Roosevelt understood, as US President, during the Great Depression (1929-1933), when he chose to pitch his tent with the poor who were most affected during the period. For this act, he was rewarded with great victories in four consecutive elections which are unprecedented and unsurpassed in US history.

This was what led the great political leader and perhaps the most influential religious figure in World Civilization, Amenhotep IV, Pharaoh of Egypt (1360-1350BC?) to say: "The glory of a king is the welfare of his people; his power and dominion resteth on the hearts of his subjects." The greatest leaders have taken heed of this eternal truth. Also, the greatest leaders are not those that lead from the mountains. They pay attention to the deepest levels of human experience.

They don't make themselves super humans; in essence, they are humble.

It, therefore, becomes very difficult to see situations clearly when one is surrounded by such luxury Nigerian leaders are infected with. All these rather make people blind hence they depend on second-hand reports from their unreliable lieutenants.

Great leaders give everything in their service to the people.

History is not in want of leaders who gave their lives in the service of their people – Mahatma Gandhi (India), Abraham Lincoln (USA), John F. Kennedy (USA), Peatrice Lumumba(Congo), Malcolm Little (Malcolm X) (USA), MartinLuther King (USA), Ernesto "Che" Guevara (Argentina), Amilcar Cabral (Guinea-Bissau), Salvador Allende (Chile) and many others paid the ultimate price with their lives. Others have endured painful punishments and assaults: Nelson Mandela (South Africa), Denis Brutus (South Africa), Fidel Castro (Cuba), Juan Peron (Argentina). Others like Ahmed Ben Bella (Algeria) and Kwame Nkrumah (Ghana) were exiled from their countries due to their defense of their people. We are indeed in a period of great triumphs and potential pitfalls.

The world is in desperate need of leadership and followership. To make the difference, leaders must set the pace for the followers. The world is in desperate need of inspirational leaders, not politicians. That is why you and I must set the pace.

Nigeria and the Symptoms of Stagnation!

John Boehner, speaker of the US House of Representatives announced his resignation, not only from his position as speaker but also from the Congress in 2015. I am not aware his resignation had anything to do with corruption or fraud, rather it was on the basis of principles which caused disaffections within his beloved Republican Party.

I am not sure if disagreeing with one's party, by which one was elected, is enough grounds to resign one's position in Nigeria. Not even a monumental case of graft and fraud will make him tread the part of honour even though he is called "Honourable". I keep asking myself if this can ever happen in my country, Nigeria.

What happens when an organism suddenly stops growing? My guess is that you know the answer. If we agree that the main purpose of life is growth, then the reason for the extinction of certain creatures like dinosaurs from planet earth could be that they stopped growing.

A cell that stops growing or fails to subdivide or die becomes cancerous and useless. When our leaders continually apply the same old, failed methods in our public life, this portends danger for the country's growth. It leads to stagnation.

Professor Chinua Achebe in his book, *The Trouble With Nigeria*, concluded that the main challenge for Nigerians today could be summed up in one word –leadership. This conclusion is valid till this day. An organisation that does not inject fresh ideas or new blood, sooner or later faces the inevitable. We do not need to be diplomatic about this fact. The best our leaders have done is to replace themselves with their children and children's children or in worst cases their cronies. Little wonder you have recurrent names like Shagari, Balewa, Akintola, Fani-Kayode, Okonjo, Nweke, Obasanjo, Buhari, and the likes who are all children of former public officials. In most cases when their children are not readily available for whatever reasons, they set sight on their godsons or *anointed* candidates to take their place.

How does a nation grow in this kind of situation? It still baffles me that we are yet to effectively develop youthful leaders to retire the likes of General Muhammadu Buhari (rtd) perhaps the only reference made to anti-corruption crusade in Nigeria at age 72. This is after his previous stint as Head of State (1983-85). The question then is: what are the likes of el-Rufai, Ribadu and Fashola doing? Can any of these boast of the virtues embodied in Buhari? Did they fall off by the way? Where are the so-called leaders of tomorrow? It is my long held view that most of our leaders are everything but creative. This was why Chief Obafemi Awolowo opined in his book *Thoughts on Nigerian Constitution* (1966) that our leaders lack "comprehension, mental magnitude and spiritual depth..." Invariably, most of them do not see beyond their noses. Like incompetent physicians, our leaders administer doses of the same drugs to different ailments or symptoms.

They live the lives of the 20th century deep into the 21st century. This explains why 20th century ideas are still fresh in their minds. An example is imperative at this point.

In October 1962, days before Chief Awolowo's treasonable felony trial began, the then Judicial Service Commission (JSC), headed by Sir Adetokumbo Ademola clearly acting on instructions from the Balewa-led government, had carefully "promoted" the Acting Chief Justice of the High Court Justice Charles Onyeama (since Justice De Leastang was then on leave) to the position of Federal Judge in the Supreme Court, leaving the more partisan Justice Sowemimo as Awo's trial Judge. In parenthesis, Justice Onyeama had been so promoted (albeit for just 21 days in which he could not even enter the Supreme Court for one day) due to his impartial role during the National Bank probe, so the authorities could not trust him to do the hatchet job of jailing Awo, hence his "promotion".

It is unfortunate that this same method was deployed twice under the Jonathan administration. First, it was used in the case of Justice Ayo Salami, when he was suspended erroneously by the NJC, and on his reinstatement by the same body, the former President suddenly became more Catholic than the Pope. It was also used against the former Speaker Aminu Tambuwal, President Jonathan's arch-rival when suddenly his case was reassigned from the presiding judge to a more partisan judge!

Still, during the Western Region crises in 1962, I saw a picture of some Parliamentarians jumping the fence to make their way into the chamber.

If we argue that our democracy was still in its infancy, can we still assume we are not growing at all when the same thing repeated itself this time at the national level for the world to see?

Are we moving forward at all as a nation? That also reminds me. The State Security Service (SSS) men also "invaded" the Akwa Ibom State Governor's Lodge. I still ask myself if we learned anything from the invasion of the All Progressives Congress (APC) Data Centre in Lagos in 2014. Or did we learn anything from the so-called Watergate break-in in the 1970s in the United States? Does it not bother people that when some talk about the best of Universities they mention the "First Generation" Universities? What then happened to the new ones that billions of naira were pumped into building them?

Last year, I went to one of those recently built "Universities" to apply for a teaching position. Had I had not seen "FEDERAL UNIVERSITY...," written at the entrance, I would have argued I was at the wrong place! Is this one of the "Universities" for which pocket-tearing money was allocated?

A friend of mine was to travel to Canada on a Student's Visa so I accompanied him to the Murtala Muhammed Airport, Lagos. I saw the beautiful British Airways aircraft. I equally admired the well- maintained Kenyan Airways just like I did, the South African Airways. I didn't come close to sighting any "Nigerian Airways". My first instinct was to loudly ask for clarifications. For the records, Nigerian Airways once served as a model for air travel in Africa (including Apartheid South Africa) but that glory has been surpassed by those that are not ordinarily supposed to be in our class at all. This is the result of stagnation or lack of growth! My take is that all the symptoms of stagnation are with us as a nation. This is why we must put on our thinking caps and be creative. Relying on the old ways of doing things is and will always be counterproductive. If in the 21st Century we still struggle with organising a free and fair election as we saw in during the bloodbath in the Rivers gubernatorial election only goes to show that of all the countries in the world there is a country that has refused to grow. I can only hope I am dreaming, that all these are not happening in my country.

Why Nigeria Needs Stalin

The Great Ife Students' Union Building (Ken Saro Wiwa Building) means different things to many people. While to some, it is a place that has produced heroes and legends; to some, it is the bedrock of student militancy; to others still, it is a house for thugs, rogues and "professional" students. Whatever it may mean to anyone is a matter of interpretation. For those, like me, who have served the union at one time or the other, it is a centre for political consciousness, analyses and education, which we will always love and cherish.

In front of that building once stood a newspaper vendor, *Abe Igi* (under a tree) where different people came to read the papers (usually for free) and in turn analyse, discuss and argue about topical issues making the news for long hours that one began to wonder if these people ever attended lectures. (I must confess I learned more politics at this point than I did in the classroom studying for a degree in Political Science in the University). It was at this place that I met the strangest person in my life!

Comrade Tony Uchendu is a young man who you would ordinarily prefer to avoid. His appearance is austere; his stature is what you would call below average. His ideas and opinions are either strange or bizarre. He professes Communism and his deep knowledge of Marxism particularly thrills me. But how would you know except you came close to him? But I had never met someone who called himself a Stalinist until I met this comrade!

In addition to lending me Isaac Duetscher's *Stalin: A Political Biography,* some days after our first meeting, he requested me to attend the meeting of his group, The Eagle Network; a group I was largely unaware of its existence on campus.

I was reluctant to read the book (I had not read any Joseph Stalin biography; all I knew about him then were from books about the Soviet Union history and politics). After hesitating for several days, I decided to honour the invitation baring any political or social consequences for attending the meeting of a strange, largely clandestine, and unknown group and at night!

It was at this meeting still that I heard further shocking message, particularly about democracy.

Noticing my hesitation, Comrade Tony allayed my fears: the group sprang from the Black Nationalists' Movement (BNM). I told him that I only knew the Movement as a political ideological group to which the Governor of Osun State, *Ogbeni* Rauf Aregbesola belonged to as a student of The Polytechnic, Ibadan.

We discussed the content of my project thesis: *The Effects of Party Politics on Nigeria's Democratic Experience* (which I dedicated to *Ogbeni*).

On seeing my work, he oppugned all my ideas about democracy and told me that all Nigeria needed was Stalin's leadership and not a democracy. It is now over 54 years that our colonial masters left us. It is also over 16 years since the soldiers went back to their barracks handing over power to politicians or *democrats*. And Nigeria has had almost equal number of years for both military and civilian regimes. The *democrats* may disagree with the points I made but no problem.

A lot of people are deliberately ignorant of the fact that two of modern history's most celebrated dictators are products of a democratic process. Benito Mussolini (Italy) and Adolf Hitler(Germany) were elected under the *Fasci di Combattimento* or Fascist Party and the National Socialist German Workers' Party or the Nazi Party respectively in 1922 and 1933 respectively, in addition to other countless dictators.

We must equally concede that elections have also produced geniuses and near-saints like Barack Obama, Abraham Lincoln, Margaret Thatcher, Julius Nyerere, Sam Mbakwe, Lateef Jakande, Sule Lamido and the likes, just as it has produced rogues and despots: Robert Mugabe, is just a good case.

Also, anyone who has studied US history would know that democracy is just a style of leadership, not a system as we may think. Franklin D. Roosevelt is a good example.

Many remember him today as perhaps the most loved American president. Few remember the *Court Packing* and attempt to flush out all his opponents from the Congress during the 1938 midterm election using his influence in the Democratic Party. All these he did to force the New Deal Program through the throat of Americans.

Few still remember he is called the lion and the fox: two creatures known for ruthlessness and craftiness. We have equally been told that democracy is built on institutions and not men. In fact, President Obama made this point clear on his visit to Ghana in 2009: Africa needs strong institutions and not men. If I am on the same page with these people, the word institution is to be taken literally: an organisation that has a particular purpose. In this case may mean courts, parliaments, bureaucracy, political parties, or electoral bodies. If that is the meaning of institution, then I submit we have them in fact, in excess. To fight corruption alone we have: Economic and Financial Crimes Commission (EFCC), Independent Corrupt Practices and other related offenses Commission(ICPC), Code of Conduct Bureau, National Agency for Food, Drugs Administration and Control (NAFDAC), State Security Service(SSS), the Police, the list is endless. Have the existence of these reduced corruption? It is on that note that I found another meaning of the word in Oxford Dictionary: a person who is well known because they have been in a job for a long time.

In the United States' Federal Reserve Board we can mention institutions like William M. Martin Jr. who served as chairman between 1951 to 1970 serving under five different administrations, both Democrats and Republicans. Also, we have Allan Greenspan who was appointed chairman in 1987 and served four different Presidents, including Bill Clinton, even though he himself was a Republican. These are institutions per excellence. And these we need! When I hear people talk about "institutions", they say it as though they will be manned by robots or X-Men. Judges can be bribed, influenced or intimidated; security agencies can compromise; other institutions can be deliberately underfunded (all these we recently witnessed in Nigeria).

The reason for all these is that these institutions are manned by weak men. Weak men cannot rise above partisanship, tribalism, nepotism, ethnicity or religious bigotry. This is where I agree with my Stalinist friend!

Irrespective of what the West wants us to believe about Stalin: he was responsible for the deaths of untold number of Soviet citizens through starvation and *concentration* camps; a murderer of many if not all his opponents and supporters (including the respected Leon Trotsky one of the leaders of October 1917 revolution); reigned terror on many through the notorious and dreaded KGB (the Secret Police); we need him to bring discipline back into our lexicon as a nation.

Stalin, it was who mechanized Soviet's agriculture; turned around its education that rural farmers were all sent to school; laid the foundation of Soviet's industrialization, and development of nuclear power which compelled Americans to treat Russians as equals in international politics; responsible for Soviet's victory over Adolf Hitler's Nazi army.

All these came with great costs. Ivan the Terrible, Peter the Great and other great reformers have been dwarfed by the giant form of the Man of Steel (Stalin) (Deutscher 1961: 294).

If we remove Stalin's contribution to Russia's history what is left? There is always a price to pay for making progress! As a developing nation, we need leaders to guide and inspire people into political, social, economic, cultural and spiritual vitality, revival and activities. History is not in want of such leaders: Napoleon Bonaparte (France), Charles De Gaulle (France), Lee Kwan Yew (Singapore), Josip Bros "Tito" (Yugoslavia), Major-General Park Clung (South Korea), Mustafa Kemal Ataturk (Turkey), Fidel Castro (Cuba) and the likes.

These will not be your first choice of *democrats* but the untold development they brought into their domains and jurisdictions cannot be quantified. Comrade Tony, I later learned, was shot by men of the Nigerian Police during a demonstration in 2012 nationwide strike, so I was not able to return his book *Stalin: A Political Biography* to him while he was alive.

During my little stay with him, I knew him to have so many ambitions. I also knew of his unconditional love for Stalin. When I looked at the book again recently, I saw the words: "If I ever meet you, Stalin," written by the Comrade at the back of the book, "I will give you a kiss."

As against what his appearance portrayed, he was just 26 years old when he was shot. Will he ever kiss Stalin?

On Federal Character and Nation Building

In the late 1960s and early 1970s, late African statesman, President Julius Kambarage Nyerere of Tanzania strongly advocated what he called "Nation building" for fragile post-Colonial African states. The fragility of these states soon became obvious and was exposed in several lights: Dr. Hastings Kamuzu Banda of Malawi declared himself President-for-Life; In Lesotho, Prime Minister Leabua Jonathan voided the 1970 election which he lost; King Sobhuza of Swaziland abolished the Parliament and the Constitution and reinstituted a monarchy. This was also the period when Zambia and Malawi were dissolving the Central African Federation, coinciding with the merger of Tanganyika and Zanzibar to form present-day Tanzania.

A large number of African States soon fell into the military dictatorship. In Nigeria, a series of events led to the collapse of democratic institutions in 1966 and subsequently, a bitter Civil War. There is the usual temptation to reduce the meaning (albeit incorrectly) of nation building to national integration, national development, political development, or the development of a national consciousness. The term includes all these, but to reduce it to any of them is to commit a "reductionist" fallacy.

Simply put, it can mean the systematic process of making a people, who hitherto are from different cultural, ethnic, religious, racial, or national backgrounds to feel a sense of belonging together within a nation.

Karl Deutch, in his book *Nation Building,* identifies five stages of achieving this "systematic process". First, the group exists as a tribe, with its distinct language and proud culture, and will resist any attempt to integrate it with other groups. The next stage is to incorporate them forcefully into other groups. The third stage is for them to minimally accept, often with the use of force or the threat of it, the new arrangement by cooperating minimally. At the fourth stage, their level of resistance is reduced to the minimum and their cooperation and obedience have risen astronomically, though they still keep their cultural identities intact. The fifth is when the group becomes almost indistinguishable from other groups within the state. This is when total assimilation is achieved. The last two stages will require minimal use of force.

As a post-colonial nation, the first three stages ended with colonialism. The last two have proven difficult in Nigeria, either due to deliberate colonial policy or shameless neglect by leaders at independence. At this point let us bring in a familiar concept, the Federal Character principle.

It was one of the post-Civil War integration efforts introduced by the Constitutional Drafting Committee (CDC) in 1978 and formed part of the 1979 Constitution. Despite it featuring in the 1999 Constitution under the Fundamental Objectives and Directive Principles of State Policy in Section 14(3) "...to promote national unity and also to command national loyalty, thereby ensuring that there shall be no predominance of persons from few states or a few ethnic or other groups in government or in any of its agencies", only a few people have bothered about it until recently when President Muhammadu Buhari made some "key appointments", leading to public outcry in some sections of the country.

We must be quick to admit that like many other provisions of the Constitution, the Federal Character principle was meant to correct some imbalances experienced in the past, but I believe it has created more problems than it has attempted to solve. Rather than promote national unity, it has disunited us more than we were before. In my understanding, the Federal Character principle assumes that in appointing a person from any part of Nigeria into a position, that person, first and foremost, must "carry his or her ethnic group along" in the scheme of things. Invariably, the appointee represents his "constituency", not necessarily his portfolio(s). It looks more like "just get someone to fill in that position, so long as it gives everyone the feeling of inclusion, not so much whether they are competent for the position or not."

I will buttress this point with the composition of the Federal Executive Council under President Goodluck Jonathan. Just in fulfilling section 14(3) of the 1999 Constitution, President Jonathan appointed Senator Musiliu Obanikoro as a Minister from Lagos. There is nothing wrong in that, but allocating the Defence Ministry to a person with dubious expertise in that portfolio only makes a mockery of the so-called Federal Character principle.

Were we really serious about fighting terrorism? There are those who argue that the Federal Character principle is to foster unity among Nigerians by giving every ethnic group a sense of belonging in the national scheme of things.

This appears as a fine argument on the surface. The "sense of belonging" is that "our son" will be in government and "our people will be carried along." If this is the "sense of belonging" they speak about with much approval, then I beg to disagree.

Rather than the Federal Character principle uniting Nigerians, it has done more division of the people in the country. It has, in the process of its operations, created a class of ethno-regional lords, local godfathers and their appendages whose sole purpose is to exploit national resources without any corresponding contribution. And that reminds me of how Jonathan's 16 years in political *offices* did not even translate to improved infrastructure (e.g. water supply) for his people in Otuoke or Obasanjo's 8 years as President which did not translate to good roads in Otta. Nation building cannot simply be reduced to national integration, on which the strength of federal character lies. In the United States of America, who cares if George Bush is President and his two sons – Jeb and George Walker – are Governors in Florida and New York respectively? Who could be bothered if John F. Kennedy is President and his younger brother, Robert is Attorney General? This is a country where one's track records and qualifications are far greater than just "where they come from" or their lineage.

This is what genuine nation building should look like. The talk of federal character reminds me of the time I was seeking admission into the university. Then, one had the greater advantage if one came from the so-called "Less Educationally Developed Areas", even when there were far more qualified candidates (comparing JAMB scores) than one, but who were denied admission on account of not coming from "Lesser Educationally Developed Areas". Do we still need to look further to know why we have so many half-baked graduates from our universities? That is what you get when you sacrifice merit for Federal Character.

Now, we must ask ourselves, "What are our leaders always thinking about when they are making decisions?" The answer to this question came recently when I thought of Professor Charles Soludo's speech at the 2012 ABTI-American University Convocation in Yola. He noted among other things that the Federal Executive Council (speaking from his experience as the former Governor of the Central Bank) is many a time like a mini-United Nations, where each member represents his state of origin or his region but not his portfolio.

When a country has systems that continually remind you of where you come from, you should ask whether it is building any nation at all. How then do we build a viable nation with an outdated ideal like the Federal Character principle? I came across the poem by a Ugandan poet, Henry Barlow, "Building the Nation", where two nation builders – a driver and a Ministry's Permanent Secretary – "built" the nation differently. Both suffered terrible stomach ulcers – one caused by hunger the other from over-feeding. If the Federal Character principle teaches us how to be "carried along" along ethnic lines, it's only a matter of time before some people begin to suffer from constipation or stomach ulcer from overfeeding.

Why State Governments Cannot Pay Salaries

In past months, about twenty of Nigeria's thirty-six states were struggling; financially unhealthy, and economically unviable states. From conservative estimates, they were not able to pay their staff salaries for at least three months. While some managed to pay at Christmas, others failed. There were accusations and counter-accusations between the Federal Government and the States over the dwindling monthly federal allocations; which most of these states depend on to pay salaries. The federal government was categorical to cite the fall in the global oil prices as affecting the reduction in federal allocations but the states were not convinced. The two positions, (depending on whether you support the federal government or you are justifying your state governor) notwithstanding went home empty-handed at the end of the month.

Before we can fully understand why the states were facing their financial challenges, we need to understand the balance upon which they exist or were created. All through the period of the National Conference, one of the most talked about issues was that of state creation.

By my estimation, there are four categories of those agitating for state creation. The first are those who want the additional state(s) in their region in order to be at par with other regions (or geo-political zones) in the country. Their region has been marginalized, so they say.

The second group, are those who just want to maintain ethnic hegemony or supremacy by having the highest number of states in the country.

Coming after the first two, are those who have apparently fallen out of favour in the political balance in their present states; so they feel marginalised, hence the call for a state of their own.

The fourth group has no identifiable positions, other than just wanting states; so, they either fit into the first three groups or just keep quiet hoping for luck to shine on them.

Common to all those agitating for more states is their silence on funding for the new states. This does not seem to matter to them because one thing they are sure of getting is monthly federal allocation. It is on federal allocations that more than 20 of the present 36 states survive. Remove the monthly federal allocations, many states will either collapse or just struggle to survive as the recent fall in allocations have shown. It is these allocations that are also increasing the agitations for state creation. You don't have to do anything to get it; it's your right as far as you are a state!

At this point let us bring in Mr. Ben Murray-Bruce, the entertainment guru; Silverbird Group owner and a Senator. He was in the news for making some hard points. I admire this man a lot because he tries to create a niche for himself. He made a point to the effect that as a result of the governors' inability to pay their workers, they themselves should not be paid, until their workers were paid. Fine point! He said all allowances to the governors must be cut. Another fantastic point if you ask me. But he missed the point altogether when he said that state governments should not blame the federal government for their inability to pay their workers. He cited the fact that if he could not pay his staff at Silverbird it would be irresponsible of him to blame his father. This is where I part ways with the entertainer.

Mr Ben perhaps forgot that at Silverbird, he runs, controls, and, in fact, owns the resources the company boasts of. If his father ever has any input, it is purely fatherly advice. He probably does not have, or will not want to have a father like Nigerian federal government who only comes once in a while and collects all the revenue of the company, and in turn, gives a stipend (13 per cent) on which he is to run the company for the month or year. This is the exact relationship between the federal and state government under the present deficient federal structure today!

We have a federal government which collects all royalties and taxes. It is responsible for all the natural resources that the states are supposed to have. Within this present arrangement, it is only logical for states to hold the federal government to account for their inability to meet their financial obligations. If we are to adopt Ben's business model; which is supposed to be the ideal situation, it means we have to amend the constitution to include resource control and abolish the primitive monthly federal allocation, which at best guarantees laziness, constipation, opportunism, and corruption. This is where we need people like Ben Bruce to help. As Senator, he owes us a duty to sponsor a bill to amend the 1999 Constitution to include resource control.

As long as we have economically and politically unviable states, we will continue to have states that cannot pay their salaries without depending on federal allocation. When we have states that are economically viable with full resource control, only paying royalties to the federal government, then states that cannot pay royalties will naturally merge with other states to become a viable one.

Having 36 weak states does not and cannot do any nation much good when we may as well have 15 politically and economically efficient states.

PART 2

2015 ELECTION/POLITICKING

Can Buhari Defeat Jonathan?

Before the 2015 presidential election, most Jonathan-supporters premised their support on one singular factor – incumbency. I had the opportunity to ask some of them if they knew that the *Titanic* was once believed to be unsinkable. I still asked them if they knew that no one ever imagined it succumbing to *on-the-sea* tragedy before disaster struck.

The deeply moving film, *Titanic* (I had seen the movie once but in a long time) shows how fatal some dangerous, arrogant presumptions can be. Like the *Titanic*, many folks, particularly, President Jonathan's supporters maintained that he could not be defeated. Their stance was premised majorly on the fact, not because he had performed excellently, but that he belonged to a party which was "too big to sink." They perhaps forgot how deep the ocean is. One good thing about presumptions (like this one) is that it blinds just as it binds. There were times in Africa when it was unthinkable to see incumbents lose elections hence this anachronistic assumption.

Perhaps these unscientific thoughts came into our consciousness because of some events in African history: Leabua Jonathan, Prime Minister of Lesotho voided the 1970 election he and his Party lost; Dr. Hastings Kamusu Banda declared himself President for Life in Malawi; Robert Mugabe of Zimbabwe who is now in his 90s is still waxing strong in power and others.

Truly this ship is unsinkable! All these were in the 20th century. The 21st century changed all those clichés, stereotypes, and puerile assumptions. We cite at least four instances of decline in the so-called incumbency factor. First, in Ivory Coast, Alassane Quattara defeated President Laurent Gbagbo (who assumed office in 2000) in 2011. Gbagbo unaware that the game was up, deployed state institutions all to avert the inevitable, but before he knew what was happening it was all over. Quattara was sworn-in in 2012 and heaven did not fall.

Second, President Abdoulaye Wade of Senegal was another man who did his best to avoid the inevitable. Incumbency could not save the 76-year old. Having been in power for about twelve years, himself defeating Abou Diouf (who assumed power in 1981) he lost to his arch rival, Machy Sall. Notice that Mr Sall had been Wade's opponent since 2000. Sall won and guess what, heaven did not fall! Bwezani Banda of Zambia, in fact, has a lot in common with President Jonathan. He was the unusual choice of late President Levy Mwanawasa for Vice President. When his boss died of stroke in 2009 he immediately assumed office as President. In 2011, the inevitable happened when faced with Michael Sata in the Presidential election. Mr. Sata won, and again, heaven did not fall. Mrs

Joyce Banda is a gender activist in Malawi. In the teeth of opposition from masculine chauvinists, President Bingn wa Mutharika appointed her Vice President in 2009. Following the death of her boss, she assumed office as President in 2012.

She is the first ever female Vice President and President in a male-dominated Malawi. She was defeated by Arthur Mutharika, the brother of late President early 2014. Again heaven did not fall!

Broken Jinx

Back in Nigeria, there was a time when it was almost impossible for incumbents to lose. The case of the Western region election in 1965 comes to mind. The Nigerian National Democratic Party (NNDP) Samuel Ladoke Akintola's government heavily relied on the incumbency factor to retain power in the election it lost.

In the Nigerian Second Republic, you were almost an endangered species if you belonged to any party apart from the National Party of Nigeria, NPN, the then ruling party.

In the Fourth Republic, you were almost home and dry as a governor in an election if you belonged to the Peoples' Democratic Party (PDP). PDP governors lost elections as incumbents; heaven has not fallen and will not fall!

Still on the movie, *Titanic*, I came across some strange observations: First, everyone in the *Titanic*, except for the architect, didn't imagine the ship could sink. Second, its builders made provisions for few lifeboats (emergency safety routes) because they did not believe it could face such disaster. Armed with all assurances, everyone including the captain went to sleep. Not until the ship hit the iceberg that the aura of invincibility disappeared and all became as clear as daylight.

Again, no one in the ruling party believed that the giant umbrella would be thoroughly broken in the 2015 elections, except the architect of the party. Its members had been lulled or hypnotized with a great dose of sleeping elixir. Well, until the party hit the iceberg then pandemonium started for an unprepared emergency. The ship's captain President Jonathan, himself boasted that he could not be defeated. The truth is that, except he was speaking for just self-encouragement, he knew the jinx of incumbency in Nigeria, which had been passed on to him by past administrations, in unwritten election codes, would fall from his hands. And not only did the jinx fall, it broke, it was shattered.

The real architects of the party (many of whom have left the party) knew that the party could, in fact, suffer a shameful defeat in an election. Just like the *Titanic*'s architect said (after hitting the iceberg): "She can sink; it is a mathematical possibility. *Titanic* will sink in two hours," President Jonathan knew of his imminent defeat, only that his advisers would not just let go easily! I don't need to relate how the award-winning movie ended because it was tragic. What I can say is that President Jonathan and his foot soldiers, like the captain in the movie and others on board, were consumed by the wreck. No one could save the ship as it sank, never to be seen again. There were only a handful of survivors, but only one could live to tell the story out of "twenty thousand souls" on board.

This ship sank. Much ado about the factor of incumbency.

The Young Party's Challenge

In his article, *NIGERIAN NATION AGAINST BUHARI*, Professor Wole Soyinka wrote "History matters. Records are not kept simply to assist weakness of memory, but to guide the future." There appear to be major similarities between the build-up to the March 28, 2015, elections and the June 12, 1993, elections. I say this because the signs as we approach the elections are ominous if you ask me. At least going by some landmark event in our history, one has a reason to worry. On the 16th of June, 1993 a group known as the Association for Better Nigeria (ABN) then led by Arthur Nzeribe approached the courts to stop Professor Humphrey Nwosu then National Electoral Commission (NEC) Chairman from further announcing the Presidential election results. While the elections were nullified, the Social Democratic Party (SDP) candidate, Chief MKO Abiola was already in the clear lead against his National Republican Convention (NRC) counterpart, Alhaji Bashir Tofa.

This is against the backdrop of the fact that the election was originally scheduled for 1989, but was shifted at least once leaving the military government in a difficult position and a big loophole for dubious groups to explore for political reasons. The 1993 situation unfolded against the 2015 presidential election. The election was moved from its original date of February 14 to March 28 with the Independent National Electoral Commission (INEC) citing security reasons justification for its action. This may equally have put INEC in a more difficult situation if the election led to a run-off thus prompting into major constitutional crises.

The strangest sign confirming my worst fear came then. A group, the Young Democratic Party got registered as a political party via a court injunction. This group had insisted on its right to participate in the March 28 elections. It also told INEC to put the elections on hold as it would have to hold its convention on the March 26 to select its own candidates and therefore allow it to campaign for votes.

In that case, the group had threatened to go to court if its prayers were not heard, thereby, putting the elections in jeopardy. My take on this young party's case is simple.

First, the fact that the party newly got registered did not give it the right to dictate to INEC on how to alter its own timetable. It is just like a candidate who just registered for an external examination, demanding the examination body to give him time to get prepared at par with the other candidates. I am sure no responsible examination body would grant this request even though it sounds noble.

Second, the election timetable cannot be altered at the last minute to suit a party or an unprepared candidate. This is only done in Mars where INEC will have to wait for all newly registered parties, who will only boast of only a handful of votes, to be prepared. Doing this will be like waiting for all candidates to say they are prepared before the exam body can say they want to administer the questions. To me whichever judge gave the injunction to register a new party at that time should have been properly checked.

Prior to the election, there were more than 15 cases in court praying for disqualification of the two main presidential candidates. Equally, INEC was yet to fully distribute the Permanent Voter Cards (PVCs) to all eligible voters. Also, the two main political parties were yet to agree on whether or not the Electronic Card Readers should be used for the election, though INEC had stated its readiness for such.

Also, at least ten cases filed by President Jonathan's supporters were in court to disqualify General Muhammadu Buhari, the All Progressive Congress(APC) presidential candidate. Two were struck out while proceedings were adjourned for others till after the elections.

My instincts tell me that some people are out to stage a judicial coup in even that the General wins. A lot of people tend to forget that the notorious Association for Better Nigeria (ABN) took advantage of loopholes like these to carry out their notorious objectives.

All that came after then was that the electoral body NEC declared the election results. The rest they say is history! For me, all these potential landmines can portend real danger to our democracy if not well checked.

This is exactly why I wrote earlier that the signs were not so good. I can only pray that we do not have to repeat the 1993 election disaster again, which almost consumed us as a nation. The election has come and gone; I pray for profound peace in Nigeria.

One thing was sure, whichever way the March 28 Presidential election went, Nigeria would never remain the same again. When Soyinka wrote that history was not just there to assist memory weakness, the Nobel Laureate knew exactly what he was talking about.

Another Look at APC's Strategy

The result of the Nigerian 2015 presidential election shows how elections are won and lost on the altar of strategies. The opposition All Progressives Congress (APC) did the impossible by unseating the ruling Peoples' Democratic Party in the March 28 Presidential elections effectively ending its 16-year dominance in the Nigerian political space. President Goodluck Jonathan and his party, the PDP, as far as some of us are concerned lost the election due to his own undoing – underestimating the APC's strategies. The APC simply discovered a new way of defeating its arch-rival with the PDP seriously suffering from constipation. The following proves the difference between the two parties:

Both parties used propaganda in the build-up to the March 28 election; it is very difficult not to! The only worrisome aspect is its tactless use by the PDP. Instead of promoting their own candidate, Goodluck Jonathan, they ended up promoting the APC candidate, General Muhammadu Buhari. They sponsored on several Television stations, personal attacks on the General, many of which largely went over the bar. They even behaved like the US Republicans, who, during President Franklin D. Roosevelt's administration, included the President's dog, Fala, in their uncontrolled attacks. There were several mentions of the General's academic qualification, his health status, and they even went so puerile to include his daughter who died of Sickle Cell anemia in their propaganda effort.

To cap it up one of the television stations airing the PDP propaganda, African Independent Television (AIT) conducted an online poll, which put Buhari clearly on the lead with 76 per cent while President Jonathan was trailing behind with about 20 per cent. Needless to say, that the poll was canceled abruptly, the message was clear – the attacks were not working!

Propaganda is not itself bad if it serves the exact purpose for which it was used. The Nazis were taught this bitter lesson during the World War II with the British superior propaganda machinery. So, if the PDP lost due to propaganda, then the APC must have had a more effective propaganda machine! Grounds covered in 2011, President Jonathan rode to power purely on the basis of strong positive public perception, winning in four of Nigeria's six geo-political zones.

The fact that President Jonathan, from South-South zone, contested against three leading Northern Presidential candidates largely divided Northern votes which all ran in his favour while he cruised home with southern votes including the South West. All that changed in 2015. The Boko Haram insurgency in the North East made that region a "No Entry" point of President Jonathan, though he won in Taraba, a Christian-dominated state, having little to do with the Boko Haram fiasco.

In the North Central where President Jonathan won in every single state, except for Niger which jumped ship, General Buhari won four out of six states: Niger, Kwara, Kogi, and Benue, leaving President Jonathan with slim victories in two: Plateau, and Nassarawa and the FCT, Abuja (a surprising victory?).

The North West, the most populous in the country is considered General Buhari's "home", so President Jonathan was expected to sweat it out seriously in this region.

Even the most optimistic of Jonathan's men would not have expected a miracle for the president in this region. It is doubtful if he even got the constitutionally required 25 percent in this region.

The South West region, which voted massively for President Jonathan in 2011, provided an unclear picture for the president's strategists. Some are of the opinion that President Jonathan won the 2011 election thanks to bulk votes he got from the Yorubas. I didn't share this view until recently.

The former president, Goodluck Jonathan, got a total of 22.5 million national votes. If we remove 8.5 million Yoruba votes from his votes he is then so close to his next contender, who scored 12.5 million votes. In the worst case scenario, the election would have ended in a run-off which its outcome is largely unpredictable. The president's loss in this region, except in Ekiti State, is largely his undoing. He did not return the favour of the region's votes throughout his tenure. Needless to say the APC appointed Professor Yemi Osinbajo from the region as its Vice Presidential candidate. This proved to be where the party hit the jackpot, winning five out of six states in the region. The Western influence there are strong indications of the United States and the United kingdom's influence on the outcome of the March 28, 2015, election.

Though this is largely difficult to prove, there are several clues to point out this fact. First, the APC's strongest point in the campaign was based on the Boko Haram insurgency. The situation largely portrayed Jonathan's administration as irresponsible, "clueless", and ineffective. To compound the problems, the Barak Obama administration refused to supply arms to the Federal Government in its fight against the terrorists.

Second, is the fall in the oil prices with the Americans refusing to purchase Nigerian oil. This led the federal government to implement "austerity measures" in the face of the "US-induced oil crises".

The opposition cleverly keyed into this slump again to portray the government as reckless.

Third, the role of the American public relations' firm, AKPD Media and Messages is another pointer to the "Obama hand" in the outcome of the election. The firm is owned by David Axelrod, Obama's confidant. Though the firm has denied it served as a media consultant to the opposition when it said it broke initial agreement it had with the APC in March, 2014, there is clear evidence to show that the firm, in fact, did the work for the APC behind the scenes.

Fourth, since he started contesting in 2003, at no time has General Buhari been granted an international audience. In fact, there were insinuations in some quarters that he is a wanted man in London because of his alleged role as Nigerian Head of State, in the attempted kidnap of ex-Minister of Transport under President Shehu Shagari, Mallam Umaru Dikko, on the streets of London in 1984, leading to strong diplomatic row between both countries. His invitation and subsequent acceptance to deliver a lecture at the influential Royal Institute for International Affairs, also known as Chatham House, London, effectively ended all insinuations. Before then, he was largely viewed as a dictator with poor human rights record and a religious bigot in the West.

The question then is: what has changed? If President Jonathan and the PDP take a closer look at their outing in the Presidential campaign they will discover that though they misfired on several occasions, they lost the battle to the fact that they largely underestimated the more vibrant, innovative, and coherent APC election strategy.

Intellectual Dwarfs and Buhari's "Illiteracy"

It is an open secret that President Jonathan has made Nigeria a big comedy movie. One can write a Nobel Prize-winning comedy film from Nigeria's experience with Jonathan's government. When one looks at characters like Doyin Okupe, Reuben Abati, Labaran Maku, Patience Jonathan and the likes, one does not need to be told that this film is a farce with characters like Aki and Pawpaw in a movie. We can pardon the chief comedian, President Jonathan for doing his best in differentiating between stealing and corruption. Let us even still spare career Jonathanians for doing their very best to justify their boss' incorrigible error. We need to pardon Doyin Okupe for his ridiculously poor knowledge of history and for trying to infect us with his abysmal ignorance in defending his principal. We equally must take it as clownish the careless statement from Reuben Abati when he did his very best to put word into General Buhari's mouth a statement another person made. This man carelessly, and erroneously, wrote in his piece that the General said he will make the country ungovernable if President Jonathan won the 2011 election.

In parenthesis, it was a PDP member, Alhaji Lawal Keita, who made that statement, yet President Jonathan was looking for who was making the country ungovernable for him. Jonathanians must be busy, even if there was nothing to do. But can we pardon a Professor who called Buhari a "semi-illiterate"?

In Wole Soyinka's *A Play of Giants*, Kongi satirically presented Kamini, a veiled reference to Idi Amin Dada of Uganda and his colleagues as power mad-men with no sophistry in politics, economy, or diplomacy. He shows how gullible and ridiculously laughable these characters are in power. They have sympathy from the academia too. They have a second-rate academic from an unnamed university, Professor Batey and an attention-seeking journalist from an obscure foreign media, Gudrun. You now see why I earlier said Nigeria is a big comedy movie. But unlike Kongi who sees these people as giants, in my own play they are DWARFS, in fact, intellectual dwarfs. I have called these ones, dwarfs, because dwarfs assume they are of "standard" height; hence, if you are of "normal" height taller than they are, it becomes abnormal. You are too tall for them hence must be cut down. Clearly, this was the position of Jonathanians and the PDP. Exhausted of their quotidian propaganda of name-calling: *Buhari is this, Buhari is that*, there was nothing more to say that Nigerians hadn't heard about the General.

One even spoke of the General's physical attributes: he is ugly. Having nothing more to say, the secretary of the party, one naughty professor, by name Wale Oladipo the then PDP national secretary called Buhari a semi-illiterate. We can spare Okupe as a mere barking dog, with very little intelligence. No qualms.

In parenthesis, he told the whole world early 2013at the formation of APC to call him a bastard if the party did not collapse by 2014. A few days to the end of 2014, the party had not only conducted its conventions, it had also waxed stronger.

Can somebody shout BASTARD (this should have been Okupe's new year greeting. He is the one who said he should be called a bastard, not me).

I will also not allow that of the naughty professor to pass. First, let us look at the General's educational background and know who is illiterate. Buhari graduated from the UK's Royal Military Academy, Aldershot. He proceeded to India's elite Defence College. As a Colonel, he was at the Army War College, Carlise, USA (1979-80) where he earned his badge as a Brigadier-General. For those who do not know, the respected American war hero, Collin Powel also attended that College in 1976. Buhari's classmates include US finest military minds: General Thomas P. Carney, General Bill Matz, General David E.K. Cooper and the likes all of whom are still alive to testify to Buhari's astuteness and dexterity in strategy. In fact, having attended that College, one receives a Master's Degree in Strategy. Well, I know very little about President Jonathan's educational background, apart from the fact that he attended the University of Port Harcourt. But to say someone who attended such prestigious institutions is a "semi-illiterate" is the peak of ignorance known to human civilization.

Since the naughty professor raised the issue, we must analyze it carefully. Well, I bothered myself to check through reputable international journals to check if I could stumble on Oladipo's publication to his credit, I am afraid I couldn't find any except the "Professor" will make one available. I wish to ask our "professor" this question: how many US Presidents bagged PhDs? If he can find a handful, definitely the greatest among them: George Washington, Abraham Lincoln, and Franklin Roosevelt none has a PhD. Only fools and ignoramuses will argue that these leaders are "semi-illiterates". I will also like our naughty professor to produce a copy of ANY publication credited to Franklin Roosevelt. This is my direct   challenge   to   him.
The problem with career Jonathanians is that like Boxer (in George Orwell's *Animal Farm*) Napoleon (their boss) can do no wrong. Some of them see him as even holier than the Pope. Their boss is just as saintly as Jesus (definitely not the Jesus of Nazareth, maybe Jesus of Oyingbo!)

Some will reign curses, even place spells on anyone who dares criticize the "anointed"; they'd prefer that heaven rather falls than their boss not win the election: their only means of survival, their benefactor, their provider, their hope, their daily bread all gone.

Some of the PDP's attack on Buhari could at best be explained as mental fatigue. I argued elsewhere that PDP had run out of ideas, hence either resulting to old crude ways as the case of the break-in into APC's Office in Lagos showed or they had nothing more to say, so frustration set in as it is evident in personal attacks as against policy.

My take is that Nigerians were tired of the *Buhari-is-this, Buhari-is-that* strategy that the PDP had deployed over the years in their bid to divert attentions from the main issue. They could have thought of something more responsible as that tactic became very boring and no longer sold. They could have been creative maybe. Like Professor Batey in Kongi's play, this naughty professor would later sink with his boss with no one to help him in the end. Intellectual dwarfs.

APC: The Question of Strategies

Since its formation in 2013, the All Progressives' Congress (APC) has proven many if not all its cynics wrong by forming the first-ever successful merger of major opposition parties in the annals of the Nigerian political history. Some of its cynics were so confident of its collapse that one of them even asked to be called a bastard if the party did not collapse before the end of 2014! I happen to be one of those who seriously doubted the possibility of the Action Congress of Nigeria (ACN), All Nigeria People's Party (ANPP), Congress for Progressive Change (CPC) merger in Nigeria because of the over-ambitious, selfish, unfocused and undisciplined nature of Nigerian politicians.

Many Nigerians, like me, have been made to hold this belief because of some events in Nigerian political history. In the Second Republic, opposition parties made up of the Unity Party of Nigeria (UPN), Nigeria Peoples Party (NPP), Great Nigeria Peoples Party (GNPP), and Peoples Redemption Party (PRP) made a serious attempt at a merger known as the Progressive Parties Alliance (PPA), which would have presented a single Presidential Candidate against the ruling National Party of Nigeria (NPN) in the 1983 elections. I need not say that the "association of hyenas" (as the then President Shehu Shagari had described them) failed to see the light of the day and what followed is now history.

Before its subsequent registration by the Independent National Electoral Commission (INEC), the People's Democratic Party (PDP) was alleged to have moved to stop the new party. Suddenly there were three different "APCs" seeking registration all in order to frustrate the efforts of the new party.

So when the Party was subsequently registered, it wasn't a surprise it took a more militant stance against the PDP which it considered its primary adversary. The APC then adopted the unconventional, strange, and offensive system of attack in tackling its opponent. No responsible strategist can fault this strategy. It was the only strategy that could defeat an opponent like the PDP. It is instructive to note that after it was formed, the APC did not hide its main and perhaps only intention: to win the 2015 Presidential Elections. This was perhaps why General Muhammadu Buhari(RTD), an APC Presidential candidate, warned the PDP to expect a very tough duel in the 2015election. In its bid to actualize its ambitions, the party's tactics were clear:

(1) To as much as possible unsettle the PDP

(2) Create major cracks, crises and divisions within the PDP with the view to disuniting it for the 2015 election

(3) To protect APC's geo-political (South West) interests thereby positioning it for the next election.

To achieve these strategic objectives, the Party did all within its powers to get under the PDP's skin, thereby putting it in a defensive and desperate position before 2015. The APC leaders were seen going after key PDP Governors, Senators, Ministers, even National Officials with the view to getting them into the APC's fold. Also, the traditional base of the APC must be protected and maintained. The Party tried as much as possible to distract the

PDP away from the South West, the Party's *home* in addition to its seeming cult-like following in the North.

These seemed to yield positive results for the Party as it took effective control of staggering 14 States of the Federation as against PDP's 20. This was an incredible start for a new party! The PDP equally responded well.

This explains why it launched a counter-attack on the APC's charges. First, the PDP welcomed with open arms all APC's decampees; even President Jonathan himself personally received the "new" members.

This explains the Presidential visit to the private residence of Alhaji Atiku Abubakar, former Nigerian Vice President and APC chieftain to lure him to the PDP.

Second, the PDP applauded the victory of other parties so long as they are not the APC or its allies as it did in Ondo and Anambra States during Gubernatorial elections which the Labour Party (LP) and All Progressives' Grand Alliance (APGA) candidates respectively emerged victoriously.

Third, the PDP deployed its "best hands" in the South West to ensure it won the region at all cost.

This was demonstrated with the elections in Ekiti and Osun States where the PDP deployed Mr. Ayo Fayose and Senator Iyiola Omisore respectively for July and August 2014 gubernatorial elections. The President's insistence on appointing Senator Musiliu Obanikoro as Minister is suspicious in this regard. All these buttress the fact that the PDP was responding equally. It would, therefore, be crooked thinking if the APC leaders assumed that things had changed in PDP's thinking since Olusegun Obasanjo's Presidency.

But as it is said, "It is good if you win, but if you lose then you have yourself to blame." The Media was never in want of speculations about APC's intentions, even before its formation.

We are in a period when the media is hardly neutral on the politics of the country (this is almost the case with the First Republic). Most media outlets are owned either wholly or partly by politicians or their cronies. It is based on this understanding that the APC adopted a more direct, aggressive and often confrontational approach to attacking its chief opponent. Just as it sought for votes on the electoral fronts, it did not neglect the media at all.

About half of APC's battles were won on public perception of its policies and programs through the media. This was what led to the reported million-dollar contract with AKPD, an American Public Relations firm, to help the APC conduct research and handle sensitive public relations issues all for the 2015elections. Though this speculated agreement led to serious verbal "war" between the National Publicity Secretary of the Party, Alhaji Lai Muhammed, and members of the elitist Nigeria Institute of Public Relations (NIPR) of which Muhammed is a Fellow.

If it is true that such agreement existed, then it is a good response to the alleged plot by supporters of President Jonathan to allocate billions of dollars to foreign propaganda for 2015 elections. The media appeared to be enjoying large largesse from full-page advertorials from both APC and PDP in the election times.

There were several full-page adverts accusing the PDP and its officials in the papers all bearing the APC's name and logos. The PDP effectively employed other groups to do its propaganda work. APC Federal Government come 2015? Though many were in doubt of this possibility, I thought it was very possible. I didn't believe the PDP was indomitable. I was proved right.

To achieve this, the APC leaders had to do more. First, the fact that APC conducted a hitch-free presidential primary, devoid of rancor and ill-feelings that were acceptable not only to the rank-and-file but also non-members of the party attest to its astuteness in strategy. This is perhaps the most important landmark the party created to convince Nigerians of their readiness to occupy the Aso Rock Villa in 2015 which it would take only a united party to achieve.

The said primary produced General Muhammadu Buhari (Rtd). Considering the fact that the 14 States the party controlled included States in different geo-political zones of the country: Kano and Sokoto (North West), Kwara and Nassarawa (North Central), Bornu and Yobe (North East), Lagos and Oyo (South West), Rivers and Edo (South-South) and Imo (South East), if the Party could hold doggedly its own in these states come what may, this could provide the turning point in 2015 for the party.

The cult-like following of Buhari in the North West and the North East which themselves account for close to 50 per cent of registered voters was just too obvious to ignore! Also, considering the fact that of all the geo-political zones the party could only boast of one solitary state in the South-East, this should be a source of worry to APC's strategists.

I really query APC's strategist in this area for not doing much in the South East though it boasts of personalities like: *Owelle* Rochas Okorocha, Senator Chris Ngige, Mr Osita Okechuckwu, Dr Ogbonnaya Onu, Senator Annie Okonkwo and Chief Mbadinuju. The party must provide answers to South East challenge. All hopes for the party to make the inroad into the zone proved abortive with the socio-political group representing the region, Ohaneze Ndigbo, rejecting General Buhari's request to meet with the Eastern leaders. The party could let go just because it looked impossible to penetrate. The state they controlled, Imo, could provide the vital key they needed to unlock the South East, after all, why is it called "Eastern Heartland"? Even if the Party would not win other states in the region it must do everything within its powers to reduce PDP's margin and comfort in that zone. It must equally be ready to stand firmly on its grounds in its "safe" areas in the South East, giving out little or nothing to the PDP. If it could at least secure the constitutional 25 percent in these states, then the party's strategists could enjoy their dinner after the March 28, 2015, election.

The Party must also undergo serious cleansing, like the palm tree or the eagle, before it went to the polls. To do this, it must identify all moles deliberately planted within its fold. After this, it must reshape those it could to its taste and route out those with irredeemable features with obloquy and then confidently approach 2015.

The party's strategists to me did marvellously during the campaigns far better than its main rival, the People's Democratic Party (PDP). As far as I am concerned the PDP strategy (before the postponement of the February 14 election) was a disaster. As a matter of recommendation, there was still more to be done.

Elections are won and lost on the altar of strategy. It was probably for this reason that a US Political consultant Joseph Napolitan writes "Strategy is the single most important factor in a political campaign. This is the most important lesson I have learned... The right strategy can survive a mediocre campaign, but even a brilliant campaign is likely to fail if the strategy is wrong."

If the party could keep it tight at the critical areas, like the South-South (and the North Central), where it got a major boost with the entrance of two former Governors of Akwa Ibom State (an important state in the South-South), Obong Victor Attah and Don Ettiebet, into the party's fold, this would be a major point if the party could take all its chances in the area.

The President Replies Tinubu

To be a presidential spokesman can be so challenging. The job involves a whole lot of complexities and risks. It may require you to offend those you once loved, including you calling your mother a dog. It may equally require you to, like Squealer in George Orwell's *Animal Farm,* call black white (as some have done). If you refuse, there are thousands of people who are ready to take your position even for lesser pay, in a country were for less than 5000 positions there are over 700,000 applications. In this job, your boss is your God who is perfect and can do no wrong! This is the situation Dr. Doyin Okupe, the Senior Special Assistant to the President on Public Affairs found himself. I really empathize with him.

It was reported in the print media (November 7th, 2014) well-captioned: NO PRESIDENT RESIGNS DURING WAR. This is the presidency's official reply to Bola Tinubu who earlier called on President Jonathan to resign in the face of poor performance. I understand the fact that the spokesman must do his job, but condescending to obvious illogicality, falsity, and embarrassing fallacies is what is not acceptable. The proposition NO PRESIDENT RESIGNS DURING WAR is a universal negative statement which denies the class of the predicate term (resigns during a war) to the subject (Presidents). This proposition is true if and only if we cannot find any subject (president) who resigns during a war or in crises situations, otherwise is false and invalid.

I want the spokesman to pay attention to the following historical facts starting with the most recent:

1. The President of Burkina Faso, Blaise Compaore, recently resigned in the face of public opposition to his 27-year regime and worsening politico-economic situations in that country.
2. Ahmed Ben Ali, President of Tunisia, resigned in the face of protests about worsening political and economic situations in the country in 2012.
3. Hosni Mubarak, former Egyptian President, resigned during the wave of protests against his over three-decade regime and worsening economic situation in his country in 2012. These spread to many Arab countries (Yemen and Syria) in what is known as the "Arab Spring."
4. Argentine President, Fernando de la Rua, resigned in 2001 over worsening economic and political situation accompanied by high inflation and unemployment rates, resulting in civil and political unrests in the country.
5. US President, Richard Nixon, resigned in 1974 over the infamous "Watergate" scandal involving the White House and the gruesome killing of students of Kent State University by the notorious poorly trained Ohio National Guard for demonstrations opposing the continuation of the costly Vietnam War.
6. Arthur Neville Chamberlain, British Prime Minister, in the thick of the World War II, after the Germans forced British troops to a bitter retreat in Norway; hence declining public confidence in his leadership, announced his decision to throw in the towel on May 9, 1940.

For constraints of time and space, I do not want to bore you with more facts of leaders who have resigned in situations not as critical as the Nigerian case. Even if the President's spokesman is not aware or moved by these, the case of US President, Lyndon B. Johnson (1963-1968) appears instructive. Like President Jonathan, his path to power followed a chronological pattern. He was a high school debating teacher; later served as secretary to Congressman Richard Kleberg. President Roosevelt appointed him Texas director, National Youth Administration; later he contested and won the vacant Texas Tenth Congressional District election into the Texas Senate. John F. Kennedy appointed him Vice President as a result of his support for the Civil Right bill while in Texas senate. With JFK's gruesome murder in 1963, he assumed the presidency. Like GEJ he completed his boss's term, contested and won his first term in 1964.

When the situation got out of hand during the Vietnam War, he withdrew his candidature for the 1968 election, unlike GEJ.

I wonder if GEJ's men ever gave him such hard historical facts. My unpaid advice to him at that point would have been that he looked for his enemies not in Tinubu, Buhari or the APC, but among the sycophants gnawing his administration. These people publicly admired his torn outfits and criticized his tastes behind his back. He should have won the war from within before attempting to do so without.

The spokesmen should have known the difference between defending a job and doing a job. Only a thin line separates the two. The inability to make this important distinction is what leads to fallacies, outright falsehoods and blatant lies as the case above. This was the reason Stalin's and Hitler's closest advisers were not spared the task of paying the ultimate price.

PART 3
BUHARI AND THE MEDIA

On Buhari's "Ban" on the Media

The media came under scrutiny. There was a "ban" on the African Independent Television (AIT), a private television station, from covering the activities of Nigerian President-elect General Muhammadu Buhari. When this was made public, our "experts" began analyzing the issue.

Our question in this matter is: What is new(s) in Buhari's action. Did Buhari ban AIT? Did he say they should not operate anymore? Did he withdraw their license? To all these questions the answer is NO. Buhari as a private citizen, being just a president- elect, he had the right to his privacy as a private citizen at least until May 29, 2015. Even if Buhari was THE substantive president, I dare ask, "What is wrong in such action?" To me, it is like me organizing a party and I told you in specific terms that you are not invited; courtesy demands that an unwanted guest stays back rather than suffer the embarrassment of gate-crashing to the event.

This was AIT's case. I still dare to ask, did Buhari break any written law? I don't know any law that is broken by "do not cover my event" order. Freedom of the press must be interpreted in the right context. A lot of people tend to forget that President Barrack Obama "banned" at least two media stations from the White House during his administration.

The pro-Republican *Fox News* and *Boston Herald* had their fair share of the White House blacklisting for their unprofessional reportage of political news. Many of those condemning Buhari did not fault Obama. This is specifically where AIT fit in. The media station's role during the election can be classified as ignoble. They were more of candidates in the election than their principal. They sponsored hate campaigns against General Buhari including broad day lies. They even went as far as insulting Buhari's family accusing him of being responsible for the death of his wife and his first daughter, Zulai, who died of sickle cell anemia about two years earlier.

After doing all these, the media station's owners didn't even bother to apologise for their below morally par role during the presidential campaign. Some opined, quite intelligently, that the General was on a mission of vengeance. They argued that he was out to take his pound of flesh on those who campaigned against him during the election. I fully agree that a leader must be in a reconciliatory mood. But let us look at it this way. Dr. Reuben Abati, President Goodluck Jonathan's Media assistant, has since apologized to the General for his abusive remarks on him during the election. The General is on record to have forgiven him even for his lousy statement in his article FOR THE ATTENTION OF GENERAL BUHARI published in *The Guardian* in 2011, where he accused him of threatening to make Nigeria ungovernable for President Jonathan. Buhari sued Abati for libel after which President Jonathan prevailed on the General to settle the matter out of court in order not to embarrass the administration.

On 12 June 12, 2012 *The Guardian* and Reuben Abati issued a public apology to the General. No one has heard any bitterness whatsoever from the General on the matter ever since. We need to also add that one of those who personally insulted Buhari during the campaign is the former Minister of Agriculture, Mr. Akinwunmi Adesina. It is on record today that Buhari forgot about all pre-election issues and became his chief campaigner for the African

Development Bank (AfDB) presidency. What more can someone ask for? The two characters above showed remorse and were, therefore, told to go and sin no more. Did AIT ever show remorse or even apologise to the General for insulting his family?

With impunity, AIT flaunted all known rules in the books, instigating hate campaigns and speeches against him. The station stopped at nothing to discredit the General. For limited economic and political gains, professionalism, ethics, and national security were sold by the station at giveaway prices yet the regulation body, the Nigerian Broadcasting Corporation (NBC) looked the other way. He who comes equity, remember, must come with clean hands. AIT did all these and they moved on as though nothing had happened. If this is what some of us call democracy, then it must be democracy-made-in-Nigeria. Apart from this, I know not what to call it!

For me since Obama broke no law in banning some media stations from the White House; since those criticizing Buhari have found nothing wrong in President Jonathan ordering the interception of newspapers for their reportage of the military's fight against Boko Haram; if all these broke no written law, Buhari's action of "banning" AIT from his personal activities is within acceptable limits.

For those who cried wolf on AIT's ban, calling the action draconian, I ask where they were when AIT displayed broad day madness.

Like the Yorubas say, *when the fly was disturbing the madman's wound, no one was concerned, but when the mad man began disturbing the fly, everyone became more concerned!* When the station was busy demonstrating its madness, no one called them to order; in fact, many applauded it. Now with just a "don't-cover-my-activities" order, they say that is draconian!

If I were one of General Buhari's media aides, I would have generally ignored AIT. The unnecessary "popularity" they got from the case was rather too cheap. It is never good to interfere in a dying man's will to commit suicide. This is my opinion.

My Fears for Femi Adesina

Inasmuch as I admire the person of Mr. Femi Adesina, the Managing Director/Editor-in-Chief, *The Sun* newspapers, for his resourcefulness, professionalism, and humility, I am at not sure whether to congratulate or sympathize with him on his reported appointment as the Special Adviser to President Buhari on Media. My fears flow from two main sources. First, Buhari has never had it smooth with the media. He is not known to be media friendly. His reputation as a dictator during his term as Nigerian Head of State (1983-1985) may pass on well as the darkest period in the Nigerian media history, with the notorious Decree 4 featuring prominently. The reported "ban" on African Independent Television (AIT) from covering his activities as president-elect strengthens this position. This is one area Mr. Adesina's professionalism and maturity are likely to be put to test.

Second, he is going to be playing very "dirty" roles. This is perhaps my worst fear for Adesina. For a man who attends a Church that places much emphasis on holiness, Four Square Church, how he plays this delicate role, going by what happened to previous occupants of the office, appears herculean!

I recently got the chance to read George Orwell's *Animal Farm* again and I cannot but sympathize with anyone in the position of Squealer, Napoleon's spokesman. Part of his job is to, with graphic details, justify ineptitude, incompetence, and corruption in the Napoleon administration as relating to the pigs and dogs that are in charge of administration on the farm. He has to make others believe the lazy pigs "...had to expend enormous labours every day upon mysterious things called 'files', 'reports', 'minutes' and 'memoranda'."

That these works were in fact "...large sheets of paper which had to be closely covered with writing, and as soon as they were covered, they were burnt in furnace." The ability to tell bold lies like Squealer is an essential qualification for Adesina's new job. Part of the job is to play the role of the Ministry of Truth (or Minitrue) in George Orwell's *Nineteen Eighty-Four,* which includes falsifying history, lying with statistics and hitherto known facts, misinforming the informed, compounding the problems for the ignorant, weakening the consciousness of the unconscious, confounding the intelligent and in fact suffering fools gladly! You will justify things like:

IGNORANCE is STRENGH, FREEDOM is SLAVERY, WAR is PEACE, NO PRESIDENT RESIGNS DURING WAR, 16 is GREATER THAN 19, STEALING is NOT CORRUPTION, and the likes.

Again, thinking of presidential spokesmen, I still remember Ron Ziegler, President Richard Nixon's spokesman. With all his sound credentials as a media genius, he was made to look silly, working hard to defend his boss during the Watergate scandal that rocked and brought down the Nixon administration in 1974. This is sometimes the sacrifice you pay for being a spokesman. By now Adesina must be a smart man. If not, he would not have survived the hostile terrain he worked in; after all, he was a Buhari supporter while working with strong pro-Jonathan*The Sun*. To survive in the teeth of opposition from people like Amanze Obi, a columnist who himself is a PDP apologist and former Imo state commissioner of information, and others who openly called on the newspaper owner Dr. Orji Uzor Kalu to relieve him of his job takes more than just scheming.

With this, he should be able to weather the storms his new job may generate.

The memories of Femi Fani-Kayode, who served as Special Assistant to President Obasanjo on Public Affairs and recently Doyin Okupe is still fresh in our minds. These people are not usually your first choice of media professionals, except you need flatterers or "attack dogs". The best description for these people is that they are embarrassment personified. The good news is that should Buhari decide to follow the tradition of the recent past administration and appoint a Special Assistant on Public Affairs, Adesina's work becomes relatively easier by placing more embarrassing functions on that office.

Even at that, the fact that President Jonathan appointed no less a person than Okupe to play his dirty role, I doubt if that ever had much effect in savaging the public image of Dr. Reuben Abati, the President's Special Assistant on Media, himself a thoroughbred professional. It is not all presidential spokesmen that have the instincts of Joseph Goebbels, Adolf Hitler's Chief Propagandist. There are those who have done remarkably well like Jody Prowell and Eleanor Clift, but this largely depended on the sound performance of their bosses. The job of a presidential spokesman is made easier when the boss himself performs satisfactorily. It is on this positive note, my fears notwithstanding, that I boldly congratulate Mr. Femi Adesina on his appointment. My best wishes are with him!

Press Freedom, Buhari and the Social Media Bill

The media came under attack, not just mainstream media, but the new or social media, no thanks to the introduction of a controversial Social Media Bill by Senator Bala Ibn Na'Allah (APC, Kebbi South) on the floor of the Senate. The bill, among other things, proposes:

1. Up to seven years in prison or N2 million fine for "anyone who intentionally propagates false information that could threaten the security of the country or that is capable of inciting the general public against the government through electronic message."

2. Up to 2 years in prison or $10,000 fine or both for anyone disseminating via text message, Twitter, WhatsApp, or any other form of social media an "abusive statement."

3. This also involves messages intending to "set the public against any person and group of persons, an institution of government or such other bodies established by law."

An amazing aspect of this bill is that its sponsor(s) did not bother to make a deliberate effort to define what they mean by "abusive statement", on which the strength of the bill lies. There are two things one can infer from this: the bill was hurriedly packaged in the light of the expositions of mind-blowing corruption allegations against some former and present public officers whose agents, the sponsors of this bill represent. Second, the sponsors of the bill do not have thoroughness as part of their daily routine for them to have made this important omission.

Acknowledged, it is on record that President Muhammadu Buhari has never had it smooth with the media. He is not known to be media-friendly. We cannot continue pretending about this fact. His reputation as a dictator during his term as Nigerian Head of State (1983-1985) may pass on well as the darkest period in the Nigerian media history, with the notorious "Decree 4" featuring prominently.

The widely reported "ban" on African Independent Television (AIT) from covering his activities as president-elect strengthens this position. The introduction of this unfortunate Bill, if passed by the Senate, could only lay credence to this fear of him becoming a dictator. While no responsible democratic government will deliberately gag the press; nothing in press freedom supports hate speeches, inciting statements or outright falsehoods. In this regard, we use freedom of the press to mean that the media can publish news items and opinions without being censored or "gagged" by any authority. When press enjoys freedom, it indicates that the press can publish news and opinions on any issues without facing any restrictions and prohibitions. But it does not mean that this freedom is absolute or arbitrary.

The media cannot just publish whatever they wish; rather they should publish things that are constructive for the society or the country and should refrain from publishing any propaganda or biased news and anything that can harm society or the state. So, the press must realize the meaning of the scope of its freedom, otherwise, their power can turn into an instrument of great public harm and damage. While such freedom mostly implies the absence of interference from an overreaching state, its preservation may be sought through constitutional or other legal protections.

Let us come back to that unfortunate bill. As far as some of us were concerned it was just another waste of time because, with the overwhelming majority of Nigerians against it, the Senate would have no option than to drop it or face public wrath. The fact that President Buhari had not even come out against the unpopular bill meant they must tour the path of honour to kill the bill altogether! This is specifically where ill-fated AIT case fits in. The media station, either deliberately or for pecuniary reasons chose murder over honour. Its role during the election can be classified as ignoble. They sponsored hate campaigns against Buhari, calling him unprintable names, including spreading broad day lies and rumours. They even went as far as insulting Buhari's family accusing him of being responsible for the death of his late wife and his first daughter, Zulai, who died of sickle cell anaemia about two years earlier. After doing all these, the media station's owners did not even bother to apologize for their below moral par role during the presidential campaign.

This would have been alright if this bill intended to curb reckless media stations like AIT rather than the wild goose chase of monitoring the social media users. This so-called bill may just be another attempt for corruption to fight back. At the risk of being accused of a fallacy of *argumentum ad hominem*, a cursory look at the sponsors and pushers convinces me of this fear. The bill, if passed, will not be at home with the Freedom of Information Act (FOIA), intending to strengthen citizens' participation in governance.

Like we earlier wrote, just as no responsible government will gag the press; no responsible citizen will support hate speeches, slander or libel. But we need to stress more emphatically that this bill is needless in the face of several laws against irresponsible speeches and reckless abuse of the media like we witnessed in the case of the AIT during the presidential campaigns earlier this year. We need to equally make some important connections here. Some people are presently in court standing trials for cases dealing with corruption. You do not expect a good soldier to just sit back and watch while you fire your missile, he will fire back. He will not only fire back, he will fire on all cylinders. It will then be foolhardy to assume that the introduction of this so-called bill should be regarded as mere coincidence. "When you fight corruption," as it is now said in Nigeria, "corruption fights back." Some of us have the fear that this bill may just be sponsored to serve as a blackmail tool against President Buhari, whose opponents have been doing their best to make his administration look "anti- democratic". The fact that the President himself came out to strongly distance himself from the needless bill leaves the sponsors to answer the moral question:

"Who sent thou?"

We have to understand that the social or new media has become a powerful medium for communication, so the senate must be very careful in its handling of it. Many, if not all the political office holders today, won their elections, thanks to the powerful influence of social media. A quick advice to those pushing this bill is for them to note with caution, that those pushing them into sponsoring this bill will readily deny them when they need them most to defend them. They are quiet now in the face of overwhelming public outcry against this new madness in town. Their silence is just so deliberate, because they are aware there will be elections in less than four years. They can look so stupid now for all they care, but those waiting to profit from their open display of madness are only waiting to strike. Senator Na'Allah and his co-travelers need not be reminded that the 2015 election battle was fought largely on the social media. We also need not tell them that most, if not all of them found themselves in the Senate today thanks to the social media. We pray earnestly that these people don't come back seeking for votes in 2019 because the social media, which they now intend to kill, will outlive them.

As Nigerian Journalists Keep Goofing!

Olakunle Taiwo of *Nigerian Tribune* made the following confession on how a disastrous interview with Professor Itse Sagay made him lose his job. He said, on getting to know how silly he had been, "speaking with the wrong person, instead of Professor Itse Sagay, I almost collapsed at the lobby of the hotel which was hosting my honeymoon. What have I done to myself, my career, my bosses, my employers, my company that feeds my family? God! I felt like asking the ground to open up and swallow me. My wife of two days was in the room oblivious of the damage that had been done to our honeymoon. With me, the honeymoon was over in just two days!"

He continued, "I joined journalism with an ambition to go far. I never knew there were deadly potholes on my way to realising my career dream. I hope and pray that this cup shall pass... While accepting responsibility for the error, I state with all sense of responsibility that it was not intentional, nor deliberate. In my almost two years in journalism, I have worked hard to build a future in the profession and serve my country, through my employers, truthfully and diligently." (*Premium Times*, December 23, 2015). This could have been me; I said to myself, had I studied Mass Communications and decided to become a journalist. But can things get simpler? This will not be the first time we will have such goofing in the media.

No less a person than Dr. Reuben Abati (whose phones stopped ringing when he lost his job as presidential spokesman) to nearly bring a newspaper, *The Guardian*, to disrepute, for his unguarded statement in one of his write-ups, "For the Attention of General Buhari". Let us quote the exact words of the editors in their apology to the General on June 11, 2013: "On April 22, 2011, The Guardian newspaper published an article on page 51 titled "For the attention of General Buhari" wherein certain allegations were made against General Muhammadu Buhari's alleged role in the violence emanating from the elections. The publication was based on information which we believed to be reliable at that time. Since the publication, however, we now have reason to believe that certain parts of the story were not verified to be correct before the publication. We assure General Muhammadu Buhari (rtd) GCFR of our highest esteem and regret any distress or embarrassment which the said publication may have caused him." There is really nothing wrong in goofing, after all we are all humans. We all are given to making mistakes, even really embarrassing ones but when we do, the decent thing for us to do is to apologise appropriately, as the Guardian did in Abati's unfortunate case.

Let us assume that Dr. Abati was just trying to be seen working hard defending his clueless boss. Like I have argued elsewhere, his job was a very delicate one. As Abati himself admitted in his "The Phones Are No Longer Ringing", he was to act as an attack dog against perceived opponents of his boss, and in some cases falsify facts just so that his boss would not look so clueless. He assumed his job descriptions perfectly well, little wonder insults, ridicule and in some cases, outright verbal abuses on his boss' "enemies" were prominent features of his tenure as a presidential spokesperson.

Can we say the same for a hustling young man, Mr. Taiwo, whose career in journalism was at stake? In the case of Taiwo, I could only pity this lad whose fledging career in journalism might have ended abruptly. Immediately his reported "interview" was published, anti-

Buhari elements on social media, even without bothering to check for facts, posted and quoted "Professor Sagay" with much approval. "Buhari is selective in his anti- corruption war"; "Buhari is witch-hunting his political opponents"; "The whole world can now see that Buhari is not sincere with the anti-corruption fight" and the likes became the favourite nursery rhymes on social media for the anti-Buhari clowns.

Not until the well-known investigative platform, *Sahara Reporters* broke the story that the Professor never granted any interview with any reporter from *Nigerian Tribune.*

Can we agree less with President Buhari who challenged our lazy pressmen on the need to do more investigative reporting? The obviously embarrassed *Nigerian Tribune* offered a watery apology on the matter. Heads "rolled", but not the "Head". The poor reporter reportedly lost his job, a day after his wedding. The line editor, also, was placed on "indefinite suspension" by the newspaper management. This was how far they could go, at least, there should be scapegoats in this kind of situation. You just have to look a little responsible, even when you are obviously stupid. One wonders why the Tribune management is yet to release the transcript of the "interview" with the man from the "other end" if truly they are sincere and want us to believe they are "innocent" and professional in their internal control. All these are just by the way. Let me now return to those who bothered themselves, or were in a rush to "nail" Buhari and his anti-corruption war. It is said that the deaf only knows the last song he heard before he became deaf.

This appears to be the situation these unfortunate elements find themselves in today. None of them even bothered to "apologise" like their sources, *Tribune* and *Guardian* did. It matters not to them since that was all they wanted to hear. Though I am on record to have lent my voice to the opposition to the Social Media Bill before the Senate, the overbearing influence of online media must be checked before things get out of hand. This is the age where investigative journalism is, for all intent and purposes, dying or dead. We live in a period in which too much information is at our fingertips, yet we are mentally lazy to utilize them. If Olisa Metuh, the loquacious People's Democratic Party (PDP) spokesman, can unconsciously refer to a statement credited to Abati which The Guardian has renounced; if we still have people who hold the opinion that Mallam Sanusi Lamido Sanusi is the "sponsor" of Boko Haram because of the report of one Reno Omokri (Wendell Simlin); if some people can report that the Chapel in Aso Rock has been closed down; it only convinces me that the "watchers" have been and are still goofing! It is on this note that I will appeal to the Nigerian Union of Journalists (NUJ); Nigerian Guild of Editors (NGE); Online Publishers Association of Nigeria (OPAN); Newspapers Proprietors Association of Nigeria (NPAN); Nigerian Broadcasting Corporation (NBC) and others to place much emphasis on professional excellence and ruthlessly root out quacks within their ranks to save the watchers or the fourth estate of the realm from becoming totally unethical.

PART 4
FIGHT BACK AGAINST THE OPPOSITION

The Fayose I Know

Sometime in November 2014, I wrote under the title, *Our Governor Has Gone Mad Again* on my Facebook wall. The title was inspired by Ola Rotimi's classic, *Our Husband Has Gone Mad Again*, which central character, Colonel Lejoka-Brown, an impulsive, irrational soldier-turned-politician was. The said article generated much interest from many of my former schoolmates, many of whom were pro-Ekiti State Governor, Ayo Fayose, back then at Ife University. Thanks to Fayoseites (as I now call them), I received the bashing of my life. Some even called me unprintable names. From all their replies to the article, two things I could make sense of was their sordid defense of the Governor.

Fayose's supporters say it to high heavens that he is a man of the people; loved by the people and because of his notorious "Stomach Infrastructure", the people can die for him! This argument only reminds me of the central character in Chinua Achebe's *The Man of the People*, Chief Nanga.

The Chief is a classic example of a corrupt, selfish and opportunistic politician that characterized the First Republic. Those who have read the novel know how the chief ended. The basis of trust for the "Stomach Infrastructure" is that life starts and ends in the stomach; hence, the people must be hungry or be made so. If not, how can one explain a state where workers are owed up to four months' salaries, and the same workers will protest against the impeachment of their employer (the Governor), no thanks to the "Stomach Infrastructure"? Still, under this notorious scheme, Ekiti is treated like a conquered territory and its people as hungry refugees who must stay on queue just to collect some cups of rice that will last them a day(s) or weeks at most! How then is this different from Amala and Ewedu politics of late Chief Lamidi Adedibu back then in Ibadan? *Truly Fayose is a man of the people.*

The second thing I could make meaning of from Fayose's supporters is that they say he is "the beauty of democracy." These people boast loudly of his victory at the June 21, 2014, gubernatorial election as an act of love from the Ekiti people. I held this opinion initially until I saw a tape which revealed how the election was "scientifically rigged." Not that I agreed the election was conducted properly, but that as a Psephologist, I could not provide any justification for the voting patterns in the state to confirm that result. The rest is now history. The Yorubas have a saying: "Ara ija leyin wa" meaning "Biting is part of the game." Invariably, rigging is part of the election. The caveat being the strict obedience to the 11th Commandment: "Thou shall not get caught!"

One is left to wonder how the same democratic process (election) that threw up legends like Abraham Lincoln, Franklin D. Roosevelt, and Margaret Thatcher, can also be the same that gave birth to elements like Adolf Hitler and Benito Mussolini. One is also left at sea as to how Africa can, on one hand, throw up giants like Julius Nyerere (Tanzania) and still at the same time nurture Robert Mugabe (Zimbabwe) even though both operated under a one-party system.

More mysterious still is the fact that a system that produced someone like Kayode Fayemi, a renowned academic, astute administrator, and strategist, and a perfect honourable gentleman still produced someone like Fayose. Such a system is inherently faulty!

Still, on the gubernatorial election, Fayose made everyone believe that he is now "Born again." Some fell for his new trick, but for those of us who know a leopard does not change its spots, we were not deceived. Almost immediately after his election, he returned to his vomit. He declared war on several fronts, first on the judiciary.

He physically attacked a judge who was presiding over the case of his eligibility to contest the election. Crises started, the courts were closed, and the state never knew peace ever since. In parenthesis, he was impeached in 2006 and by law, he is not expected to hold any public office for ten years.

He launched another round of attacks again this time on the legislature. It took seven members out of the twenty-six-member state House of Assembly to approve Fayose's list of Commissioners and "impeach" its speaker Dr. Adewale Omirin under the protection of the Nigerian Police! In parenthesis, 7 out of 26 does not even constitute the Constitutional requirement of one-third to form a quorum. Only Fayose and his loyal supporters can explain the new formula that makes 7 out of 26 to equal one-third.

It would have been alright if Fayose remained a local embarrassment. He took his cause too far when early 2015 he sponsored front page advertorials in several Nigerian dailies which were calculated at discrediting the All Progressives Congress (APC) presidential candidate, General Muhammadu Buhari. He listed the General with one of the former Nigerian Heads of State who died in office just because of the General's age, 72. It took the maturity of Nigerian political leaders particularly those of Northern extraction, for the matter not to degenerate to the fracas. Need we add that his party, the PDP which he thought he was doing a favour by the advert, quickly distanced itself from it and Fayose was alone than ever. Even his family rejected him for bringing their name to disrepute. To all these, he insisted he had no apology. Embarrassing himself, his state, his people, his family, even his mother is not a big deal to our Governor. If this is not madness, then I don't know the meaning of the word. I haven't heard from my schoolmates at Ife for a while now to know if they have changed their opinions about Fayose.

I was informed that one of them openly criticized him since the March 28 presidential election which Buhari won. If this is true, then I take it as a vindication of my earlier stand in my article, *Our Governor Has Gone Mad Again*.

As far as I am concerned like I have always said, the Fayose I know will never bring anything good to Ekiti. He is an embodiment of contradictions and mediocrity. This is the Fayose I know!

Is Fayose on the Loose Again?

In an article, *The Fayose I Know*, I chronicled the several dishonourable acts of the Ekiti State Governor, Mr. Ayodele Fayose. As soon as the article was published, I received an email from a young man, whose address reads, "TMoney", querying my knowledge of Ekiti and my right to talk about a State I am not from. For the records, I am a Nigerian, my father is from Kwara and I was born in Lagos. I am not aware anyone must be from Ekiti to be embarrassed by rabid acts in a state that pride itself as the Fountain of Knowledge.

I deduced from "TMoney's" reply that he is a Fayoseite (as I often refer to his supporters). He accused me of being blinded by my admiration for Kayode Fayemi, the former Governor of the State.

My reply came on two fronts. First, as a political scientist, I cannot but admire the astuteness and academic dexterity of Dr. Fayemi. Who wouldn't? Second, I told him that as far as I know, Fayemi never brought the glorious name of Ekiti to disrepute at any time during his administration. I made him understand that the choice between Fayemi and Fayose is that choice between virtues and vices!

Just some days after the said article was published, Fayose in his usual manner again ejaculated: He alleged he had evidence that Alhaji Adamu Muazu worked for the All Progressives Congress (APC) during the 2015 presidential elections. As at when I read this piece in the news, I suddenly knew that Fayose's problem is more than just political. It is psychological. To me, he is suffering from a post-conflict psychological trauma which only a professional psychiatrist can explain. If not, he would not have publicly made the statement credited to him on his official media account.

Except he will come out to deny this statement, he alleged that Alhaji Adamu Muazu the National Chairman of the People's Democratic Party (PDP) the same party on which platform Fayose rose to become Governor, suddenly started working for APC. He even alleged he had "evidence" to back up his allegations. Except Fayose will also provide, in addition to his allegation, the "evidence" that an air ambulance lifted the President-elect, General Muhammadu Buhari, to London for a medical check-up in the heat of the presidential campaign, I insist he took a dose of hallucinogen or is mentally deluded. A Yoruba proverb says, "Oro asiwere ni ma yato" meaning "Only a madman talks differently from the rest."

Fast track to the presidential campaigns, we can conclude that only Fayose had the "evidence" of Buhari having cancer; it was his own private hospital "Amadu Bello Teaching Hospital" that diagnosed General Buhari of cancer; it was Fayose's London hospital that diagnosed Buhari would not survive being Nigerian President.

Now, we recall that at some point, the PDP and its Presidential campaign team distanced themselves from Fayose making him more alone, more than ever, in his notorious attacks on Buhari. Can you now see why it is Fayose who needs a medical check-up?

Let us still apply the concept of like attracts likes. I have seen Fayose and the company he keeps. Ekiti State prides itself as the Land of Honour; I am still looking at this contradiction in having a Fayose as governor of Ekiti. The state boasts of people that have contributed in no negligible ways to the development of the Nigerian society in academics, politics, military and a host of others. You will agree with me that Fayose is a misfit when we use any of these parameters of measurement. I only see Fayose celebrated by those with whom he shares the same philosophy, for example, Otunba Iyiola Omisore.

The old English saying, "Show me your friend, and I will tell you who you are", perfectly applies in this case.

For people like "TMoney" who had invited me to visit Ekiti to see how people are "enjoying" under the notorious "Stomach Infrastructure" programme of Fayose, I only sympathize with their limited understanding of what the serious business of governance is all about. The recent rants of his party's boss on the loss of his party at the presidential poll can only be an expression of a frustrated child hitting his feet on a stone. If not, how else can one explain this? Is he letting loose?

Still on Fayose's Stomach Infrastructure

Nigerians by now must be getting used to one of the latest additions to their glossary of political terms – "Stomach Infrastructure". If Chinua Achebe's, *A Man of the People*, which was written in the 1960s, is still relevant today and been copied and repackaged under new names by some high profile politicians then it only proves that it will take a longer time to win the war against piracy in Nigeria. Some policies are nothing but the repackaging of the "fat-dripping, gummy, eat-and-let-eat" scheme under a new name. The most recent version, under its proper name, was made popular or reignited by the PDP candidate (now Governor) Ayodele Fayose during the Ekiti Gubernatorial campaign in June 2014.

We must concede that the "Stomach Infrastructure" scheme is the unofficial political programme adopted by different Nigerian politicians with varying degrees; it is today the official economic/developmental agenda of Ayo Fayose's administration in Ekiti State. Only few people have heard Fayose publicly articulate his economic policy strategy for development, apart from when he goes public to spring up controversies. We didn't come close to hearing him discuss his programme for job creation, industrialization, agricultural development and the likes. Save for his vivid description of "Stomach Infrastructure", his government aims to provide against Kayode Fayemi's investments in Infrastructural facilities aimed at attracting investments into the state during the gubernatorial campaigns.

True to his words, (Fayose is known to keep his words, I admire him for that), he kept the scheme "Stomach Infrastructure" alive after he won the election. The first or one of the first official appointments Fayose made as Governor after he was sworn in on 26 October 2014 was a Special Assistant on "Stomach Infrastructure", Mr. Sunday Anifowose, with a cabinet rank. Can you now see why I said it is the official state policy in Ekiti? Supporters of the scheme argued that it is progressive and development-oriented. They have equally done their utmost to compare it with the Welfare system in Western nations, even though they starkly contrast both in content and intent. Their argument is premised on the Yoruba saying, "Ti ebi ba kuro ninu ise, ise buse" meaning "If we remove hunger from poverty, poverty vanishes". They perhaps forgot that the poverty-induced proverb (if proverb it is indeed) does not address matters of food security, job security, and the full realization of human potentials. The fact that you have eaten this morning does not mean you are ever sure of the next meal. One, therefore, need not look further to see the folly in this argument!

The main thrust of the "Stomach Infrastructure" is that life starts from and ends in the stomach. The stomach must always be pacified, otherwise, it will complain. This is why you must build an infrastructure on the stomach and for the stomach alone. The scheme does not presume any limit to satisfying the stomach even when you suffer from constipation. You are only living to eat under the regime of "Stomach Infrastructure".

Sometimes in 2015, Ekiti State workers, under the auspices of the Trades Union Congress (TUC) and Nigerian Labour Congress (NLC), held a strange rally. The rally was not to press for the payments of their months-long unpaid salaries, which Fayose's administration did not pay for over 5 months after he was sworn in. It was also not to press for better working conditions and conditions of service. It still was not to press for the implementation of the

N18,000 minimum wage in Ekiti. The rally was "in solidarity with the people's governor" against his impeachment for abuse of office.

If this is not "Stomach Infrastructure" for the labour leaders, I know not what to call this.

Can we blame the poor workers? They are but civil servants who must work for every government in power, at least from the last time we checked. In a state that is largely agrarian, if you don't keep the job you have, getting another one is like trying to milk a rock, except of course you are to return to your village farm because there are only a few industries. For the labour leaders who mobilised the workers for that strange rally to support a drowning man who had caused them a better-imagined hardship through unpaid salaries, I can only think of the Yoruba saying, "Owun ti a ma a je, ki je ka gbon" –*what we intend eating will not make us wise.*"

While thinking about the words "Stomach Infrastructure" as I prepared writing this piece, I reached for my dictionary once more to check the meaning of the two words. I found out the "Stomach" (which has no sustenance, save for constipation) coming up with "Infrastructure" (which has sustainability) makes "Stomach Infrastructure" a perfect oxymoron!

Why Should Kemi Adeosun Cover Her Hair?

Religion is one of the greatest institutions created by man. For instance, Islam is defined as a "religion of peace" but you will find in the Quran some passages as violent as this: "And when the sacred months are passed, kill those who join other gods with Allah wherever ye shall find them; and seize them, besiege them, and lay wait for them with every kind of ambush", even though you will find in its hallowed pages many passages urging mercy toward others, tolerance, respect for life and so on. Most interpreters of the Koran find no argument in it for the murder of innocents. It would be naive to ignore in Islam a deep thread of intolerance toward unbelievers, especially if those unbelievers are believed to be a threat to the Islamic world.

The use of religion for extreme repression, and even terror is not restricted to Islam. For most of its history, Christianity has had a worse record. From the Crusades to the Inquisition, to the bloody religious wars of the 16th and 17th centuries, Europe saw far more blood spilled for religion's sake than the Muslim world did. Christianity defines God as love but the Holy Bible contains a verse like "I have brought you not peace but sword." (Matthew 10:34).

Perhaps the most important thing for us to realize today is that the defeat of each of these fundamentalisms required a long and arduous effort. The conflict with Islamic fundamentalism is likely to take as long. For unlike Europe's religious wars, which taught Christians the futility of fighting to death over something beyond human understanding and so immune to any definitive resolution, there has been no such educative conflict in the Muslim world. Only Iran and Afghanistan have experienced the full horror of revolutionary fundamentalism, and of the two only Iran has so far seen a reason to moderate its religious inclinations to some extent. From everything we see, the lessons Europe learned in its bloody history are yet to be absorbed within the Muslim world. There, as in 16th-century Europe, the promise of purity and salvation seem far more enticing than the mundane allure of mere peace. That means that we are not at the end of this conflict but in its very early stages.

Faith cannot exist alone in a single person. Indeed, faith needs others for it to survive – and the more complete the culture of faith, the wider it is, and the more total its infiltration of the world, the better for it. It is hard for us to wrap our minds around this today, but it is quite clear from the accounts of the Inquisition and, indeed, of the religious wars that continued to rage in Europe for nearly three centuries, that many of the fanatics who burnt human beings at the stake were acting out of what they genuinely thought were the best interests of the victims. With the power of the state, they used fire, as opposed to simple execution, because it was thought to be spiritually cleansing.

A few minutes of hideous torture on earth were deemed a small price to pay for helping such souls avoid eternal torture in the afterlife. Moreover, the example of such government-sponsored executions helped create a culture in which certain truths were reinforced and in which it was easier for weaker people to find faith. The burden of this duty to uphold the faith lay on the men required to torture, persecute and murder the unfaithful. And many of them believed, as no doubt some Islamic fundamentalists believe, that they were acting out of mercy and godliness. One can guess rightly the reason religion is so misunderstood.

Questions that I often wonder about are: why is religion so misunderstood by those who should even know better? Is culture not supposed to be part of religion? Why do some people do negative things in the name of religion? There was an outrage on the social media about President Muhammadu Buhari "forcing" the Minister of Finance, Mrs. Kemi Adeosun, to cover her hair during a meeting in Qatar. The pictures that surfaced online showed the Minister, with her hair covered, signing a bilateral Agreement on Avoidance of Double Taxation and the Prevention of Fiscal Evasion with Respect to Taxes Income in Doha.

The perception of some Nigerians who saw the picture was that the president actually mandated the minister to cover her hair, a supposed directive which some interpreted to mean that Buhari was on the verge of "Islamising" the country.

Those who have been following the thread of discussions since the 2015 presidential elections will not be surprised to hear the phrase *Islamising Nigeria* from Buhari's opponents. Leading the pack in this is no less a person than the Ekiti State governor, Ayodele Fayose who, for reasons best known to him, decided to capitalize on the fears of some Nigerians to accuse the president of setting in motion the process of *Islamising* the country.

The first thing that came to mind on reading this piece on the social media was that some people were only doing their utmost to make the minister look like a minor who has no sense of decision of her own. I say this because even my 5-year old niece knows when to say "no" and mean it. If my niece knows when and how to stand her ground, why should a 48-year old woman not know how to, especially in a sensitive matter pertaining to one's faith?

The second thing that came to me was the question of why the president would even be interested in "forcing" her to cover her hair. Can it be a condition from the Qatari government to get the sought deal? Is it an act of sheer patriotism or desperation or religious bigotry? Does covering one's hair in a foreign land simply translate to "Islamising" your country?

As confusing as these questions appear, the answers are easy to find if we look well enough. I have seen the picture of Mrs. Ellen Johnson-Sirleaf, the President of Liberia with the Emir of Qatar, His Highness Sheikh Tamim, on one of her visits to that country with her hair fully covered. I am not sure of the level of "Islamisation" she has subsequently pushed in Christianity-dominant Liberia. I have equally seen the pictures of Mitchelle Obama with the Chief Imam of Jakarta Mosque, Ali Mustafa Yaqub, during her visit to Indonesia. Her hair was fully covered, just as it was when she met Pope Benedict XVI during his papacy.

Some went as far as telling us that Buhari visited a Church once and did not bother to take off his cap. My direct reply to this, having read my Bible, is that I have not found any portion or verse that tells us to take off our caps as men while in Church. If my Church doctrine tells me to take off my cap and I do so, it is my business. I have never seen the Pope or any other priest with his head uncovered. My Bible yet tells me that women should cover their hair during worship. But again, if my Church permits a woman to leave her hair uncovered during service, it has little to do with my business!

Aside from our "too religious" friends, what I think Adeosun should have done was to have asked President Buhari or whoever "forced" her to cover her hair: "Sir, why should I cover my hair?" Maybe this would have saved some of us the stress of having to speculate.

Buhari: The Second Coming

Turning and turning in the widening gyre,

The falcon cannot hear the falconer;

Things fall apart; the centre cannot hold;

Mere anarchy is loosed upon the world,

The blood-dimmed tide is loosed, and everywhere,

The ceremony of innocence is drowned;

The best lack all conviction, while the worst are full of compassionate intensity.

(W.B. Yeats *The Second Coming*) William B. Yeats' poem shows the Nigerian situation in 1983 before General Muhammadu Buhari and his colleagues struck on December 31, 1983.

False historians are at work. Femi Fani-Kayode(FFK), doing the job he was paid to do as President Jonathan's Campaign spokesman, tweeted on his official Twitter account, on 2015 New Year Eve, that General Muhammadu Buhari, the APC candidate "truncated democracy and took away our peace on this day 30 years ago." I agree fully with FFK that since Buhari came the forces of reaction have murdered sleep. They have known no peace. In parenthesis, FFK's job, like the Ministry of Truth in *George Orwell's Nineteen Eighty-Four* involves large-scale propaganda. You hear things like FREEDOM IS SLAVERY; IGNORANCE IS STRENGHT; WAR IS PEACE; 16 ISGREATER THAN 19; CORRUPTION IS VIRTUE, VIRTUE IS VICE. Don't be surprised, they justify these before their gullible followers. This dirty job also includes malicious distortions of hitherto plain historical facts (and in some cases falsifying them) in the process confounding the pseudo-intelligent, confusing the gullible, compounding the problems for the ignorant and permanently weakening the consciousness of the unconscious.

This is FFK's job; no one should blame him as he is well paid for it. My own job, on the other hand, is to put the records straight, fill in where FFK missed it, and clarify the points where FFK appears confused so that confused people like him may understand. In 1983, like now, things had all fallen apart. Orders were no longer in order. The government had corruption stamped in gold. In fact, corruption became a virtue with irredeemable features, as it is now. The economy was, like now, battered with a high rate of inflation, unemployment, huge debt profile, reckless devaluation of the naira, mismanagement and wastes and ill-thought austerity measures as a result of fall in oil prices. The list is endless.

There were ethnoreligious crises everywhere Madakeke/Ife, Kano, Kaduna, Maiduguri, Bauchi and so on and the Shagari government was helpless and hapless. The final straw that broke the camel's back was the massive rigging of the 1983 general elections in favour of the National Party of Nigeria (NPN) leading to a breakdown of law and order in the country. Clearly things were falling apart, the centre could not hold.

This was the "democracy" and "peace" FFK and his colleagues enjoyed so much (they wouldn't let go of) that he boldly tells us that Buhari put (and still intends to put) an end to in 1983. It was a crime for Buhari to have ended their party. Do you now see how WAR IS PEACE? Any curious observer will quickly strike the similarities between what was happening during Shagari's time and what is happening now. The second coming of Buhari discomforted them. They worked round the clock to avert it. The intervention of General Buhari in 1983 implemented immediate changes to the country's then multiphase challenges.

The administration's responses were immediate, manifesting in the following: The Buhari Administration recovered all ill-gotten wealth from politicians and other public officials, no matter how highly placed and irrespective of tribe, religion or political affiliations, through special investigative tribunals. The administration's spirited anti-corruption campaigns went far beyond the experiences of Nigerians when a detachment of the Nigerian secret service went to London (where ex-Minister of Transport under Shagari was living before the coup) to literally "abduct" Dikko back home to face trial. This mission was largely unsuccessful but the intent was well noted and admired. I wish to note that in fighting the monster of corruption, innocent people might sometimes suffer, just as removing a tumor from the body sometimes affects healthy cells to save the entire body.

The administration restored order and discipline in public life clearing the country of the stranglehold of corruption, impunity, indiscipline, immoralities and other social ills with the formation of the War Against Indiscipline (WAI) which till date is still a landmark. WAI brigades were set up in schools to instill discipline, order, patriotism and other national values among our young ones.

Concerned by the growing rates of social vices, the Buhari administration promulgated decrees carrying long jail terms and death penalties for crimes ranging from economic sabotage, drug and currency trafficking, examination malpractices and the likes, to serve as deterrents to potential criminals. Under these decrees, which may be applied retroactively, many were prosecuted, and in many cases sentenced to death. These executions were boldly carried out. Enforcing discipline where indiscipline prevails requires bold, detribalized, decisive, and "tough" leadership. In November 1980, Mallam Muhammadu Maitatsine led an extreme Islamic sect in an operation to wipe out other Muslims and non-Muslims. This group was extremely intolerant, and the Shagari government watched helplessly as this group killed Nigerians in broad daylight in Kano, Kaduna, and Maiduguri.

The Buhari administration wasted no time in flushing the sect and all its remnants out in 1984 and normalcy was restored. This is the primary responsibility of the state. There is no excuse for failure. Referencing W.B. Yeats' poem, *The Second Coming*:

> *Surely some revelations is at hand*

> *Surely the Second Coming is at hand*

> *Troubles my sight: somewhere in the sands of the desert,*

We have to understand that our present situation in Nigeria is in a worse case than it was in '83. These were the "revelations...at hand" that reactionary forces are afraid of and will do anything to suppress.

The General "Troubles my sight" (Apologies to W.B Yeats) as they see him coming to take away the feeding bottles from their mouths. Was this why they raised 21 billion naira for elections? They would gladly pay you $2000 per tweet just to discredit the General. The sacred time was slow but finally, it came. They knew they could run but not hide. They could postpone the inevitable, but could never avoid it. They were only postponing *their evil day* from February 14 to March 28. Alas! The Second Coming.

I will not end this piece without saluting the courage put up by numerous Buhari volunteers on social media, too much to name. Despite the financial inducement in the period of economic hardship, you stood your ground. When others were roasting their mothers, you kept yours. For these wonderful people, I share these beautiful P.B. Shelley's lines:

To suffer woes which Hope thinks infinite;

To forgive wrongs darker than death or

night; To defy power which seems omnipotent;

To love and bear; to hope till Hope creates

From its own wreck the things it contemplates;

Neither to change, nor falter, nor repent;

This like thy glory, Titan, is to be good,

great, and joyous beautiful and free;

This is alone Life, Joy, Empire, and Victory.

(Percy B. Shelly, *Prometheus Unbound*, 1820)

I thank you for you did not falter, fear or brake. You kept the spirit high; sustained the momentum; fought like true soldiers of fortune and faith; and in the end Victory!

Buhari's Second Coming we know brings hope and victory.

May we all find profound Peace.

"Amandla!Awethu!!"

Fani-Kayode: Saying "Yes" When He Means to Say "No"

When the All Progressives Congress (APC) was formed, one of the immediate challenges that came up was dealing with the ultra-conservative elements that had found their way into its ranks. At that point, the party could not provide satisfactory answers to the question of the presence of reactionary elements like Femi Fani-Kayode within its fold. Perhaps, the party leadership thought they could be reformed and reconstructed into the party's ideological dispositions only to be proven wrong before long. This was why I wrote in my article, *APC Crises: Is the Table Turning?* that apart from the unifying ambition of defeating former President Goodluck Jonathan, it appears the party had no further ambition. Even though my views, like many Nigerians at that time, were in tandem with the APC, I have never been comfortable with persons like Fani-Kayode in the party. To me, his presence can only guarantee monumental embarrassment (which I think he represents) to the party. I told my friend Kitan Omole, who like me, was a Buhari sympathizer but unlike me, he admired Fani-Kayode for his attack on Jonathan in the early days of the party that the man is only on holiday in the party and should be taken seriously. My friend did not agree with me because he was carried away by his [Fani-Kayode] criticisms of President Jonathan on social and print media and was enjoying his undeserved popularity.

On this, FFK, as he is known among his admirers, is a very smart guy who knew what he was doing. Everything worked for him in the APC. He used that platform to rain personal abuses on President Jonathan (not sparing the Igbos who support him). His diatribes against the Igbos in no small ways contributed to the branding of the APC as an "anti-Igbo" party. Surprisingly, many pro-Jonathan Igbo writers who earlier criticized FFK and APC, saw wrong in his views, no more, when he started "revealing APC secrets" later on. All was well to these ones as long as you supported Jonathan even if you had earlier insulted their mother.

Like I said, FFK is a smart man, or a con man if you like, who knew well what he was doing. All these he did till he had a strange dream– the APC fielding a "Muslim-Muslim" ticket for the 2015 presidential election. I am not aware till this day, which position the APC gave FFK for him to be privy to such information. I am equally not aware that the APC that I know like my palms, will ever take FFK so seriously knowing fully his antecedents, or ever give him any serious position in that party. When FFK slept and had such a strange dream remains a mystery to me till today. Well, not only did APC field a respected staunch Pentecostal Christian Pastor, Professor Yemi Osinbajo, as its Vice Presidential candidate (as against FFK's strange dreams), it also won the March 28 presidential election. This leads me to my main point– FFK is the baby that will not grow. Babies cry for everything, especially for food. You can easily know when baby FFK wants to eat.

He cries the loudest when he is hungry. He dances at his best when his belly is full. He does not know how to call it quits when it comes to eating. This is why former President Obasanjo beautifully described him as a dog that will bark at his boss' enemies (real or imagined) and shake his tail or sing your praises when he is given food. It hurts, but very true!

FFK was largely silent after the presidential election. He was busy going from one court to another for trials on money laundering charges against him. Later, he was in the news again. As though in victory mood (from his money laundering case), he launched attacks (as he usually does when he feels like eating) on Buhari's administration for its inability to tackle the humongous Boko Haram challenge. He restated his traditional argument that Buhari was, in fact, a "silent sympathizer" and financier of the deadly group. It takes no less a person than FFK to manufacture such made-in-Ife revelations. I will say this for the records: FFK told the world as at the time he re-joined the People's Democratic Party (PDP), that General Buhari is the prime sponsor of the dreaded group (obviously one of his several lies). He opined that the North was using it to frustrate the Jonathan administration when he wrongly claimed that the General said he would make Nigeria ungovernable for former President Jonathan.

The fact does not matter to FFK, (just like it didn't matter to his role model, Joseph Goebbels, Adolf Hitler's Minister of Propaganda), as long as the lie sounds good and big enough. One would have expected that this baby would grow from sucking breast to at least chewing solids. If Buhari, taking FFK's infantile logic, was the one behind Boko Haram, to frustrate Jonathan, except FFK stays in the Mars, he would have known that the Buhari who fought Maitatsine to a standstill in the 1980s will never have supported terrorism. My unsolicited advice to President Muhammadu Buhari is to be aware of this hungry baby now that he is idle with no food in sight. This is his natural way of seeking employment and the President must be on guard against considering his uninviting resume.

This is exactly what his attacks on Buhari's administration were intended to achieve. It is on record that he led several opportunistic attacks on former President Olusegun Obasanjo before he was invited to join the latter's administration as Special Assistant to the President on Public Affairs and later as Minister of Aviation. This tactic was then deployed to get former President Jonathan's attention before he was appointed presidential campaign spokesman for the 2015 election.

Fayose can at best be ignored; those who have learned to do so, he largely left alone. President Buhari should consider taking Obasanjo's advice by taking him as a dog which barks and when it tires out, it maintains its peace! Perhaps, FFK did not properly understand the lyrics in the old school matching song which goes thus:

Wherever you go;

Wherever you are;

Do not say "yes";

When you mean to say "no".

In parenthesis, please don't add "Baba Ibadan", which is usually the most exciting part of the song. Can we still recall that before the Independent National Electoral Commission (INEC) could commence collating the election results, the same FFK, the "INEC Chairman", went on air and announced that his party, PDP, was leading in 23 states of the federation? Need I say more that he says "yes" when he means "no"?

If he tells you it is raining, it is imperative that you go outside to check the weather yourself. Like Squealer in George Orwell's *Animal Farm*, if he calls something white, it is time to check well to see if it is not black. This exactly is why no responsible person should take him seriously because he is known to say yes when he means no!

Joe Igbokwe on Biafra

If you are familiar with events in the Nigerian political sphere, the man, Joe Igbokwe, needs no introduction. Depending on how you view him, he is an activist, publisher, journalist, politician, a dogged fighter, and a writer. Joe is seen within the All Progressives Congress (APC) circles as a patriot, nationalist and a dogged publicist having been the party's, perhaps, most vocal state publicity secretary. But to the ethnic chauvinists, he is nothing but a rebel, infidel, or a traitor.

His only offense to this latter class of people is his strong loyalty to his party's cause and the fact that he holds his views and is never ashamed to defend them. His latest of these views is the controversial topic of Biafra. Hardly does a week go by without Joe making the news. Who can fault that, after all, is he not a party publicist? If he is not putting the records straight on behalf of his party, he is airing his views on an issue of national importance. He is a Nigerian, hence, entitled to his views.

His article, *Biafra: Truth Be Told*, is surely one that many pro-Biafrans will not like to read or talk about. To them, it shouldn't have come at the time it did. To these people, Joe (who hails from Nnewi in Anambra state) is not, or no longer, an Igbo. To these people, as long as you do not support Biafra you are less, or not, Igbo. Also, to these ones, you have automatic "Biafra" citizenship so long as you can call for the release of a certain "Nnamdi Kanu" who himself holds a British citizenship and claims he is not Nigerian. Igbokwe automatically falls into the category of those Igbos, many of whom I know, do not support Biafra.

Having laid the above premise, we think it is rather fair to say that there are some genuine issues raised by some Biafra agitators, but what some of us are against is the opportunism and the opportunists who intend taking advantage of genuine issues for their own limited political and economic gains – there always are.

This is where I agree totally with the salient thesis in *Biafra: Truth Be Told*. It is on record that people openly campaigned using ethnic appeals for one candidate or the other during the 2015 election. The majority, if not all, of those presently calling themselves, at the risk of saying the obvious, campaigned vociferously for former President Goodluck Jonathan. They never in their lifetimes believed the man could lose the last presidential election and even concede. No sooner had the man lost and moved on, then some of them began wearing their Biafra agitator-uniforms.

Let us put the issues into proper perspective, for us not to be misunderstood. Many of the so-called "Biafra" activists saw nothing wrong with Nigeria when they were compensated with juicy appointments under the former president. They controlled the nation as though it was their personal property. In fact, one of them, Emeka Wogu, then Minister of Labour and Productivity, made it clear that they were "the ones ruling" hence the "Do not disturb" sign was boldly displayed on the door.

Let us look at Joe's profound statement in the article: "When they fail in national politics they go back to play ethnic politics and they resort to blackmail, primordial sentiments, ethnic preoccupation, intimidation, harassment, and subterfuge." As obvious as this statement seems, many find it difficult to see. But I want to expand the discussion a bit. Let us take a look at some pseudo-Biafra supporters who suddenly found their voices recently.

The first and perhaps the most loquacious of them all is Femi Fani-Kayode. One may argue that he suddenly found his strange love for Igbos, after telling us *The Bitter Truth About the*

Igbos. Though few will agree with this, but it appears FFK as he is often called is still suffering from the excruciating defeat of his paymaster and boss during the March election.

One thing about FFK is that he sees history in relative terms. He owns – and only him has – the license to murder history, rape history, abuse history, defile history or even re-write history all with reckless abandon. Like his role model, Josef Goebbels, who served as Adolf Hitler's Chief propagandist during the World War II, he believes all humans have weak memories.

Facts do not matter to Femi as long as the lies are "Big enough" for his gullible disciples to believe. When he writes about Biafra– he now has the authority to do so – his epistles are taken as gospels to those who classify themselves as Biafrans and music to those who choose to cry more than former President Jonathan for his electoral defeat.

Who dares blame them? After all, the enemy of my enemy is my friend, as a Chinese proverb says. My candid advice to Igbos is to know who their friends are. "Keep your friends close," as the Buddhist saying goes, "and your enemies closer." Let us leave FFK alone before we are accused of giving him too much-undeserved attention.

Need we add that some of the neo-Biafrans who themselves know next to nothing about the matter, only know what they were told? This is a part some people will not like to hear, but we will say it here for historical purposes. When the great Biafran leader, Col. Dim Emeka Odimegwu Ojukwu was granted a state pardon by President Shehu Shagari in 1982, the Ikemba soon contested for Senate under the then National Party of Nigeria (NPN), but did his people vote for him? Lest we also forget, he contested for the presidency, how many votes did he get even in Anambra?

Let us bring in Chief Alex Ekweme. We recall he, despite being a founding member of the Peoples' Democratic Party (PDP), contested for the party nomination for president in 2002. We all remember how the South-East governors then strived to outdo themselves to be seen to be more loyal to President Olusegun Obasanjo than even his own ministers. There was nothing wrong in all these for these people as long as it guaranteed fat bank accounts and unmerited rewards. No one talks about Biafra when contract figures are inflated; Biafra makes no sense as long as "our son" is given a juicy political appointment; Biafra could wait a little had Azikiwe won the presidency. Or that Biafra must go if "our daughter" is alleged to have stolen and sacked from office; "Biafra or death" when "our son" leaves a position and the same "son" must replace him; it has to be Biafra because "our son" comprises the majority of those in the team that won the U-17 World Cup, but everything is wrong if the team is composed of those that are not "our sons".

Did Joe Igbokwe really say anything new about Biafra?

Why the Phone No Longer Rings

Every introductory year student of Political Science is told that power is central to any political discourse. Once you have political power, you are told, you have everything.

There are many things you can do when in power that others cannot do. You are made to understand that if you are not in power, you are really an endangered species. While you are in power, you make important political appointments (and terminate them in some cases); you write a book which almost certainly becomes a bestseller; you have guaranteed news coverage on daily basis; you are made guest of (dis)honour at social functions; your community proudly associates with "our son's" accomplishments; somehow, everyone gets your number and the phone is always ringing! These are some of the things that make power exciting. How dare you tell Robert Mugabe to consider retirement at 90? Where do you want him to go? Activities in political spheres keep the likes of President Mugabe eternally young so there is no question of living the boring life outside power. Let's face it, will he still be physically active if he retires to Matibiri, his village, even to enjoy his loot? Will he not die before his time if he leaves Harare?

At this point, let us bring in our dear Reuben Abati, former President Goodluck Jonathan's Special Adviser on Media when he wrote recently what can be best termed, a post-power "lamentation", "The Phones no Longer Ring". For someone like Abati, power can be an interesting adventure, just as it can intoxicate. You get away with a lot of things just because you are in power. There is a saying in my village that if you want to know a man's true character give him two things– money and power. All you need to test a literary giant like Abati to come up with a fat lie like one of his articles in *The Guardian*, "For the Attention of General Buhari" is for him to be appointed a Presidential spokesman. For those who do not know, it was in the said article that he accused General (now President) Muhammadu Buhari of being the cause of post-election violence having earlier said he "...will make Nigeria ungovernable for President Jonathan". The General quietly approached the Courts for a libel suit against him, and the rest, as they say, is history! Still on the article, "For the Attention of General Buhari", Mr Abati may just be trying hard to be seen working hard defending his clueless boss. Like I have argued somewhere else, his job then was a very delicate one. As Abati himself admitted in his "The Phones Are No Longer Ringing", he was to act as an attack dog against perceived opponents of his boss and in some cases falsify facts just so that his boss would not look so clueless. He digested his job descriptions perfectly, little wonder insults, ridicule and in some cases, outright verbal abuses on his boss' "enemies" were prominent features of his regime as a Presidential spokesperson. Does he still wonder why his phones stopped ringing? Insults don't win arguments; just like propaganda do not win wars. Insults can only exacerbate the issues, leaving several scars, not heal it. If propaganda ever wins, with the monumental German propaganda machine put in place by Joseph Goebbels during the World War II, the World should probably have been living under a Nazi rule today. If the former columnist is still wondering why his phones stopped ringing, he needs a definite lesson in history!

I happen to be one of those who believes that former President Jonathan was the architect of his own failure. Praise singers, flatterers, court jesters and the like were enough to damage the ground for him. Working with people like Femi Fani-Kayode and Doyin Okupe in his media team, a professional like Mr Abati is sure to be sorely embarrassed. What could he have done to save the drowning ship?

As I made this point I remember Ron Ziegler, US President, Richard Nixon's spokesman. With all his sound credentials as a media genius, he was made to look silly working hard to defend his boss during the Watergate scandal that rocked and brought down the Nixon administration in 1974. This is sometimes the sacrifice you pay for being a spokesman. What could Abati have done to save President Jonathan, save for his enjoyment of the melodies of his ringing phones? Since Mr Abati wrote that I must confess I have had to sympathize with him. Maybe if he had worked with better people, his phones will still be ringing, if not louder by now, I thought to myself. I don't honestly share the view that he should have rejected the offer to serve President Jonathan. After all, there are others who served the same administration, like Dr Akinwunmi Adeshina, the former Minister for Agriculture, whose phones are still ringing today as President of the African Development Bank(AfDB). I still do not share the view that he should have avoided the public service like a plague because it is the same service that produced eminent persons like Simeon Adebo, Jerome Udoji, and the likes whose phones were still ringing long after their retirement from service. I still do not agree with those who said his phones stopped ringing because he didn't do his job effectively (perhaps for Jonathan's loss). In my opinion, he did his job very well, to the extent he was ready to go down with his boss, so there was no question of loyalty. If there is any reason his phones suddenly stopped ringing, it was because he came up against the Nigerian people. This one lesson, Mr Abati must learn, and quickly!

Why Bishop Kukah Goofed!

It appears to me that a set of Nigerians took a while to get used to the fact that Goodluck Jonathan is no longer Nigerian president. Before the March 28 election, in their bid to show him their "love" they threatened to make the country ungovernable should their benefactor get sacked from his job. Watching closely, some Jonathanians (incorrigible supporters of the former president), still carried on even after he had been defeated. These are the most loyal supporters you will find anywhere in the world. After he had "conceded" defeat to his arch-rival, General (now President) Muhammadu Buhari, this class of Jonathanians made him their "worshipful master" or hero who is infallible and untouchable. As far as this writer is concerned, these are nothing but tribal pirates, religious Buccaneers, and ethnic bigots. This class was created thanks to Jonathan leading "our son's" government. Since President Buhari has not or is yet to appoint "our son" into his government, Jonathan is regarded as "the best President Nigeria has ever produced". This is logic, as far as Jonathanians are concerned!

Bishop Matthew Hassan Kukah needs no introduction. His credentials as a social critic are quite glittering, though he cannot fall into the class of giants like Desmond Tutu. His role as a member of the National Peace Committee during the tensed moments of the March 28, 2015 election is also not to be swept away by the wave of the hand. These are his exclusive privilege which no one can take from him. The question I asked myself only when I heard of Bishop Kukah's widely-reported interview is: "What went wrong?" The National Peace Committee led by former Head of State, General Abdulsalam Abubakar in 2015 paid a courtesy visit to the President. There were several rumours as regards the intent of the visit. The issues became clearer some days after when Bishop Kukah, who incidentally is the spokesman of the Committee, gave a shocking interview.

Before I wrote this piece, I had to read the Bishop's statements severally. Please permit me to quote him (on the then on-going probe by Buhari's government): "There is no such thing as probe in a democratic setting like ours. What obtains is investigation, and once people lead and things are not right, investigation becomes necessary.

"However, in doing that we must never be distracted from spectacular actions undertaken by former President Jonathan. He is an individual.".

In the same interview, he gave an unsolicited advice to President Buhari to "face his work". If I had not known Bishop Kukah well enough, I would have sworn he is an incorrigible Jonathanian or GEJite as they are sometimes called. If not a Jonathanian, who will argue this way? For Kukah's records, part of Buhari's job on which platform he was elected, is a fight against corruption, as contained in Section 15(5) of the 1999 Constitution and I quote, "The State shall abolish all corrupt practices and abuse of power." This is a bold political objective which any sane President will be willing to pursue. So, we agree with the clergyman on this: Buhari is busy with his work and he is not distracted at all. Again, with due respect to the "spectacular actions undertaken by former President Jonathan" this writer insists he is not insulated from taking responsibility for the administration he presided over, so President Buhari has a constitutional responsibility, and it must be carried out!

In my search for what the clergyman meant by "spectacular actions undertaken by former President Jonathan", an insight came when I read the transcript of another interview he recently granted. Many watched Channels Television's breakfast show, *Sunrise*, where he appeared as a guest on Saturday August 13, 2015, where he spoke really like the Jonathanians I know. Among other things, he criticized the Buhari administration and called Jonathan a hero. How faithful a Jonathanian can one be?

Let us bring the clergyman's interview on Channels Television into clearer perspective. On the said interview, he echoed two traditional pro-Jonathan arguments. First, he criticized Buhari for being too slow. Need we to remind the Bishop about Aesop's fable, *The Hare and the Tortoise*? The moral of that story is very simple: Thoroughness and quality count far more in the long run than speed. The race is usually not to the swift as there is no sense in starting fast and ending poorly. How often has the Bishop heard this told?

His second point – perhaps the Jonathanians' strongest – is that Jonathan is a hero. He is a hero because he conceded defeat in an election he clearly lost. This perhaps was what he meant by "spectacular actions" he took. He is a hero; therefore, should not be investigated. He is immune from being called to account for his stewardship just because he accepted he lost an election. Apart from this argument being jejune, I find it even more ridiculous coming from a clergyman.

For the purpose of clarifications, former President Jonathan did Nigeria no special favour. If there was any favour done, it was Nigerians that did him a great favour. Nigerians gave him the privilege to lead them for about 6 years; they gave him shoes he once did not have. If the same Nigerians that gave him shoes say they don't want him anymore, does he have any other choice than to vacate that office? Maybe the clergyman meant that Jonathan did himself a favour by choosing to leave peacefully. In any case, since he lost the presidential election, he is duty-bound to leave. All those who have lost elections in Africa have left office, so Jonathan did nothing special. Laurent Gbagbo is facing the International Criminal Court (ICC) for refusing to vacate office peacefully in Ivory Coast in 2012. Maybe Jonathan is only trying to avoid that embarrassment. If heaven did not fall in Gbagbo's case, it will not fall in Jonathan's.

In any case, we thank him a lot for his contributions, but he must be called to account for his stewardship. This alone is beyond emotions. In fighting corruption, corruption fights back, as a new saying in Nigeria goes. You must get your footings right in dealing with the systemic corruption that has brought us backward. We should know how many jobs can be created with $20 billion missing from the NNPC coffers. We are interested in the number of industries that could have been created with that amount. We want to be in the comity of responsible nations so that we can have investors' confidence. We are interested in preventing goats from finishing our hard-harvested yams. My unsolicited advice to President Buhari at these trying times is to vet the advice he listens to. As far as I am concerned, Bishop Kukah is only playing Jonathan's cards with the likes of Ayo Oritsejafor in the self-appointed National Peace Committee. Maybe he has genuine intentions, one may not be too sure. This is only a personal opinion.

Doyin Okupe: Don't Cry for Us...

Dr. Doyin Okupe is one Nigerian that needs little introduction. He means different things to different people depending on one's political persuasions. Having served as spokesman for former President Goodluck Jonathan, no doubt, he made many enemies just as he made new friends. Wearing a new hat, he came public his account of why the former president lost the last presidential election. I really empathize (or sympathize) with whoever serves as a spokesman for a grossly clueless administration. The task can be very challenging defending an obviously clueless boss. It is not made easier when the spokesman himself is always under the heat. This job involves a whole range of complexities and avoidable risks. This job then may also require you to offend those you once loved, including you calling your mother a dog. It may equally require you to, like Squealer in George Orwell's *Animal Farm*, call black, white (as you will sometimes do). If you refuse, there are thousands of people who are ready to take your position even for lesser pay in this country were for less than 5000 positions there were over 700,000 applications. In this job, your boss is your God who is perfect and can do no wrong! This was the situation Dr. Doyin Okupe, the then Senior Special Assistant, on Public Affairs, to the President Jonathan, found himself.

Now he, like a loyal employee, has to cry for his former boss. Let's spare him for being excessively loyal to his boss. Let's also understand the fact that his job, a thankless one at that, required one to do his best to look stupid as it may often require. In order to be seen to be too busy in his job, he said on November 7, 2014, that NO PRESIDENT RESIGNS DURING WAR, when the heat became too much for his boss to bear. This was the presidency's then official response to Bola Tinubu, the All Progressives Congress (APC) national leader, who earlier called on President Jonathan to resign in the face of poor performance. One can understand the fact that the spokesman must do his job, but condescending to obvious illogicality, falsity, and embarrassing fallacies is what is not acceptable. Those who know Okupe very well probably know he airs his views even when they make him look silly (at 60 years plus). Later, he released his missile on the reason his boss, whom he once boasted would win, lost. He wrote in one of his Facebook posts, the "errors" committed by Jonathan that made him lose the election. According to him, "If any error was made it was first the failure of the PDP administration to sack the unfair and compromised electoral officer who was allowed to conduct the election in spite of his obvious and profuse partisanship." It is understandable when an examination candidate fails a paper and then blames the examiner. Even though the candidate returned his answer scripts blank, he wants the examiner to be magnanimous enough to have mercy on him to grant him a passing grade. When the examiner insists on standards, the candidate sees nothing wrong with his ridiculously poor performance, but sees everything wrong in his "unfair" examiner! Let's bring this analogy to Okupe's diatribes.

The former presidential spokesman wanted us to believe that "the unfair and compromised electoral officer" was the beginning of the end of the PDP's administration in Nigeria. Like the poor performing candidate in an examination, Okupe chose to see everything wrong with the examiner, in this case, the electorate and the electoral umpire, the Independent National Electoral Commission (INEC). Doyin Okupe perhaps had forgotten so soon that his boss was even scared of participating in the election itself. He had to be "begged" by some of his ambassadors, stylishly called "Transformation Ambassadors of Nigeria". This man also cornered the truth by refusing to tell us that his boss was even scared of losing even his own party primary. The party came out later to tell us that every incumbent everywhere in the world has "the right to first refusal." The party's mercenary writers will murder history; defile history; even rewrite history just to satisfy their ethnopolitical ambitions. Perhaps, Okupe is either sincerely ignorant of the fact that the same "unfair and compromised electoral officer" was appointed by his boss who also conducted the first and perhaps only election he will ever win, in 2011. In case Doyin forgot, Jonathan was never contesting against Attahiru Jega, but he was so unfortunate to have come up against the Nigerian people.

The second "error" according to him was the inexplicable acquiescence of the PDP government to the use of the infamous card reader which was "skillfully manipulated to the disadvantage of the PDP presidential candidate." On reading the quoted words, I had to be sure it was an adult who wrote it. I even did my best to try to confirm the possibility of the writer writing under the strong influence of alcohol. The statement apart from the obvious fact that it lacked logic, one need not look farther to see the foolery involved in those words. I dare ask, how powerful was the APC, in opposition, to have made it possible, in the face of the well-known PDP desperation during the election to have "skillfully manipulated" the card readers without the PDP crying foul? In this digital age, how easy would it have been if "informed" persons like Okupe did us a favour to present credible data analyses to support his claims? When the card readers were prevented from being used in Rivers, Akwa Ibom, Delta and other states that Jonathan and PDP "won" did the APC also "skillfully manipulate" the process in those states as this man claims? Why did the military under Jonathan arm-twist the "unfair and compromised electoral officer" into postponing the election by six weeks and what role did the PDP play?

The third error, according to Okupe, is that the PDP fielded "a good, God-fearing and patriotic man who in spite of his enormous power, the avalanche of deployable arsenal of war at his disposal, transformed himself to be the victim and refused to fight so that his countrymen may live and his nation survive." This is Jonathanians' strongest argument, so let us be quick to put it to bed. For Okupe's records, former President Jonathan did Nigeria no special favour. If there was any favour done, it was Nigerians that did him a great favour. Nigerians gave him the privilege to lead them for about six years; they gave him the shoes he once did not have; if the same Nigerians who gave him shoes said they do not want him anymore, did he have any other choice but to vacate the office? In any case, we thank him a lot for his contributions, but we insist he did us no special favour!

What people like Okupe should know in their lifetime is that Nigerians voted against his boss specifically for the goats to be kept, as much as possible, far away from the yams. Those "regretting" General Muhammadu Buhari (Rtd.) becoming president never voted for him in the first instance, so they should not cry for those who did.

A Letter to President Goodluck Jonathan

May 29, 2015

Your Excellency Sir,

I had to publicly write you this letter because I know you probably didn't read the one I personally sent you early last year. By this time next week, you will probably be resting in your hometown at Otuoke or anywhere you have chosen.

I need to remind you of issues I raised in the letter and more. In 2011, I was one of those Nigerians who saw you as a man of like passions; one who understood our experiences because you shared them. Like most Nigerians then, I thought because you shared our experiences, you would understand us better; hence, I voted for you. Without collecting a dime from you, we voted for you. We too had no shoes; we wore torn school uniforms and had to trek long distances on empty stomachs to school. We bought your mantra of once having no shoes to mobilize massive votes, though your campaign was not one of the best. Once you were sworn in as President, your public perception as an embodiment of hard work and humility, and your best efforts at tackling the security situation in our dear Nigeria, began to wane.

You were unfortunate to have surrounded yourself with people who apparently did not share your vision. They were quick to blame your opponents or the "enemies" they created for you for the deteriorating security situation in the country. But whether you believe it or not, the All Progressives' Congress (APC) or the so-called Boko Haram or the North (as you might have been made to believe) are not your greatest enemies, but those that presently surround you. I will justify this point with several empirical facts in this letter.

Sir, you may recall in 2012 that you said the dreaded Boko Haram has infiltrated your Cabinet. Many have interpreted this statement differently since it was made. Whether you made this statement in the heat of the moment or just to evoke public sympathy or whatever motive you had in mind, if you watch carefully you can link this statement to that which I made earlier. Sir, to buttress my point above, I say whoever advised you to proceed to Kano to welcome Mallam Ibrahim Shekarau into the People's Democratic Party (PDP) at the time of great national mourning cannot be your well-wisher.

Also, whoever organised the Shameless Women Rally to "demand" for your re-election in 2015 at the time the mothers of the kidnapped innocent Chibok girls were demanding the release of their children in Abuja is never your friend. Yet these were the people you trusted for advice on how to run the country.

Sir, though they were meant to be doing what was delegated to them, some of your aides, ministers, advisers, and other self-appointed praise singers are not only over-ambitious, officious, and high-handed, but also tend to get involved in activities which are not directly related to their job descriptions.

They simply engage in eye service, flattery and sycophancy just to get your attention. Surprisingly, you appear not to be calling these people to order even when they display a public show of shame! Some of your lieutenants have done particularly well in advising you, but what became of them?

I recall former National Security Adviser (NSA), late General Andrew Azazi, was given marching orders for boldly telling the truth on the security situation in the country. I was told that your men were angry with the General and then prevailed on you to sack him. The unwanted fate of Gen. Azazi may also await others who may have wished to be so bold; hence they chose to rather be your praise singers, flatterers and court jesters.

Also, Sir, recall that when the Adamawa State government, led by Murtala Nyako, refused to approve the use of Ribadu Square for a PDP Unity Rally which you were to lead, your lieutenants cried foul at the top of their voices. They were quick to see the politics of the situation. But do you know that the government's reason for its action is that you cannot hold a political rally while the nation is still at the shock of the missing Chibok girls? Do you also know that when you harkened to the voice of wisdom to call off the rally even the APC, Gen. Muhammadu Buhari, and other well-meaning Nigerians applauded you?

Do you also recall that the APC had to reschedule its state congresses for its governors to attend the National Security Meeting? If you check well, it is not all your lieutenants that are happy with this patriotic decision of yours so you can now see those that mean well for you and those who don't! On March 28 election; please permit me to remind you that in 2011, when you led the PDP rally at Mapo Hall, Ibadan, you insulted Yoruba leaders. But as a peace-loving people, we not only pardoned you after you apologized for the unguarded statement, we rewarded you with a large chunk of votes, except in Osun. We did this for you without any cost on your part.

After your dismal performance, you returned to us in 2015 to clamour for votes. This time, you chose to insult not just our leaders, but the entire race. You distributed money openly to local scammers, drug addicts, praise singers and charlatans in public glare in your desperation for undeserved Yoruba votes.

You didn't stop there; you practically did your best to colonize the region and appointed your trusted lieutenants over a tribe that places much emphasis on hard work, honour, and virtue. Your team, comprising drug dealers, murderers, political jobbers, Buccaneers and blood-sucking Vikings: Musiliu Obanikoro, Iyiola Omisore, Ayodele Fayose, Buruji Kashamu, Jelili Adeshiyan, Femi Fani-Kayode and the likes, who are themselves of no electoral value, cost you, your honour. These aides played their part much as you played yours in the March 28 debacle. Your aides personally insulted the person of General Muhammadu Buhari, the APC candidate, not sparing both his late wife and daughter.

I initially thought these actions were products of your overzealous aides wanting to get your attention not until I witnessed your campaign in Enugu. I do not need to remind you of your 'unpresidential' remarks on a retired General in the Nigerian Army. If it were to be a boxing match, this was a below-the-belt hit, which can lead to loss of points on your part.

Regardless of how you handled yourself in the past, I must end this on a positive note. By simply not consulting your aides before conceding defeat on March 31, 2015 to Buhari, you showed that there remains in you some good. Had you consulted them, the nation will probably be witnessing what is presently going on in Burundi. This perhaps has been the only thing you did right in your 5-year reign as President.

Had you watched well for enemies within, maybe things would have been different today. My best wishes for you are those you wish yourself.

Femi Aribisala: Time to Recover from Trauma!

Nigerians made history proving to the world again that peaceful transition was, in fact, possible in Africa. The election having been won and lost, it appears some people still feel the scars of the pains of defeat as though it happened yesterday. One of such persons is a political commentator, Femi Aribisala.

If you notice, I called him a political "commentator", not an "analyst", as he wants many of his readers to believe he is. In order to be seen as scientific in his write-ups, he sometimes taught us *How to Lose Presidential Elections Four Times* not minding the fact that he would later tell us *Why Buhari Will Never be President of Nigeria*. As funny as the premises on which some of his arguments were based, there are those who based their "analyses" on many of his unscientific conclusions.

At one point, in one of his articles, he paraded his "credentials" of being an authority in election analyses. He told his readers: he has been a student of elections for over 40 years. While studying for a degree in History and Politics at the University of Warwick, he obtained a scholarship to visit the United States to study the circumstances behind the 1973 election of Maynard Jackson as the first African-American Mayor of Atlanta. These reasons were just enough for his readers to believe whatever he told them as gospel. Needless to say, that it was in that same article that he gave a famous verdict: Goodluck Jonathan will win the 2015 presidential election by a landslide!

In parenthesis, this prediction reminds me of former Soviet's leader (Nikita Khrushchev's) famous statement, "We will bury you" speaking to Western diplomats about Soviet's confidence of "burying" their rivals in the heat of the Cold War in 1956. After winning a gold medal for his woeful predictions, Femi needs to save his face. To do this, someone or something had to be the scapegoat. I later read his article, "*How Jega Defeated Jonathan For Buhari*". After reading this, I concluded that he, after searching all over for whom to blame for his wrong diagnosis (if he ever did any), chose Professor Attahiru Jega, the then INEC Chairman, as his perfect whip boy.

Like a typical public school pupil who failed his papers, he blames his dismal performance on anything and everything but himself – his teacher, his parents, his friends his foes, the test questions or anything that can easily justify his point! Let me be quick to admit, writing from firsthand experience working as a psephologist, that the job of predicting the outcome of elections could be murcky, complex and dangerous (requiring you sometimes to put your career on the line). Predicting elections requires some level of dispassion. When you get too involved and end up with a wrong prediction, you end up frustrated like Femi because there are often too many variables waiting to alter your experiment and get you frustrated.

The lack of emphatic details led to the famous _Literary Digest_ fiasco in 1936 which wrongly predicted a defeat for US President Franklin Roosevelt. Many will equally not forget the case of Gallup Poll which predicted a victory for the Republican candidate, Mitt Romney, against President Obama in 2012.

I cited these cases to show how complicated predictive analyses can be sometimes. If these reputable institutions can err this much, Femi needs neither rant nor look for scapegoats since no one is infallible. All that was expected of him was to be professional by updating his system of analyses like Gallup and others have done. This should not be a platform for reminding brother Femi what is and what is not political analyses but, I will say that every political analyst (except if so-called) should know that some experiments cannot be performed for ethical and practical reasons in political analyses. We cannot, unfortunately, re-run the 2015 presidential election under another INEC chairman to test for differences in outcomes. If someone else, instead of Professor Jega, was the Electoral Commission boss, whether the outcome of the election would have been significantly different is, to say the least, counter-factual or virtual history.

Because we consider it futile to engage in virtual history, let us go back in time to compare data that are real. To argue, like Uncle Femi did, that Jega "rigged" the election for Buhari is to note that the 2007 elections would have had a different outcome had Professor Maurice Iwu not been the then INEC chair. Or that had Femi Aribisala been the chairman of the National Electoral Commission (NEC) during the June 12, 1993 election, Chief MKO Abiola would have been sworn in as President!

Consider his postulation that Jega, not APC "defeated" Jonathan in the 2015 election. Perhaps, Femi needs to be consistent since he told us in another article that just immediately after the same Jega he criticized, announced the postponement of the election by six weeks, that the party was low on cash and therefore, in shambles and crumbling. Where is consistency? Where is coherence in your "analyses"? Was it also Jega that "rigged in" Jonathan in 2011? Mr. Femi!

I am aware that some people will bring in the point that the APC appeared stronger than the Congress for Progressives Change (CPC) or the Action Congress of Nigeria (ACN) was in 2011 making it comfortable enough for it to be rigged into office in 2015. If we take this at face value, then our firm conclusion will be that the APC won the 2015 presidential election because it was stronger in all intent and purposes has grown massively over a period of four years as against its PDP counterpart.

Looking at the three-party game that played out in 2011, one will see that Jonathan won due to some complications. I do not expect many people to agree with this but had the ACN entered into any form of agreement with the CPC then, the election would have ended in a re-run which outcome is highly unpredictable as the events in 2015 clearly show.

The same situation played out in 2015, the only difference being that the progressive forces achieved what many doubted as a possibility – the formation of APC. It should therefore not surprise objective political analysts why the party won. The professional thing expected from Femi Aribisala after making such wrong prediction was simply to apologize to his readers and move on rather than look for scapegoats. His post-election rants against Buhari and the

APC, including his display at an event in the University of Lagos, showed that he was yet to recover from the trauma of 2015 electoral defeat of the "hero of democracy". I hope he has recovered now?

Could this be why there was so much campaign from Jonathan's supporters to sack Jega just weeks to the 2015 elections?

#iStandWithBuhari and the Limits of Political Opportunism

Nigerian citizens desperate for a new dawn and swept by the euphoria of the "Change Mantra", went all out to support, perhaps the most persecuted presidential candidate, General Muhammadu Buhari. We were told severally how the General intends to "Islamise Nigeria"; we were told he was a member of the Islamic State (or ISIS); we were equally told of how he once promised to make "Nigeria ungovernable for Jonathan". All these notwithstanding, we shunned every obvious temptation for ethnicity or religious bigotry to support and vote the most hated man in certain quarters as president.

Since he became president, Buhari seems to have gotten new supporters who seem to love him more than those who endured the worst conditions to support him during the election. These neo-Buharists, many of whom never attended his campaign rally nor donated financially to his effort at the exalted office, suddenly found their lost love.

After the election, traditional Buhari's critics, also known as the Wailing Wailers, started several hashtags on Twitter, such as #BabaGoSlow, #100WastedDays, #BudgetOfYams, #TyrantBuhari and more recently and embarrassingly, #BringBackCorruption. To all these, Buhari's supporters responded well too. They launched counter attacks like: #GoOnBuhari to counter the accusations of his critics that he is a dictator. Apart from this, noticing the loss the seeming defencelessness of Buharists on social media, neo-Buharists regrouped and decided to do "something unique." They launched what they called, #iStandWithBuhari.

The group promoting the hashtag became vocal on social media. Seeing the group's sponsored advert, I immediately called its secretariat. I was told the group intended mobilizing a whopping 9 million Nigerians to a rally in support of President Buhari. I asked if there was any election in sight which the President was participating in. To this, the receiver of my call answered in the negative. He only told me of the president's war against corruption and the commencement of operation of the Treasury Single Account (TSA). The question I asked myself after ending the call was: Why the rally?

Inasmuch as I have no personal issue with showing affections to one's country leader, this effort suffered from two obvious deficiencies. First, the poor timing of the rally especially at a time when Nigerians are facing harsh economic realities is at best uncalculated. Second, is the fact that it only exposes political opportunism and the insincerity of those behind the hashtag.

Calling Nigerians out for a rally at such time is obviously a bad Public Relations strategy. The people pushing the hashtag are obviously no experts in PR, otherwise, they would have seen the futility of their effort even before it materialized. The message is shabby, just as its medium is tactless. It appears some idle political aides wanted to be seen as working hard on their job. It may also be true some of those people who hate the president so much are behind this mess.

This leads me to my second issue with this poorly-thought-out rally. Where will the funding for the rally come from? Who are the overt and covert sponsors of the event? In critical periods, it will not be so difficult to mobilize unemployed people to execute one's selfish ambitions. These people are easily found gathering in groups at newspaper stands or other conspicuous places to attend such rallies. Let us assume each of those mobilized was paid a stipend of N1000 or given a meal, this will cost (using conservative estimates) a whopping N90 billion. My God!

If this money can be channeled into building industries, these rally attendees will be gainfully employed.

There is nothing new in rallies of such nature. The fact that it is the same people that are behind groups like: Daniel Kanu's Youths Earnestly Yearn for Abacha (YEA); #BringBackGoodluck; Ifeanyi Uba's Transformation Ambassadors of Nigeria (TAN); Goodluck Initiative for Transformation (GIFT); Neighbour To Neighbour (N2N) and others too numerous to mention adds to my suspicions that these are nothing but professional praise singers, flatterers, charlatans and– to say the obvious – scammers.

But the true intentions of the group became manifest. Its National Coordinator Mr. Mustapha Ramalan resigned, thanks to the schism within the group. Ramalan's reason is that "...the nine million-man pro-Buhari match should be postponed because the government is still trying to pick up and hence should be given more time to justify the nine million-man march." Do I dare ask, at what point did he recover his senses?

If I was in a position to advise President Buhari on this matter, I would suggest he considers taking Niccolo Machiavelli's advice in his wonderful book, *The Prince* about dealing with these charlatans. The Italian philosopher wrote: "...*a wise prince ought to hold a third course by choosing the wise men in his state, and giving to them only the liberty of speaking the truth to him, and then only of those things of which he inquires, and of none others; but he ought to question them upon everything, and listen to their opinions, and afterwards form his own conclusions. With these councilors, separately and collectively, he ought to carry himself in such a way that each of them should know that, the more freely he shall speak, the more he shall be preferred; outside of these, he should listen to no one, pursue the thing resolved on, and be steadfast in his resolutions. He who does otherwise is either overthrown by flatterers, or is so often changed by varying opinions that he falls into contempt.*" (*The Prince*, Chapter 23)

The Presidency or any other government needs to understand that it should never keep mum in the face of well-known political opportunists. The President's media team must come down hard, issuing a strong "Caveat Emptor" on the matter. While we understand that the administration needs public support, getting support from these ones whose intentions are purely to embarrass, malign and ridicule his modest achievements will further dampen, not construct, the administration's image. There has to be limits to political opportunism.

On Kogi "Inconclusive" Election and Other Matters

Depending on one's political persuasions, many stayed glued to their radio or TVs in anticipation of the declaration of the much-anticipated election result in Kogi on November 21, 2016. The social media was awash with all manner of projections about who the eventual winner of the gubernatorial election would be between two political gladiators Idris Wada of the People's Democratic Party (PDP) and Abubakar Audu of the All Progressives Congress (APC). As important as the election seemed, it was, and still is, my view that Kogites must be the most unfortunate people having to choose the lesser between two evils. So, having followed the campaigns of both candidates as objectively as I could, I posted my verdict on the election on my Facebook profile that APC's Audu stood 51 percent chance of winning a "closely contested election" some days to the Day of Decision. It only appeared to me that Audu's chances kept increasing as the polling day approached, with that of the then incumbent governor, Wada, progressively declining!

I was in the middle of my reply to Jude Ndukwe's article, "Kogi Governorship Election: Avoiding Nigeria's Costly Mistake" (published in The Premium Times), almost immediately when Audu must have been declared the winner of the election, before I stepped out to see the "El Classico", a match between two most successful Spanish (if not the World's) Football Clubs – Real Madrid and FC Barcelona. I need not remind the *Galaticos* fans of the 4-0 thrashing by Barca. All that turned to a labour of love when the election was declared "inconclusive" by INEC and the death of the leading candidate (at least going by the rigorous psephological analyses of the result) the same day.

It appeared events simply overtook all pre-election matters to deal with other unexpected issues that were thrown up. In parenthesis, Jude Ndukwe, must look beyond his obvious ethno-political views and look at issues more factually. He argued, "Kogi State made a mistake by voting for APC at the presidential election thinking that APC was a credible alternative, having seen that APC is only a shadow of what it paints itself to be, it would amount to political suicide and avoidable self-destruct that would leave an indelible mark of regrets and sadness in the lives of the people if they make the same mistake a second time. It is always better to prevent the flood with the umbrella than waste resources, time and energy trying to sweep it away with forlorn-looking brooms".

One is not then in doubt about this young man's loyalty. He probably didn't support or vote for President Buhari during the March election, so he should learn to live with the consequences of his own choice.

Those that voted Buhari did so for a reason: *for him to keep the yam tubers safe from the rampaging goats; recover the lands invaded by the locusts; "witch-hunt" the witches that boldly devoured the community in the daytime and to allow the farmer to reap bountiful harvests*. If President Buhari is doing this satisfactorily then no one made a "mistake" as Ndukwe wants some gullible elements amongst us to believe! As far as I am concerned, Ndukwe's tone throughout the article sounded like the badly beaten boxer who received a knock-out and is struggling to recover. Having turned himself to Wada's campaign manager with his write-up (mind you, I did not support Audu like I said earlier) he was either doing his best to sincerely blow the trumpet of his own ignorance loudly or was just being mischievous!

Let us leave pre-election matters for now, and consider the other issues brought up after the election. Since the APC's candidate died at almost the same period INEC was announcing the election as "inconclusive", legal and constitutional issues arose. I am not a lawyer, neither do I lay claims to the technicalities of the law; therefore, I will be looking at the issues, not as "technically" as lawyers would, but from a political standpoint. There has been no shortage of legal position(s) on the matter. I will do my best to look at all of them on their merits. Let's forget about INEC's initial decision to declare the election "inconclusive" for now. The first position, common among PDP supporters, is that since Audu died before the conclusion of the election, the party candidate, Wada, should be declared the winner.

This must be a strange legal interpretation because, the fact that a candidate, who has a running mate dies, does not automatically translate into the next "leading" candidate being declared the winner. Let's assume the election under dispute was, say, a Senatorial election where there is no running mate, this argument may look more tenable!

A second position is canvassed by a faction of the APC.

This group stands on the ground that since Section 181 of the 1999 Constitution maintains that since technically the "Supplementary" election can at best be described as a "mere formality", the running mate to late Audu, Mr James Abiodun Faleke should naturally "carry on the flag". This group argued that INEC erred by not declaring Audu Governor-elect, which would have made things easier for Faleke to have stepped into his shoes. As nice as this position looks on the surface, it comes with some obvious flaws.

First, before he died, Audu was yet to be declared "Governor-elect" by the Electoral body, so the question of Faleke declaring himself "Governor-elect" by virtue of the fact that Audu was "leading" before he died is out of place. Second, there are more technical issues concerning party politics than just simplifying the whole matter down to Falake "stepping" into Audu's shoes. If the APC fell for this simple trap, then it may as well not have fielded any candidate for Kogi polls at all!

I made this last statement because in making this error, the opposition could easily go to court (and win), this time not to contest the fact that APC won the election, but to contest its faulty presentation and substitution of candidates. Let us take a moment to agree, albeit in principle, that it is that simple in this case. The APC had submitted Faleke' name originally to INEC as Deputy Governorship candidate. That could not change mid-way through the process, save Faleke himself must be ready to submit himself to a rigorous process of party primaries. True, he was nominated by Audu as his running mate, a constitutional provision, but since he did not participate in the primaries, he was ineligible to be declared Governor-elect, except the APC thought otherwise.

We must not fall for the argument that Faleke participated in the primaries indirectly while Audu participated directly. This argument holds no water because nowhere in the constitution or Electoral Act, is it explicitly provided for that the Deputy Governorship candidate must participate in party primaries.

That leads me to the third point I want to make – it is political parties, not candidates that actually contest elections. Strange as this looks, it is the fact. The 1999 Constitution has no provision for an independent candidacy. In fact, in the letters and spirit, it is against such. The case of *Rt. Hon. Rotimi Chibuike Amaechi vs. Independent Electoral Commission & Ors (2) Celestine Omehia (3) Peoples Democratic Party (2008)*, now popularly known as

Amaechi v Omehia, proves this fact. The APC and the APC alone can nominate or substitute its candidate for an election in which it is participating. It is a given that INEC must have acted in error by declaring the election "inconclusive" in the first instance. With about 49,000 votes remaining, it is our considered view that the APC had satisfied the Constitutional requirements of one-quarter of votes in all the 21 Local Government Areas in the State. The Chief Returning Officer, Professor Emmanuel Kucha, can at best be described as just too officious. We say this in the light of the fact that it is almost, if not totally impossible using the electoral patterns in all the areas of the state, difficult for either party to achieve near 100 per cent of the disputed votes. Let us forget the fact that only a little over 25,000 voters had the legal voting instrument – the Permanent Voter Card (PVCs)–in the remaining polling units. I also maintain that the Attorney-General of the Federation(AGF), Abubakar Malami, should have sought the proper interpretation of Section 181 of the 1999 Constitution and Sections 33-35 of the Electoral Act from the Supreme Court before giving a public advice to INEC to request the APC to substitute its candidate. This makes the situation more complex and pre-emptive. It is our considered view that, however the case goes; it will surely expand the scope of electoral discussions in this country.

Igbos and Buhari's Government

The Igbos appear not to have hidden their contempt for the All Progressives Congress (APC) since its formation in 2013. The party's image has not been redeemed among Igbos with the APC Government, led by President Muhammadu Buhari, delayed a bit in appointing anyone from the South-East, the home of the Igbos into his government. It doesn't appear pleasing to Igbo ears that Mr Emmanuel Ibe Kachikwu from Delta state was appointed Nigeria National Petroleum Corporation (NNPC) boss. This is perhaps why the *Ohaneze Ndigbo* (the apex Igbo group) Youth Council accused the President of "hatred for the Igbo nation". Words like "federal character", "marginalization" "Biafra" and the likes have been used frequently in public discussions especially among many "Igbo" writers who have suddenly found their lost voices! While no responsible person should support the marginalization of any ethnic, religious or national group in Nigeria, we must consider jettisoning our support of the so-called federal character. Igbos, in particular, have a lot to learn from other Nigerians and must be ready to do away with Civil War mentality to really prosper in a united Nigeria. On the federal character which was introduced in 1978 and became part of the 1979 Constitution and subsequent constitutions, we need to know if it has added any value(s) to our lives as a nation. After Chief Obafemi Awolowo lost the 1979 Presidential election, Yorubas who voted massively for him playing the role of opposition in Shehu Shagari's administration. The Vice President, Senate President, Speaker of the House of Representatives were all non-Yorubas and heaven did not fall. No one mentioned federal character or "marginalization of Yorubas". Much ado about federal character!

If Yorubas did not go into extinction outside mainstream politics for about 40 years under different platforms – AG, UPN, AD, AC, ACN – I submit the Igbos must learn, like Yorubas did, to develop unique political character outside political power! From a little observation, it appears some Igbos are yet to jettison their Civil War experiences when others have moved on. It is no longer a secret that Igbos made their choice clear during the presidential election and that was not General Muhammadu Buhari, but whether they stand with him through thick and thin is yet to be seen. One of the questions that came up during the campaigns was General Buhari's role during the Nigerian Civil War. This question was raised by no less a person than the People's Democratic Party (PDP) campaign spokesman, Chief Femi Fani-Kayode. Needless to say that Fani-Kayode or FFK as he is sometimes called would have committed "genocide" considering his earlier views on Ndigbo while he was in the APC. How he suddenly become a "beloved Igbo" when he joined the PDP remains strange to me. This only convinces me that anyone can be a "friend of Ndigbo" if he can just oppose Buhari or the APC!

In parenthesis, what role does a soldier play during a war? Does FFK expect Buhari to come out and say he did not fight according to command? At the risk of sounding immodest, though I was born over two decades after the end of the War, I have read several Civil War books from both sides; I didn't come close to any specific command led by General Buhari. Those that played prominent roles were: T.Y. Danjuma, Murtala Muhammed, Benjamin Adekunle "The Scorpion", and later, Olusegun Obasanjo and the likes on the Nigerian side. You can mention people like Joseph "Air Raid" Achuzie, Alexander Madiebo, Emmanuel Ifeajuna and others on the Biafran side. I am yet to find any Civil War document on Buhari's specific role(s) during the war!

This leads me to my next point – Igbos do not appear to know their real "enemies".

They supported former President Jonathan, himself an Ijaw man from Bayelsa State even adding "Azikwe" to his name just to make him "our son". Jonathan himself did not disappoint, he rewarded the Igbo nation with "juicy appointments" in his government. But as at the last time I checked, Ijaws fought alongside the Federal army during the Civil War. People like Isaac Boro and immortal Ken Saro-Wiwa both from "minority areas" fought the Biafrans to a standstill during the war. I am not sure if Ijaws will proudly call themselves Biafrans anytime soon!

An Advertorial titled "APC is Dead on Arrival in the South East" sponsored by an unknown group in the eve of the launch of the party in Anambra sometimes in 2014, cites the "deportation" of 14 destitute persons of Igbo Origin to Anambra and Imo States as a case for Igbos not to support the APC. I wish to say that while I condemn this act by the Lagos State Government in its totality, I am not losing sight of the present security challenges in the country necessitating such actions by the Government. Lagos is not one of those States that harbors destitute Almajiris. Apart from this, before this action by Lagos State, the PDP Government of Abia State has adopted the Indigenization Policy leading to thousands (mainly Igbos) non-Abians losing their jobs in the State Public Service. Nothing was wrong with relieving Nigerians of their jobs but everything was incorrect with clearing the streets of beggared and impecunious fellows!

Igbos must accept their present reality and fast. Buhari is the President of Nigeria at least for the next four years. There are, for me, few options left for Igbos in the Buhari administration considering the fact that they boxed themselves into a tight corner. They can either play the role of a responsible opposition standing with the PDP or join the APC Government, the latter which will make them negotiate from the position of weakness. If Igbos decide to play the role of opposition, that is, standing their ground till the end then they will be taken more seriously in the political schemes in the future. This can also lay the foundation for Igbo Presidency sooner than we may think.

The second option will be that Igbos will join the Buhari government through their "rejected stones" – Ogbonnaya Onu, Rochas Okorocha, Chris Ngige and the likes. This will also mean that pan-Igbo groups will do more than just praise singing of President Buhari and his lieutenants in the region to win him over for their past "sins".

I do not know how General Buhari must have felt early this year when he wrote to Ohaneze Ndigbo, requesting a simple audience. The response of the organization, in my opinion, portrays that of a disoriented body in desperate need of reformation. The group did not even deem it fit to acknowledge receipt of the General's letter! In all these, I think all hope is not lost. President Buhari must, through the state his party controls in the region (Imo), provide the lead. The President must shun shallow thinkers and flatterers in the region by building the Second Niger Bridge which has been in the realms of dreams over the years. The administration must also ensure that Ports are located in the region for improved revenue and job creation. I know little of Igbo needs except those I am told by my Igbo friends. The time to build a Nigeria where Igbos can be proud once again to be Nigerians is now. Buhari can do this and more. My only advice to Igbo leaders is for them to drop their Civil War lenses and look at issues more clearly within the century realities!

A Reply to a "Wailing Wailer"

I received an email from one Mr. Sam C. Okudah, containing an attached document replying my article, IGBOS AND THE BUHARI GOVERNMENT. With the manner the document was sent, one would have thought it was just a private mail for my viewing only to later learn that it had been published on some online media. Though I took exemptions to many of his saccharine remarks against the write-up, I thanked him and sought his permission to publish the article on my blog nonetheless. But I think I need to set the records straight so that we do not get confused. On reading his piece, RE: IGBOS AND THE BUHARI GOVERNMENT, my first conclusion was that either Mr. Okudah didn't read the article at all or that he just chose the parts that he could understand from it. I say this because if he truly read and digested the piece, he would have known that my main thesis in the article is that Igbos should henceforth be more tactical when it comes to political issues.

From his diatribes, I could only make sense of a few points he raised which I am going to put straight here. The first point Okudah made was that I wrote about something I knew little about – the Igbos. He quoted me when I wrote that I knew very little about Igbos and what may be their peculiar needs which the Buhari government may wish to address.

On this, he pointed out: "Don't you see that what you have tried to do was to obfuscate your gullible readers? Your article is one of the worst cases of dis-ingenuity and mendacity I have ever read."

Let me say this clearly, I made the statement "I know little of Igbo needs except those that I am told by my Igbo friends" in relation to what Igbos stand to benefit if some of them can just drop their toga of Civil War defeatist mentality! I will equally add that it is never a sign of weakness if you play the Socratic ignorance- "I know one thing: that I know nothing". What is wrong in admitting you have limited knowledge about something? How would the situation have been, if the *Ohaneze Ndigbo* leadership had just granted a simple audience to General Buhari during the campaigns even if they wouldn't vote for him? What excuse will Buhari be having about not being "well-briefed" on Ndigbo had some people being more civilized in their approach? What right have you to tell a man who went into the forest to kill an elephant how to share the meat? Mr. Okudah may find the quote by Amenhotep IV, Pharaoh of Egypt, (c.1250BCE) interesting when he said,

"The wise man doubts often, and his views are changeable. The fool is constant in his opinions, and doubts nothing, because he knows everything, except his own ignorance". Invariably, all wise men admit to their degree of ignorance! Another point, perhaps his strongest, Mr. Okudah made in his article is on Buhari's "lopsided" appointments. One cannot expect much from a man whose hatred for Buhari is written all over his face even in his article. Let me be quick to admit that I am not impressed with the balance of President Buhari's appointments, but I insist on supporting anyone that is qualified to fit an appropriate position, not just where they come from! On those wailing on "regret" for voting Buhari among which he included the Yoruba socio-cultural group, *Afenifere,* I think Okudah needs some tuition-free political lessons here. Senator Femi Okunrounmu and his cohorts were former President Jonathan's supporters who obviously overrated themselves politically. If there is any political lesson the former president must learn, it should be that he selects those he must avoid like a plague and this includes people like Senator Okunrounmu. It was

Okunrounmu who went public to declare that "Yoruba will regret voting Buhari". As at the last time I checked, Afenifere, Oodua People's Congress (OPC) and the likes publicly supported former President Jonathan during the 2015 election. In fact, Yinka Odumakin, its spokesman supported the People's Democratic Party (PDP) Gubernatorial candidate, Mr. Jimi Agbaje in Lagos. Still, I ask, what right do these people have to "weep" for millions of Yorubas who trooped out to vote Buhari? (I think the best song here should be Don't Cry for Me Argentina). Can we still say these people speak for the Yoruba nation?

At least the *Ohaneze Ndigbo* directed all Igbos to vote for Goodluck Jonathan and they did so without mincing words. Can we say the same for Afenifere? That still reminds me, Odumakin was Buhari's spokesman during the 2011 election, the turning point was when he stopped "speaking" for Buhari and "spoke" for Jonathan in 2015, but unlike in 2011, Buhari won. Can you now see how contagious failure is? I think Buhari must be thanking God that Afenifere, OPC and Odumakin didn't support him in 2015! Let me still recommend the wonderful political bible, Robert Green's *The 48 Laws of Power*, to Mr. Okudah. The 10thlaw in that great book, Infectious: Avoid the Unhappy and the Unlucky, states among other things: "Recognize the fortunate so that you may choose their company and the unfortunate so that so that you may avoid them. Misfortune is a crime of folly, and among those who suffer from it there is no malady more contagious. Never open your door to the least of misfortunate for, if you do, many others will follow in train...Do not die of another's misery." For those who do not know, the Action Congress of Nigeria (ACN) won all states in the South-West, except Ondo, without the support of Afenifere. Smart Yoruba politicians have paid important attention to avoid these unfortunate elements. That former President Jonathan fell a victim of their deceit and chose to consider their unflattering resume should bother lovers of the former president. Does anyone still wonder why the APC National Leaders like Bola Tinubu, Bisi Akande, and the likes avoid them like an infectious disease? It was just so unfortunate that former President Jonathan did not pay attention to this important Law, rather he chose to enjoy the company of flatterers like Fani- Kayode, the same people Niccolo Machiavelli urged The Prince to avoid like a plague! It still bothers me why anyone will write with much frustration against an article containing harmless advice which contents are nothing new to public knowledge. Maybe Mr. Okudah is just a perfect replica of those that Femi Adeshina, Buhari's Special Adviser on Media and Publicity, once referred to as "Wailing Wailers". Will this man and people like him ever stop wailing? Was he even expecting a reply?

Are Buhari's Critics in Early Lead?

Victory is sweet and defeat is avoided like a plague; no one wants to be associated with it. Not wanting to be classified as "failures" after their "hero" lost the presidential election, President Muhammadu Buhari's opponents or better still critics appear to be cruising off with an early lead. The most recent his critics have done is to label him "Baba Go Slow" referring to his seeming lack of activities. But is it all about an early lead? Watching from afar, I have come to realize that Buhari's critics can fall under any of the following categories: first, are the career Jonathanians or GEJites as they are now popularly known. Leading this pack is our dear Femi Aribisala. In fact, one of these people had openly written that he will not accept Buhari as his President. These people were so sure that their boss or hero would win no matter the cost. They "prophesied" that Buhari will never "smell" Aso Rock. In fact, Aribisala once wrote under the headline: *How to Lose Presidential Election Four Times* in one of his columns stating why Buhari would lose the fourth time. If wishes were horses, they say, men will ride. How time flies. Anyways, he is foremost among Buhari's critics.

Not all Buhari's critics are pro-Jonathan as many may think, though it is very difficult to vouch for this distinction. We can have a second group as those having issues either personally with Buhari himself or his party the APC. This group accommodates people like a former Governor of old Kaduna state Alhaji Abdulkadir Balarabe Musa and a renowned writer Okey Ndibe. One really cannot explain Balarabe Musa's issues with Buhari considering the fact that they are from the same state, Katsina. He was noted to have criticized President Jonathan vociferously at some point and I am not aware he has rescinded on his opinion about Jonathan. His criticisms of President Buhari is what one finds hard to explain, other than the fact that he may probably know something about Buhari that is not to public knowledge. On the other hand, Okey Ndibe's case can be because he had issues at some point with the way the APC was being run. I am not sure Ndibe will be your first choice of a Jonathanian or GEJite. Either way, they constitute a pack of their own.

The third group is perhaps the most reckless. They are nothing but tribal pirates, ethnic Buccaneers and religious Vikings. In this group we boldly include Radio Biafra and its sponsors. They are myopic in views; tactless in approach and reckless in criticisms. On one hand, they urged their "people" not to vote in the election; on the other hand, they want Jonathan to win in an election they forced their people not to vote. I find it difficult to reconcile these contrasting objectives.

More confused was I when I knew that former President Jonathan is Ijaw, a tribe that proudly supported the Federal Army during the Nigerian Civil War. It was only this radio that broadcast the news that President Buhari authorized the bombarding of "Biafran territories", by which they mean Cross Rivers and Akwa Ibom. While they told their listeners that "Igbos are not Nigerians", one is left to wonder at what point did the Efiks, Ibibios, Orons, etc. (whom they also claim as part of "Biafran territories") became Igbos? Apart from this pirate radio which, I later knew, broadcast from London, no other credible news medium reported the "bombardment"!

The fourth group can be neglected as mere "professional" critics, wanting no more than mere attention or patronage. Some of them may have good intentions you never can tell! The most brilliant of these criticisms is "Baba Go Slow". I only laugh anytime I hear these critics on social media make this argument. I have carefully avoided taking part in these discussions because once you air your views you will most likely either get insults or get intellectually-insulting answers. While not making excuses for sluggishness, I think these critics must get their facts right. First, they have done their very best to compare Buhari to Jonathan. They tend to forget that Jonathan's early missteps were just enough to turn Nigerians against him. Second, they also tend to forget that unlike Buhari, Jonathan had close to two years before his election in 2011 so there were no issues about "smooth transition".

Third, Jonathanians, in particular, must by now be aware that the Buhari transition committee did not submit its report immediately because Jonathan's administration would not cooperate with the committee. When they hammer the argument that Buhari's administration is slow, two things come to my mind. The first is Aesop's fable, "The Hare and the Tortoise." The moral of that story is very simple: thoroughness and quality count far more in the long run than speed. The race is usually not to the swift as there is no sense in starting fast and ending poorly. Alas! This is one of life's terrible lessons.

Also, I remember Franklin D. Roosevelt, the 32nd United States' President. Like Buhari, Roosevelt defeated an incumbent President, Herbert Hoover, in 1932. In the weeks following the election, Roosevelt withdrew from public glare leaving the space for his enemies in the Republican Party to criticize him. "He is not prepared for the challenge," so they said. Their criticisms became even more personal and aggressive. At his inauguration, he gave a rousing speech which is now known as "Hundred Days", that served as a major blow to the GOP leaders' attacks. Roosevelt then went to win the next three presidential elections, which is unprecedented and unsurpassed in US history. This appears to me to be the position of Buhari's critics today! For those celebrating Buhari's "sluggishness," it is only a demonstration of the fact that they are bereft of political wisdom. They are revealing their cards too early into the game. They perhaps need to be reminded that the People's Democratic Party(PDP) had congratulated then President Jonathan for "early lead" as the results for six states were being announced.

In fact, the loquacious Femi Fani-Kayode, the PDP Campaign spokesman, had told the world that the party was in "early lead" in 22 states. This is how "early lead" wins.

This is my humble opinion; I may be wrong.

PART 5

INSURGENCY AND ETHNIC NATIONALISM

Early Warnings, Political Risks, and Democracy in Africa

In my article, *Are Things Fallen Apart in Burundi?* I argued for the importance of effective early warnings in the management and prevention of avoidable conflicts in African countries. In the said article, I also argued that conflicts don't just manifest in their elaborate forms; there were early warnings which were largely ignored by those who should know better. Little things we hitherto take for granted might often turn out to be the most decisive. This is why early warnings must always be taken seriously, if not for anything, to minimize the effects of needless conflicts. Permit me to quickly quote the great Prussian strategist, Carl von Clausewitz; in his classic, *On War*, he said, "Everything in war is very simple, but the simplest thing is difficult." Invariably, the simplest things or warnings if unheeded to, more often than not turn out to be fatal!

Let me quickly bring in the pirate radio station, *Radio Biafra,* at this point. The station, I am told has been broadcasting for about three years with only a few people cognizance of its existence or even taking it seriously. Its sponsors must be aware that the project is a journey to nowhere in particular. Its financers might as well be those who are in need of political patronage or to say the obvious, attention-seekers.

It was only recently that the radio station began to enjoy its "popularity boom". Why?

In its series of attacks against the "president of zoo" or "the occupational Nigerian government", the station in one of its programmes accused President Muhammadu Buhari of making "anti-Igbo comments" on BBC Hausa Service. The statement from the radio's patrons should have been treated as insignificant, but the Presidency out of tact bothered to respond to a station that is supposed to be non-existent. Buhari's government went ahead to publicly announce the "jamming" of radio signals. While I am for the liquidation of the notorious radio, I had expected the government would have been more strategic in its systemic annihilation of the pirate radio station.

The dangers portent by this radio station can be likened to the station formed by Hutu extremists in Rwanda, Radio Television Libre de Millie Collines (RTLM) which was formed mainly to broadcast messages of hate, racist propaganda, obscene jokes and music to "spur Hutus to action of flushing out the cockroaches (Tutsis)". This notorious radio station was perhaps the most influential in the systematic extermination of the Tutsis. This, to me, is what Radio Biafra is trying to achieve given its main operator's boast of training militias in firearms "to counter the Occupational Government of Nigeria". To be forewarned is to be forearmed!

Still, in East Africa, two countries that share historical affinity are Burundi and Rwanda. Both countries have gone through needless bloody wars having their own fair share of ethnic conflicts. In 2015, violence erupted in Burundi as a result of President Pierre Nkurunziza's decision to run for a third term in office in violation of the Burundian constitution. At some point, there were rumours of Military coup in that country. The President made good his threat to run, in a poll largely boycotted by the opposition. Analysts, including me, feared that the violence witnessed in recent times since the President's declaration for the illegal third term might continue.

Rwandan President Paul Kagame's supporters urged him to amend Article 101 of the Rwandan Constitution to seek a third term in office. It is yet to be seen what becomes of both post-conflict societies after these, but political risk analysts are unanimous in their views that both ambitions portend danger and possibilities of renewed conflicts in the East African countries. The East African region is known for its volatility, considering the ease and speed at which conflicts spread. This is why the African Union in particular, and the United Nations must do just more than condemning the election as "not credible", they must act, as the signs are ominous. Innocent lives have been lost to sheer self-interested ambitions of few individuals already; losing more lives than can be accounted for. I have cited these to show that despite the Nigerian presidential election, incumbency still plays a critical role in African democracy. Laurent Gbagbo's experience in Ivory Cost, 2011/12; Robert Mugabe's in 2008 and the likes still remind us of the fact that incumbency is still a political risk factor in African democracy.

After the much-celebrated 2015 Nigerian presidential election, crises were largely averted with former President Goodluck Jonathan quickly accepting defeat. There were strong indications of plans to foment trouble in some parts of the country should the election go another way. The quick intervention from some Western nations might have prevented much bloodshed in the aftermath of the Nigerian presidential election.

This is why I appeal to Western nations to consider exerting the same pressure they put on former Nigerian President Goodluck Jonathan on Nkurunziza and Kagame and future incumbents to drop their toga of pride and personal ambitions and embrace peace. In both Burundi and Rwanda, oppositions appear non-existent as a result of harassment, intimidation, or in some cases outright murder. About 200,000 people have fled both countries to neighbouring Congo, Tanzania, and Kenya. The media remains under permanent ban with Nkurunziza's government shutting down African Public Radio for political reasons. All these have even made the opposition weaker.

The experience of the 1993 Civil War in Burundi and the 1994 Genocide in Rwanda are still with us. The latter was what United States' President Bill Clinton called his worst failure over his administration's inadvertence to intervene or at least prevent the genocide. We have a chance to correct that especially when the warnings are clear!

Can Biafra Be Achieved Through A Referendum?

I made a new friend at an event at Golden Gate Restaurant, Ikoyi. His name is Charles and as he told me, he is from Arochuckwu in Abia state. As we began talking, I fell in love with his deep knowledge of history and politics. He seemed to have a firm grasp of several political cum historical topics, ranging from terrorism to US politics. We both agreed on every topic raised, until one of us brought up the issue of Biafra. I wasn't surprised to discover that Charles, like many Igbos I know, is a pro-Biafra supporter, when I asked about his views on the arrest of the director of the Pirate Radio Biafra, Nnamdi Kanu. But unlike most pro-Biafran agitators that I know, he has read several books written about both sides of the Nigeria-Biafra War, before coming to conclusions on the matter. On Kanu's arrest and continued detention by the Directorate of State Service (DSS), my new friend brought out the traditional pro-Biafran argument of "marriage incompatibility." He argued: "If a marriage is no longer working, the best solution is to part ways or divorce peacefully." For my friend Charles, he told me, he didn't witness the war, but bloodshed is way out of the cards as far as achieving "self-determination" for Biafra is concerned. He argued that the solution is just too simple.

The solution he proposed is for Nigeria to conduct a United Nations (UN) supervised referendum to decide the future of Biafrans. I made him realize that I am not really against Biafra as such, although he found this difficult to believe. I informed him that what I am against is the fact that the agitations by people like Kanu are only filled with political opportunism, which the Jonathan-led administration represented. I quoted Carl von Clausewitz, the great Prussian general, in his classic, *On War*, "Everything is very simple in war, but the simplest thing is difficult. These difficulties accumulate and produce a friction, which no man can imagine exactly who has not seen war."

I reminded my friend that the struggle for Catalan independence in Spain dates back as far as 1640, with the unsuccessful first Catalan Republic after the Reaper's War. In the subsequent War of the Spanish Succession, Catalans hoped to salvage their institutions of home rule, in the face of a centralising Bourbon pretender, rather than outright independence. And support for Catalan independence, unlike that of Biafra, is based on the thesis that from the 19th century Catalonia has been a nation derived from contemporary political and cultural ideology based on the Catalan history, its language and unique culture.

If things were that simple, an independent Catalonia would be existent today. Still on Catalonia, I informed him that if it were by conducting a referendum, the Catalan Government had conducted a referendum on independence on November 9, 2014. And, since the Spanish government had refused to recognize the outcome of the referendum which returned over 80 percent "Yes" vote in favour of independence, a "Republic of Catalonia" would probably have to wait longer.

In 1973, a referendum was held on the question of Northern Ireland's continued existence within the United Kingdom (also known as the Border Poll). That was the first time a major referendum had been held in a region in the UK. The vote resulted in an overwhelming majority stating they wished to remain in the UK. The nationalist, Catholics and other pro-independent groups boycotted the poll which led to a turnout of only 58.7 percent of the electorate. Gerry Fitt, the Social Democratic and Labour Party (SDLP) leader called on his supporters "to ignore completely the referendum and reject this extremely irresponsible decision by the British Government". In addition to taking a majority of votes cast, supporters of the "UK option" received the support of 57.5 percent of the total electorate.

The Scottish Independence Referendum Act 2013 is an Act of the Scottish Parliament, which was passed on November 14, 2013 and came into force on December 18. Together with the Scottish Independence Referendum (Franchise) Act 2013, it enabled the Scottish independence referendum of 2014.

On November 14, 2013 the Scottish Independence Referendum Bill, setting out the arrangements for the referendum, was passed by the Scottish Parliament into the Scottish Independence Referendum Act 2013, coming into force on December 18, and enabling the Independence referendum of 2014.

There were serious fears in other parts of the UK that should Scotland attain its independence, Northern Ireland, with a history of violent attacks against British authorities, would likely go as well. One wonders why the Westminster government granted the Scottish government's request for such referendum which it could not grant to Northern Island. Ulster is, after all, far more of a Scottish colony than an English one, demographically speaking. From the reign of King James VI of Scotland (who also became James I of England in 1603), Ulster was disproportionately colonized by the Scots (many of whom later left for America to become 'Scot-Irish'), which explains why Presbyterianism was always a more popular denomination in Ulster than the Church of Ireland.

The Scottish legacy is also reflected in efforts in recent decades among Protestants to cement an 'Ulster-Scots' culture and language. While you will see the Scottish saltire at Orange Order marches, you won't see an empty-handed Cross of St George. The two lands are united in their love of and hatred of Glasgow's two football teams and by simmering sectarianism. The Scottish National Party (SNP) was very keen to jump on the Braveheart bandwagon. Why not go even further back in time? Parts of Ulster and Scotland were once united in the sixth and seventh century in the kingdom of Dalriada. The revival of this ancient kingdom, should Scotland vote "Yes", would make much more sense than Northern Ireland's continued bondage under England.

After all, most English people are notoriously ignorant about Ulster. During the Troubles, the English regarded the province with a mixture of irritation and indifference, which is why the Irish Republican Army (IRA), in the 1970s, knew that England would only take notice if there were bombs on the mainland. "They're both as bad as each other" and "fancy fighting about religion" were the two common reactions. To the English, the Northern Irish are a foreign people, which is why they found the grating, mangled accents of John Cole and Ian Paisley so amusing.

So, if it is about agitation, or referendum, we probably would have seen Northern Ireland join their brothers under the Dublin government or form a sovereign state of its own.

After several years of conflicts, some say since 1955, the Sudanese government approved the request for a referendum for Southern Sudan in 2011, on whether the region should remain a part of Sudan or become independent. The referendum was one of the consequences of the 2005 Naivasha Agreement between the Khartoum central government and the Sudan People's Liberation Army/Movement (SPLA/M). Expectedly, the final results of the referendum show that over 90 percent voted in favour of South Sudan's independence.

No one prays for the situation the new country finds itself today. Most people will probably not recall that it took over 20 years of protracted conflicts for the country to part through a referendum. If things can be so simple!

Let's focus on Quebec, a province in Canada. It has always been the sole majority French-speaking province. Long ruled by forces that focused on the affirmation of the province's French and Catholic identity within Canada, the Quiet Revolution of the early 1960s prompted a surge in civic and economic nationalism, as well as voices calling for the separation of the province and the establishment of a national state of its own. After arriving in power in 1976, the government held a referendum in 1980 seeking a mandate to negotiate "sovereignty-association" with Canada but it was decisively defeated. It is instructive to note that the Canadian Supreme Court, in 1998, ruled that Quebec has the right to secede (which is not unilateral), but one can easily say "Twinkle, twinkle little star"; Quebec remains firmly part of Canada. The American Civil War (1861-65) was fought to determine the survival of the Union or independence for the Confederacy.

Among the 34 states in January 1861, seven Southern slave states individually declared their secession from the United States and formed the Confederate States of America. The war had its origin in the fractious issue of slavery, especially the extension of slavery into the western territories. After four years of combat, which left over 600,000 Union and Confederate soldiers dead and destroyed much of the South's infrastructure, the Confederacy collapsed and slavery was abolished.

It will be difficult to compare the Confederate fighters with pro-Biafran agitators. The colonies, the 11 states that wanted to secede joined the Union VOLUNTARILY, like the original 13 states, so one would argue they had the "right to secede" voluntarily. The fact that the gallant US Military rose to its duty cannot be faulted. Can things be that simple? Like the statement I quoted earlier from Clausewitz, things look so simple, can be said so simply, can be looked at as "simple", but they are not always so simple. This was what I told my friend and I hope he agreed.

Buhari and the Challenge of Terrorism

The reality, today in Africa, is that Terrorism remains a challenge. We have had to cope with the deadly acts perpetrated by the notorious al- Shabab in Somalia, Tanzania and Kenya. What about the ruthlessness of Boko Haram in Nigeria, Cameroon and Chad? We need not forget so soon the havoc wrecked by the Lord's Resistance Army (LRA) in Uganda for many years. In the centre of this reality is the question of overcoming this monster of terrorism.

During 2015 presidential election campaign, President Muhammadu Buhari made it clear that top on his priorities, when elected as Nigerian president, is his promise to see the end of terror and its attendant evils. This was at the period the dreaded Boko Haram was at the peak of their nefarious activities in Nigerian North East region. It is on this note that President Buhari gave an unusual order in his inaugural address to the nation on May 29, 2015 for the Military High Command to, with immediate effect, relocate to Maiduguri, the ancient capital of Nigerian northeastern region which is also the terrorists' stronghold. This order has been given different interpretations from several quarters within and without Nigeria. Irrespective of anyone's interpretation(s) of the order, one thing is clear: fighting terrorism requires taking some hard and tough choices like moving the entire military brass to the terrorists' stronghold. Like I have always said on this matter, terrorism poses unusual challenges and defeating it will require some radical, unconventional and in some cases strange decisions from the politico-military leadership. No one recalls terrorism being a "Nigerian" issue some two decades ago.

Terrorism was almost missing from the Nigerian glossary over a decade ago but it features prominently today. This is why it must never be taken lightly. It is on this note that the formation of the Multinational Joint Task Force (MNJTF) led by Nigeria against Boko Haram makes a lot of sense. Since the swearing-in of the Buhari-led administration, the terrorists have not relented in their attacks on the region, rather, they intensified their assaults wreaking more deaths and havoc and challenging the Nigerian state. In doing all these, the terrorists may only be taking the very chance that President Buhari's government is yet to properly form.

This is why I will advise President Buhari to get to work before things get out of hand. On my part, I will advocate that Nigeria must wake up to his historical role of providing leadership at the continental level. The formation of the MNJTF is welcome but that alone will not be enough to defeat terrorism. Nigeria provided leadership during the struggle against colonialism. Nigeria must canvass for the African Union (AU) to take a stand against terrorism. It must insist the Union puts its feet down and roars ferociously against the insurgents. President Buhari must, in his capacity as AU Chairman, canvass for an AU High Command, a special Anti-Terror Squad, or under any appropriate name, comprising volunteers from member states in our bid to conquer insurgency.

For so long, it appears the AU fell asleep immediately it achieved its mandate of "eradicating colonialism in Africa." One would have thought that since all African countries are now politically independent, the AU would have sought a new mandate, which should naturally be, "eradicating terrorism, insurgency and poverty in Africa." One will equally have thought that the change of name from the Organisation of African Unity (OAU) would have meant a change in approach, philosophy, tactics, mandate and perspectives.

The Union must come to the realization that the rise of insurgency on the continent is a direct attack on the corporate existence of the AU.

This is where President Buhari must prove to be different! Some may question the workability of our proposal. We would then be quick to point out that Nigeria is on record to have funded the powerful OAU organ, the Liberation Committee. The Committee, with its secretariat in Dar es Salaam, Tanzania trained guerrilla fighters in their determination to achieve the core mandate of the defunct OAU. Nigeria supported groups such as the Popular Movement for the Liberation of Angola (MPLA), the South African National Congress(ANC), the South West African People's Organisation (SWAPO), Front for the Liberation of Mozambique (FRELIMO) and the likes. Probably OAU's support for these groups made it difficult for it to give a definition to the word "Terrorism" at that period. If the same passion deployed to fight colonialism was deployed in our war against insurgency, it would have been only a matter of time before we prevailed!

This is just a piece of advice to President Muhammadu Buhari on this matter.

Why We Are Missing the Point on Terrorism

On 26 June 2015, the world watched with horror, shock and disdain the unprovoked terrorist attacks claiming the lives of about 50 people and leaving many others injured in three countries – France, Kuwait and Tunisia. This deadly act came few days after Jens Stoltenberg, the North Atlantic Treaty Organization (NATO) scribe spoke on CNN concerning the bloc's policy on containing the Islamic State – the group that claimed responsibility for the attacks. The confidence with which Jens spoke, one would have been lulled to sleep with his or her two eyes closed if not for the attacks on the French factory. Can we assume we are then missing the point? There appears to be an assumption among many anti-terrorist analysts that since the Islamic State fighters are "mainly Muslims" they will honour their earlier "ceasefire" agreement during the Ramadan fast. Apart from the group's attack on a Kuwaiti Mosque negating this misguided view, we appear not to be learning from history!

The US military got everything right in Vietnam until a ridiculous tactical blunder in 1968. The US military had erroneously assumed that the Vietcong- North Vietnamese militia would, in fact, honour the "ceasefire agreements" during the Tet – a day highly revered in Vietnam when, during a war, it is traditional to declare a truce. Needless to say, it was on this same day that the Vietcong shipped in arms, using the Tet holiday as a cover, to South Vietnam, an area then under full US military protection. The rest, as they say, is history.

This same mistake we still make today. One should be amazed if we cannot see a progressive return to the Cold War era. The only difference this time is that it is not between the world's superpowers or ideologies, but between the world's deadliest terrorist groups! The Islamic State which claimed responsibility for many attacks on those three countries can be seen as a direct response to the Al Quaeda Islamic Magreeb (AQIM)-linked al-Shabab attacks on the AU base in Mogadishu, Somalia.

The Garrissa University (Kenya) attacks in April 2015 and others in East Africa may just be a direct response to the rising profile of Boko Haram (an Islamic State ally) notoriety in West Africa. One needs to see the patterns of these attacks as battles for control of "spheres of influence" between these two dangerous groups. In parenthesis, during the Cold War era, Africa was really a battleground. To further confirm how far we have missed the point, we are paying lesser attention to the timings of these attacks. One of the issues that traditionally dominate every US Presidential election is Foreign Policy. Shaping the US foreign policy is global security and terrorism. We must not forget that the two leading parties have been at loggerheads over what is responsible for the rise of global terrorism. While Democrats have been quick to point out that George W. Bush administration's tactless invasion of Afghanistan and Iraq in 2001and 2003 respectively is responsible for the rise in world terror; Republicans provided the counter-argument that Barack Obama's indecision to prevent the spread of the "Arab Spring" is the reason for the rise of a notorious group like the Islamic State (ISIS). Irrespective of which side of the divide one belongs, these terror groups have much interest in US election than most people may think!

The Vietnamese fighters or Vietcong with their poor training and orientations understood the simple fact that 1968 was a US presidential election year. With that at their disposal, they acted promptly by doing all they could to shape the US public opinion in an election year and take full advantage of the shifts in public opinion. This remains an error President Lyndon B. Johnson (who was defeated in that year's Democratic Primary in New Hampshire to anti-war campaigner Senator Eugene McCarthy) will never forget!

It is more than mere coincidence that the attacks came on the same day the US Supreme Court handed its judgment in favour of "marriage right" (a fairer way of saying homosexual, gay or same-sex marriage right). Again, this is perhaps one of the hotly debated issues in US politics today. The Islamic State fighters are known to have murdered those they identified as "homosexuals" and "infidels" with impunity.

Being an issue that is sure to generate much heat as the presidential campaigns heat up, one needs to look well to see the connections. To this writer, these attacks may not be unconnected with parts of the terrorists' intentions to shape the outcome of the US presidential election! We are either overrating or underestimating these terrorists. It also appears we lack proper diagnosis of their intentions. We need to divest emotions from our analyses of terrorism and their activities if we are really serious about winning the war against terror. Terrorists think the way(s) we do not think; they do things we won't ordinarily do; their understanding of human nature and experiences differs remarkably from ours. They are not the ghosts or spirits they want us to believe they are neither are they the beasts we take them to be. They are but mortals with their own fears too, only playing on our own fears and spreading their fears through us. This is the point we are missing!

The Nigerian Military and the Fight Against Terrorism

It is heart-lifting to receive the news of the advancement of the Nigerian Army against the dreaded group, Boko Haram. This is coming at the time when public support for, and the confidence in, the Military is at an all-time low. We can only pray for more morale for these young men working day and night to defend our dear nation. Given this background, it is pertinent to remind us of the issues raised by Boko Haram activities in the North-Eastern part of Nigeria. The memories of over 10,000 lives lost to nefarious activities of this group are still with us. Over 200 Chibok girls are still with their abductors. We can still hear the cries of the internally displaced persons (IDP). What better time do we then have to have a national military debrief? Holding a debrief is a standard military practice in advanced countries, even during a war. There was a national military debrief, in full public glare as recently as the 2006 Lebanese war following the kidnap of Israeli soldiers, and subsequent attacks on Israel by the group, Hezbollah.

For some people, setting up a commission amidst fighting was a dubious, questionable decision given the distractions it portends on the military hierarchy. In Israel, the debrief is as important as the fighting!

Also, after the Iraqi invasion controversy in 2003, the Westminster government set up the Chilcot Inquiry, also known as the Iraqi Inquiry to look at the role of the British army in the debacle. Therefore, military debriefing is not an unusual affair, except if we decide to make it so. Sometimes in 2014, about 97 soldiers faced the court-martial for various offenses that could be classified as mutiny. While we agree that discipline, order, doctrine and combat readiness are the hallmark of the Nigerian military, we mustn't turn a blind eye to the germane issues raised concerning institutional decay and corruption within the military high command by these unfortunate fighters.

One is left to wonder how foot-walking local hunters in Michika, Mubi and many parts of northeastern Nigeria record more successes against the Boko Haram than the army. One is still left to wonder why the lesser-trained Chadian, Cameroonian and the Niger armies will have to come to the aid of the almighty Nigerian army in battle against Boko Haram. These issues should bother all patriotic Nigerians. A military debrief would have revealed all these and saved us from the monumental embarrassment caused by the "exposition" of the helpless and hapless soldiers. We are aware some people will raise eyebrows about our proposal for a national military debrief at this time. These people will raise their most potent argument – the debrief will distract the soldiers from their primary duties. It was this same argument that was used to justify the military's unpreparedness for the February 14 presidential election before it was shifted to March 28. But these same people did not find anything unusual in the Court Marshal of 97 soldiers in the heat of the military onslaught against Boko Haram. It was alright for soldiers insisting on military standards, professionalism and best practices to be executed but the issues they raised are secondary. What a country!

As against the familiar, if our proposal will be accepted, the Nigerian military must consider making some ground-breaking changes. It must consider changes in its orientation and doctrine. It must be willing to sacrifice discipline for flexibility; organization for the initiative; and predictability for innovations. These must also be included in the terms of reference for the proposed national debrief. In addition, we suggest our sailors, soldiers, and pilots should be kept busy either in peace or battle. Idleness is lethargic. Use makes functional. Whatever is unused is either misused, underused or abused. In peacetime, our soldiers should be used for physically-demanding jobs like road construction, bridge building, farming in the rural areas and other socio-economically beneficial duties.

Apart from the physical benefits they provide our fighters, these tasks would prepare our soldiers; they would prepare them mentally for battle. This also boosts good civil-military relations. This may appear strange to some people but it was practiced in Tanzania in the 1970s which successfully kept the soldiers busy effectively after the unsuccessful mutiny in the army in 1964. This explains why Tanzania is one of the few countries in Africa that never fell into a military misadventure. No one needs to be told that the successful Tanzanian army invasion which disposed of Idi Amin's dictatorial regime (Uganda) in 1979 was thanks to the excellent training and leadership in the poorly-equipped Tanzanian army.

In order to have our military perform optimally and professionally, we must first insist on having a full national military debrief or a public commission of inquiry to trace the root cause of cases of under-performance of the army in the face of Boko Haram's onslaught leading to the loss of lives of untold thousands; rendering many homeless and permanently incapacitating millions.

Can Buhari Relocate the Military Command Centre to Maiduguri?

In his inaugural address to the nation, the Nigerian president, Muhammadu Buhari gave a strange order for the Military Command Centre or the Headquarters to immediately relocate to Maiduguri till terrorism is defeated. Since he made this speech, many so-called military "experts" or analysts have suddenly sprung up to voice their opinions on the matter which has the capacity or otherwise to solve or deter our efforts at fighting terrorism. Of all the opinions I have read or heard, either for or against it, I must confess I saw little or no logic in most of the opinions offered other than ethnopolitical arguments. I soon saw how quickly ignorance spreads.

Before we go further, let me make some clarifications. I am not a military expert, neither do I lay claim to being one. I have no military experience or training save for my three weeks camping experience. I further applied for the Nigerian Army Short Service Combatant (SSC) Commission which I couldn't make the final list in 2014. If there is anything I know about the military it is purely from my interactions with my soldier friends when I joined the National Youth Service Corps in Adamawa State in 2013 and stayed briefly at a military barracks in 2013. Having said that, let us get back to our task. In my opinion, most of us, or perhaps our military "experts" are missing out on some basic points which are crucial to our understanding of the fight against terrorism. The issues are not made easier when we continue to look at them from purely ethno-emotional lenses. First, we need not be reminded that Muhammadu Buhari is the Commander-in-Chief of the Nigerian Armed Forces by virtue of his position as President of the Federal Republic. The 1999 Constitution under which he took his oath of office, confers upon him certain powers under section 218(1) to "determine the operational use of the armed forces of the Federation." My simple, layman understanding of the term "operational use" includes but is not limited to the establishment of bases, formations, command, divisions and subdivision in any component of the armed forces in any part of the federation.

If the commander-in-chief, in his wisdom, chose to relocate the command centre to any part of the federation for operational efficacy, this writer sees nothing wrong in that!

Perhaps, some fears are due to geographical factors. One of the arguments is that moving the military headquarters out of the Federal Capital Territory (FCT) will not prove effective. They support their argument with the fact that the command centre is not the infantry, hence a waste of time to relocate. I immediately reached out for my copy of the 1999 Constitution again, I am sorry to announce that nowhere in the constitution lies a clause that made the President's action regarding this matter illegal. A prominent military analyst has defined a commander-in-chief as someone who keeps himself abreast of the situation, makes expedient decisions for an operation or battle, assigns combat missions opportunely and completely, disseminates decisions to units and sub-units, organizes interactions, renders total support to troop operations and puts decisions into effect resolutely. We are not used to these types of radical decisions made by a true commander-in-chief, rather, we are used to pot-bellied generals, commanders and lazy soldiers as products of a below-efficient military brass.

Moving the higher echelons of the military to the troubled spots will make them have quality briefs, reports and field orientations, which is about all that is needed in the fight against terrorism. We must be quick to admit that there are no hard-and-fast rules to fighting groups like the Boko Haram. This is where we must quote the great Prussian military strategist, Carl von Clausewitz, in his classic, *On War where* he writes, "Everything in war is very simple, but the simplest thing is difficult." On the surface, fighting Boko Haram and defeating the terrorists looks easy, but fully conquering terrorism involves a lot of complexities which are too detailed to be written in a single article or chapter. If we had observed carefully we would have found out that the group is not as strong as it has been depicted; but for the reckless (in)decisions by the politico-military establishment, the group would just have existed in the footnote of history.

If Boko Haram militants can flee on the advancement of the Chadian and the Cameroonian Armies but find comfort on Nigerian soil under the full glare of the "almighty" Nigerian army, then there are things we are not just doing right! It is at this point that the risky decision to relocate the full presence of the Nigerian army to the troubled areas makes some sense. If Boko Haram can after then prove stronger than the entire army, then the time has come to take a long, hard look at the army itself!

Napoleon Bonaparte is considered one of the greatest generals in history. He achieved this feat, not by sitting at the comfort of his command or headquarters in Paris, he always leads the battle himself. His entire military campaigns were directed by a single commanding mind. He received quality field reports, intelligence, and battle briefs thanks to his presence on the battle ground. We might not have remembered him today had he just sat at his high command barking out orders like we have today in the Nigerian military. Adolf Hitler missed out on Napoleon's great strength by relying too much on information from his high command in Munich during World War II. He and his generals were almost never on the battlefield. They sat comfortably at the headquarters to analyze contradicting field reports. Little wonder the well-equipped German army fell like a pack of cards. The rest is history. I cited these two examples just to show how long our generals have slept. Like I wrote in one of my articles, *How to Fight Terrorism*, I argued that there are no conventional rules when it comes to fighting terrorism. Several minute details often prove critical or decisive which is part of the complications which Clausewitz wrote about. Roads get clogged, troops refuse to report to their assigned stations for mobilization (or leave and return home after they have reported), equipment is inadequate or out of date, troops are not trained to use equipment which is up to date and so on. All these notwithstanding, we are aware relocating the military command to Maiduguri might not end the menace of Boko Haram overnight, but it can be part of the solution. This is my humble opinion on the matter.

ISIS: The Challenges of Global Terrorism in Post-Cold War

In an amazing display of bravery, an unnamed Tunisian street hawker set himself ablaze (some say it was out of frustration) on a sunny afternoon. This singular heroic act soon led to series of riots which ultimately brought down Ahmed Ben Alli's regime and things were never the same again. As the world watched the "Arab Spring" extend to Yemen, Egypt, Syria, Libya and many other Arabian territories, arms freely flew into the hands of "freedom fighters" and pro-US regimes' foot soldiers which later became deciding issues in world peace and security. Ever since the world left us to find solutions to our problems they left us alone and went silent. Keen observers of international affairs will probably know that not much has changed in the United States' foreign policy thinking since the end of the Cold War era in 1990. The role of Washington in the so-called Arab Spring shows that the White House still views international relations strictly from Cold War lenses. The role of the "World Powers" in Syria specifically calls to question the supposed end of the Cold War.

Ever since communist China and former "Soviet" Russia supported Asa'ad Damascus's Government, Washington found a way to oppose the same regime hence supporting the "freedom fighters". Not minding the fact that the US supported Hosni Mubarack's over three-decades-old regime, US-led NATO forces brought down the seeming popular anti-Western 42-year-old dictatorial Libyan regime led by Muammar Gaddafi. Suffice to say, both countries have known no peace ever since!

There is a school of thought that Washington's reluctance to intervene in Syria's crises was because the country has no Crude Oil (an important geo-political resource) unlike proximate countries in the Middle East. There is still another school that says, had the Obama-led administration intervened at the early stages of the Syrian crises, it might not have exploded or in the worst case, human casualties would have been very minimal. The two views cannot be wrong, if Washington had dropped its Cold War lenses and viewed the issues from more realistic standpoints.

The decision of the US and its allies of initial "non-interference" have proven costly. The new dimension of global terrorism and insecurity accounts for this rather unfortunate decision. The disturbing nature that international terrorists now take which has led to the agitation for Islamic States of Iraq and Syria (ISIS), the Islamic States of Iran and the Levant (ISIL) and other Islamic States (for short) affiliates and their nefarious activities in the region explains the conspiracy of world leaders as these groups rein terror on countries and innocent lives. The Washington government supplies arms to its "Freedom Fighters" in Syria, Libya, and in other places to fight governments they do not support as part of their foreign policy objectives, forgetting that the so-called "freedom fighters" soon turn "terrorists" after they are left alone. This was exactly the case with Western-trained Osama bin Laden and the likes. The same "Freedom Fighters" they armed are now the new Islamic State (IS) fighters that have been killing people with impunity and the world is silent!

Even if we concede that the US is protecting its economic and political interests in the Middle East (Oil and Israel), doing it at the expense of monumental loss of human lives is uncharitable, considering the fact that the US was a major causative factor in the imbroglio. The fact that Washington singularly accounts, far more than any other, for the escalation of the ISIS crises, US it is that must take the lead in bringing an end to all these needless killings. The world cannot remain silent as innocent lives are being lost. As a matter of recommendation, State Department's strategists must get off this Cold War mentality. The world is in the 21st century and the Great Wars went with the 20th century. The fact that either Russia or China supports or opposes an issue does not automatically mean the US must take an opposite action on the same issue. This will only make international relations filled with tension, suspicions, distrust, and hatred. Human lives are at stake. The whole world, not only the United States, must stand firm against the ugly trend of ISIS. This is not the time to remain silent. Our people are dying daily for daring to profess their faith. We must not be passive. We must not be silent. If you are silent now while these atrocities go on then you are part of the world that was silent while we died. We died for what we know nothing about. We died because of the profession of our religious beliefs. And as ISIS operated; burning and killing children, murdering "infidels" and maiming innocent and harmless citizens, the world went silent. It all started in Tunisia.

Africa: The New Challenge of Terrorism

The terrorist attacks on Garissa University, Kenya on 2 April 2015 which resulted in the death of 148 students by a group, al-Shabab, calls for worry on the part of African leaders, under the African Union system. African leaders must devise a new way of looking at the monster of terrorism in the 21st century. With pomp and a collective sense of fulfillment, African nationalists gathered in the historic city of Addis Ababa, Ethiopia on 25 May 1963 to witness the birth of the African regional bloc, the Organization of African Unity (OAU). Amidst the euphoria, the immediate mandate of the new Organization was clear decolonization. It was with this mandate that the OAU, now African Union (AU) looked at the issues on the continent.

In order to achieve its immediate objective, any means to see this done will do just well as far as the OAU is concerned. One important organ of the OAU was the Liberation Committee which headquarters was in Dar es Salaam, Tanzania. This explains why several guerrilla movements like the Popular Movement for the Liberation of Angola (MPLA), Mau Mau Movement (Kenya), South West African Peoples Organization (SWAPO) in Namibia, Front for the Liberation of Mozambique (FRELIMO) and the likes all trained under the guidance of the Liberation Committee. It is no longer a secret that most, if not all countries that gained independence in the 70s, 80s and 90s did so with the force of arms. With this, it was very difficult for the OAU to precisely define "Terrorism". If it did, there is no way its definition will not include acts perpetrated by groups like the African National Congress (ANC) in South Africa, for instance.

The ANC itself was granted an observer status in the Organization. The same ANC was defined as a dangerous terror group by the Apartheid regime in South Africa. This was the OAU dilemma. All countries in Africa are now politically independent, so the perspective of the African leaders must change. There are no more colonial masters to deal with at least. The changing of name from Organization of African Unity (OAU) to the African Union (AU) in the beginning of the century does not mean change in philosophy. The change in name will only be meaningful if African leaders themselves change their way of looking at the present challenge confronting the continent – Terrorism.

Before we go further, let us digress a little. During the Cold War, Africa was a battleground for Shylock European and Western powers for "spheres of influence". Crises in Congo DR, Angola, Algeria, Sudan and the likes all have Cold War undertones. The question then is: "Why should Africans be made to suffer from what is not theirs?"

This is not to say that Africa does not have issues of its own. At least groups like Boko Haram (Nigeria), al-Shabab (Somalia), Lord's Resistance Army (Uganda) have African roots, but we can make a bet they would not have been so sophisticated if not for their affiliations with the notorious Islamic State of Iran and al-Sham(ISIS) and the Al-Quaeda Islamic Maghreb (AQIM), two groups which intend to turn Africa into a battleground for their rivalries.

This is perhaps the case with Boko Haram and al-Shabab with the former pledging allegiance to the Islamic State (IS) fighters and the latter to Al-Queada. The rivalry between the IS and al-Queada has been well documented so it needs no recounting here. It is our take that the

Garissa attack is just a show of relevance by al-Shabab to wade off the growing influence (with the recent allegiance oath by Boko Haram to the ISIS) of the Islamic State on the continent which al-Queada once boasted of. This is our logical explanation for the attacks. We, therefore, call on African leaders to act fast: Africa cannot be a battleground for another "Cold War" between ISIS and Al-Quaeda. If not for the reckless indecision of some African leaders, groups like the Boko Haram would not have attained their present notorious dimensions. Failed state institutions in Somalia can best explain the rise of al-Shabab. It is at this point that the AU must seek a new mandate by coming in fully to save the continent. It is happening in Kenya today, we do not know the next port of call. If Africa cannot tame these groups with roots in Africa how then can we deal with foreign groups like ISIS and AQIM? The Yoruba proverb says: "The thief at home is the one which brings the thief from outside."

With the same vigor the OAU now AU fought colonialism, it must deploy a spirited fight against the monster of terrorism. It is time the AU established its own High Command, with volunteers from member nations in its bid to conquer the monster. The Command must have a special operation force, or an Anti-Terrorism Department (ATD), with its own separate secretariat and staff. The ATD must be given the powers of "Unrestrained Entry" in any African country where there is an early warning of impending terrorist attacks.

Also, the ATD must establish bases in all member states of the African Union as part of its operation. We are aware of the old question of "territorial integrity" or "sovereignty" that some might raise. Since terrorists respect no territory or sovereignty, so must every counter-terrorist effort. It is just like fighting cancer; to save the body, the cancerous cell or tumor must be removed to every of its slightest trace. So, must terror and every trace of it must be expunged from our domains. It takes more than conventional approach to fighting terrorism. It is an emergency with no "normal" connotation!

In addition to the noted challenges of AU system, there are other challenges the African leaders face ranging from lack of institutions, processes, and proper conflict analyses mechanisms in member states. A good example is Nigeria where the fight against the notorious Boko Haram has been clouded by political opportunism, sycophancy, and clear institutional weaknesses/decay. The fact that the poorer Chadian, Niger and Cameroonian Armies had a successful onslaught against the group relative to a fairly richer Nigeria confirms serious institutional decays in the Nigerian defence system ridiculing the Nigerian so-called fight against Boko Haram. It is on this note that African leaders must wake up from their self-induced slumber to the new challenge of terrorism. The Garissa University terrorist attacks must be the very last.

How to Fight Terrorism

It is no longer news that terrorism is an, if not the main issue in African politics today. The terrorists carried out a deadly assault on April 2, 2015. The Garissa University terror attacks in Kenya, by the notorious al-Shabab terrorist group, which left 148 innocent students dead, should convince even the most ridiculous doubting Thomas of the reality of the threat posed by these groups on our existence as a continent. The question then is how to fight it – terrorism.

There have been various suggestions on how to deal with this disturbing trend. One central aspect in all the suggestions is the role of the Military. The, perhaps only point of disagreement, is methods or mode of its (Military's) involvement. Before we proceed, let's make some important clarifications. Using the military to tackle terrorism can at best provide mixed results. This is the fact that the military operates on conventional principles in prosecuting conventional wars. National Armies are expected to observe certain laws in war such as treaties governing "Prisoners of War" and the likes. Professional Armies are by law prevented from training under-aged as soldiers. Extraterritoriality is often extended to friendly or allied militaries, particularly for the purpose of allowing that military to pass through some territories during a war.

All these do or may not apply to unconventional groups like guerrillas or terrorists. It is therefore illogical to fight unconventional elements using conventional means! It is time for a more pragmatic approach to tackling this issue. The successes recorded by local hunters, in Nigerian towns of Mubi, Michika, and Madagali, and the efforts of the local group called Civilian Joint Task Force (CJTF) in rolling back the notorious Boko Haram in Nigeria provides a vital clue to kick start the process. The success recorded by these efforts proves that the military may lack thorough analyses as a result of poor institutional and system processes, to really root out this menace. To curb the menace of terrorists, there is the need for a trans-border approach. I maintain this because terrorists are groups without territories of their own. This is where the African Union (AU) and other sub-regional blocs come in.

Like I argued in my article, "Africa: The Challenge of Terrorism", the AU needs to do more than depending on army recruits from member states. It must, itself, have its own standing High Command for its own specific operations and enforcement of its sanctions. The Union which has a rich history of armed struggle against colonialism, having through its powerful Liberation Committee, trained guerrilla groups against colonial and apartheid regimes, must rise up to its new challenge without much ado. The Union must ignite its historic spirit of struggle, and face this monster of terrorism. It is on this note that I recommend an Anti-Terror Department (ATD) or any other suitable name under the direct supervision of the African Union(AU) for the specific purpose of combating terrorism. The ATD must be well-funded by member states, voluntary donations from individuals and organizations with objectives similar to those of the African Union. It must have a secretariat of its own, and an effective means of propaganda. You heard me right "Propaganda" in the fight against terror.

We are equally recommending the ATD be trained under the guidance of professional soldiers in the art of conventional warfare. The ATD must be granted the full powers of extraterritoriality throughout the continent. This condition is not negotiable.

In some cases, some governments for foreign policy reasons or any other politically-motivated reasons sponsor or harbour terrorist groups. This is where the efficacy of the propaganda machinery of the ATD will be put to test. The AU must do all within its powers:

political, economic, social or any other to put pressure on such government by cutting off its arms supplies. Volunteers for operations for the ATD must be regularly paid from funds available at its disposal. They must all be of African descent. Their camping base must be in strategic places in North, Central East and Southern Africa for effective operations. The Garissa University attacks should be seen as early warnings by the AU for further attacks which next port of call is highly unpredictable.

We are aware some may take our recommendations as too simplistic. I agree. But a quick reminder here is that the United States-led North Atlantic Treaty Organisation (NATO) has for more than a decade been in Afghanistan fighting Al-Queada and the Taliban; the only mistake, however, has been, fighting terror using conventional methods!

How to Fight Terrorism with a Lean Purse

Apart from those who witnessed the Mallam <u>Muhammadu Maitatsine</u> riots in the '80s, many would have beaten their chests that terrorism cannot be an issue in Nigeria as we know it today. These people have obvious reasons to support their optimism. Added to the spate of attacks is the attack of Garissa University in Kenya, leaving 148 innocent students dead in the process. The al-Shabab claimed responsibility for the attack and has grown even bolder and more daring than ever.

Boko Haram has constituted itself into a regular menace in Nigeria's northeastern region gaining notoriety for the death of tens of thousands and injuring more others. ISIL's activities has gotten it world attention good enough to convince the ridiculous doubting Thomas of the reality of the threat posed by these groups on us. The question then is how to fight it.

The threat of terrorism is one that transcends any conventional solution. The military alone cannot, just as I have written in the past, win the war against terror, in this case, <u>Boko Haram</u>. Supply of Western arms has proven to be useless as the rise of ISIS attests to. Improved budgetary allocations to the military and joint military actions against terror without corresponding support of the "civilian sector" will just be as futile as pouring water into a basket.

As hard as this may sound, it is true. What we must understand is that funds allocated to fight against terror more often than not glide their way into private pockets as <u>DasukiGate</u> has proven in Nigeria. If they are not siphoned, they often turn out not to be enough, no matter the face value of the currency. If it were for huge allocations, the United States will not be spending millions maintaining their soldiers in Afghanistan fighting a lost war against the Taliban. What about the Vietnam debacle in the '60s?

If we are truly serious about winning or sustaining the victory against Boko Haram and other terrorists, there is the need for a strong civilian component in the fight. By "civilian component", I mean thoroughly-oriented, organised and systematic efforts at integrating the public in the fight against insurgency while in the process of improving <u>civil–military relations</u>. Improved image of the <u>Nigerian Army</u> and its civil-military relations will do a lot of good in the fight against Boko Haram. This is where, I think, the media will play a key role.

Presently, there seems to be a major disconnect between the Army on one hand and the public on the other hand. My best guess is that insurgents are taking advantage of this gap. Even in conventional wars, the Army still needs the civilians. This may be why there is often militia who are themselves not professional soldiers but are trained by the military during conventional wars. If the military needs civilians during war; why then the disconnection in the fight against the insurgency? The truth of the matter is that it is cheaper to engage the civilians in our efforts at sustaining momentum and hopefully the total eradication of terror in our land!

During one of his visits to the Theatre Command of the Operation Lafiya Dole in Maiduguri, Bama, Konduga, and other areas affected by the crisis, Nigeria's Minister for Information, Alhaji Lai Muhammed, recognising the need for civil engagement, spoke about the need to have his ministry inaugurate a national security campaign against insurgency to sensitize Nigerians on the need for active participation of individuals in security matters. In the minister's own words, he said, "No nation succeeds in the fight against insurgency without the civilian component; so, we will let Nigerians know that the fight against insurgency is a national issue…" Before I proceed, let me be clear that I am not a fan of Lai Muhammed as Information Minister, though I once applauded him as APC spokesman and in that capacity alone. But even if I don't agree with his appointment in that portfolio, I have to on this matter.

Many people tend to have forgotten the fact that Britain once had the challenge of terrorism just like Nigeria. Northern Ireland used to be a troubled spot thanks to the violent activities of the <u>Irish Republican Army </u>(IRA) and its affiliates. The group terrorized people in the region with reckless abandon in the 20th century. This is where I propose "Attrition by Charm" launched by the Royal Irish Regiment to seek a permanent solution to the Irish problem in the late '90s.

What did they get right? First, the British anti-terrorism strategists understood the fact that the regiment, which is an amalgam of the Royal Irish Rangers and the Ulster Defence Regiment, had a particularly poor image among nationalists, making them vulnerable to attacks in spots with strong Dublin or Catholic attachments. Second, the fact that the soldiers were largely seen as "foreigners" which reminded the locals of colonialism (which most Irish resent) led to a decision by a number of soldiers to take lessons in the Irish language and the Gaelic culture to improve their image in the nationalist community.

If we adapt this into our own fight against terrorism, we can achieve the similar result with a minimal budget. What we should do are the simple, minutest things. Our soldiers fighting in the northeastern part of the country should be made to take lessons in Kanuri language. I say this because it is spoken by about 500,000 people who use it as a second language. Since the most troubled areas are Borno and Yobe, speaking the language of the locals, other than simply Hausa, will make the soldiers no longer appear as strangers whom the locals should not trust. When this is done, our anti-terror strategists should consider seeking the support of local opinion leaders and farmers and make them "feel" being part of the solutions to the challenge of Boko Haram. The support of media platforms like *Aboki News* and the likes may also be sought on behalf of the military.

As useless as muddy water is when compared to tea, so is media without a message. The message in this regard should be simple, easy to understand and ruthlessly effective. We can have a message as simple as making the locals and civilians to be *"part of the solution, not the problem"*.

Civilian engagement can help the military in identifying insurgents, providing critical intelligence reports and spotting supplies and logistics to the insurgents. This is why many nations during war engage in powerful propaganda just to mobilise their people to support the military efforts. They do this because they know the military alone cannot win the war. War can be costly in terms of human and material resources, but if we adopt the right tactics and strategies – two key elements of any successful war – we can see the end of terrorism in our nation.

PART 6

CORRUPTION, INDISCIPLINE AND IMPUNITY

The APC and the National Assembly Drama

It was with great relief that I received the news of the All Progressives Congress (APC) acceptance to work with Bukola Saraki and Yakub Dogara as Senate President and Speaker of the House of Representatives respectively. This was against the earlier stance of the party when it, in fact, "rejected" both men, and the entire process that produced them in the first instance. This singular act not only affirms my earlier position in my article, *National Assembly "Crises": Searching Seriously for Answers!*, but also shows that the party is, in fact, "maturing" into a ruling party after many years in opposition. Every political party, except it is so-called, seeks to acquire political power. There is no sense in permanent opposition, though we talk of "permanent power". Acquiring political power is never easy, but more difficult it is to maintain yourself in power. This appears to be the APC's challenge today. Having spent so many years in opposition, it is finding it difficult to accept the reality that it is now the ruling party, no longer the "opposition" party it used to be. Should we then agree with the school of thought that the party is not prepared for power? Are we to agree that it is a "fragile opposition" as a United States' think-tank described it before the presidential election?

Since the National Assembly drama began, which reached its climax on June 9, many APC supporters (if they are not properly so-called) must have thrown caution into the air in their response to the outcome of the National Assembly leadership election. I had my fair share of insults from fire-emitting APC supporters after making my opinion public on the issue in the article cited above. Despite some of them acknowledging my earlier support for President Buhari during the elections, some of my APC comrades did not spare my "honour" as some went as far as raining curses on even the memory of my late father all because he hails from Kwara state. The most printable of all the adjectives they used to describe me are "turncoat, renegade, betrayer." I could only hope that all these would have ended with the party National Chairman, Chief John Odigie-Oyegun, on behalf of the party, accepting the result of the June 9 National Assembly leadership. To me, this is the most mature position the party has taken since the March 28 presidential election. The National Assembly drama has certainly revealed some things to the party and to all.

First, the APC must come to the realization that it is no longer the same party that controls just one state (Lagos). The party is now in control of over fifteen states in the federation. The fact that the party did the unimaginable on March 28 shows that a lot has changed in the party's body chemistry. It, therefore, must "grow" to its new reality very fast. The utterances of the party's spokesman, Alhaji Lai Muhammed, must reflect those befitting of a ruling party. It appears he is yet to shed off his "militant" posture he had as opposition spokesman!

Secondly, the party supporters must maintain magnanimity either in victory or defeat. The over ambitiousness displayed by some of the party supporters in the closure of the National Assembly complex in the morning of June 9; the "ban" on African Independent Television (AIT) from covering the activities of President Buhari; the alleged prevention of top ranking

People's Democratic Party (PDP) supporters from travelling abroad and the likes all attest to the overzealousness of some APC members. They need to improve on their attitude and orientation especially now that they are in power. This point was made recently by Professor Rufai Alkali, former political adviser to President Jonathan. The APC must avoid the tendencies to condescend to impunity. This was one of the reasons PDP was voted out of power!

Thirdly, the APC must understand the culture of negotiation as a standard practice in civilized climes. You don't get to win all the time just as you don't lose always. The present Speaker of the United States House of Representative John Boehner, is a Republican, while President Barack Obama is a Democrat. It is no big deal even if PDP "controls" the Legislature, it is only part of the maturation process.

And that reminds us, both Saraki and Dogara, the last time we checked are members of the APC. The only error is that the party overestimated its own power while underestimating the chances of its rival, PDP in the Legislature. There were so many early warnings the party did not pay heed to! The party need not be reminded that PDP relied too much on flattery, eye services, and praise singing from its supporters especially during the Goodluck Jonathan years. This is one of the pitfalls the APC must avoid like a plague. There are still many more grounds to cover; more battles to fight; more territories to conquer and more elections to win with 2019 just close by!

APC Crises: Is the Table Turning?

There is disquiet in the once-peaceful house of the APC. To put it more lightly, all does not appear to be well. After the March 28 presidential election, most people (including this writer) only imagined "doom" for the party's bitter rival, the PDP after it lost the presidential election. The APC strategists must have thought that with the presidency in the bag, all will be well after all. But this was never to be. Can it be the case that the tables are turning fast? This writer has written severally on the need for the party to review its post-presidential election strategies and attitudes. Like I have always maintained, it appears the party overestimated its position against the PDP. Another possibility is that some APC "optimists" might have felt the PDP would have given up just because they have lost the presidential election. But if recent events are anything to go by, it appears to me that the tables are turning, and fast against the APC except things are done now – fast!

Even the most optimistic party supporter cannot deny the existence of "irreconcilable" differences within the APC today.

There were early warnings which the party strategists for reasons best known to them simply chose to ignore. The only logical explanation one could find for this is that beyond winning the 2015 presidential elections (defeating the PDP), these factions or "trends" within the party had no other ambition hence, the post-presidential election crisis. Bad enough, in not more than a month after President Muhammadu Buhari was sworn in, Nigerians were left in the realm of speculations about the administration's cabinet selections, ideological colouration, and policy direction. To me, this confirmed that we are to agree with those who observed that the party was not prepared for the presidency.

If we take the face value of this position from the standpoint of events in the National Assembly crises and that the APC government was yet to properly form months into its swearing-in, then we may not be too far from correct. In parenthesis, it was reported in a/some national newspaper(s) in the heat of the presidential campaigns that the party had, in fact, given up winning the election and had decided to mortgage the presidency for winning the gubernatorial elections in some states.

Like I wrote earlier, the warnings of the escalation of crises within the party went largely unheeded to. They were expressed in the National Assembly crises. This does not mean the PDP doesn't have its own set(s) of internal contradictions; the only difference is that the latter was able to properly diagnose its problems and root them out ruthlessly while the former pretended all was well. Can you now see how the tables turn? Immediately after the presidential election, there was a loud noise from the former ruling party over its loss of power. Suddenly "factions" arose as to who was to blame for the party's loss. The situation calmed down with the "removal" or "resignation" of the party's erstwhile National Chairman-Alhaji Adamu Mua'azu.

At least for now, there appears to be a boost of morale for the PDP following its control of the National Assembly with which it could use as a protective shield for itself, at least for the next four years. All these the PDP did while our APC strategists were on holiday enjoying their honeymoon. One should be surprised the APC strategists could not see or preempt the crises with a view to preventing this mess. One would equally have doubted the party's foresight for thinking the well-known PDP would just give up a fight after losing in the first round. If the party did not see the fact that the PDP infiltrated its ranks before the elections, then one is left to wonder if they did any proper diagnosis of the PDP at all. If the APC missed out on all these, then my unsolicited advice is that the party leaders should by now be in the market shopping for strategists!

Some things can be very painful. It can be more painful when you are beaten in your own devices, your own game. About four years ago, the Action Congress of Nigeria (ACN), one of the merging parties in the present APC, openly celebrated the victory of Aminu Tambuwal as Speaker of the House of Representatives which the PDP had to live with for four years. For those who know, the APC's position was strengthened by the PDP's loss of that position. The APC has every right to kick; to weep; to make a loud noise or to scream because the tables are turning and fast.

I will not end this piece without the mention of the chorus in the beautiful lines from the British songwriter, Adele Laurie Blue Adkins' (better known as Adele) song *Turning Tables* which goes thus: "*I won't let you close enough to hurt me, no I won't ask you, you to just desert me. I can't give you what you think you gave me. It's time to say goodbye to turning tables, to turning tables. Turning tables, yeah, turning.*" So, whoever must turn the table must always be in the position of strength. If the APC must take any advice I gave or have given, it must be this one.

Forming Buhari's Cabinet

After his election into power in March, President Muhammadu Buhari has been taking pains to choose those he would work with to deliver his campaign promises, at least, in the next four years. The task of choosing ministers is never an easy one in Nigeria or in any other part of the world for political and technical reasons. Considering that Buhari was elected on the platform of the All Progressives Congress, he is duty-bound to protect the interest of the party that got him to power –*at all times*. He has become the leader of the party; therefore, he must deal with crises that may arise from within the party.

He must also take into consideration the fact that there will be elections in the next four years. In choosing ministers who are, more often than not, party members, the President must identify a potential conflict that his appointments may cause so that the party's unity is preserved ahead of the next general elections. In doing this, the President should look out for persons with a history of party loyalty. In Nigerian politics, people with long years of party loyalty are rare. Since the President is the leader of the party, he must defend the party ideology and manifestoes, by appointing party men and women to his cabinet for the formulation of policies, guidance, and implementations.

The second factor the President must consider is that apart from being just the party leader, he is the father of the nation. In some cases, he may want to look outside the party for some appointments when it appears no party member is thoroughly suited for a particular portfolio. He can find loyal technocrats to head ministries like Finance, Foreign Affairs, Justice, Education, and Science and Technology that must not be left for "professional politicians". The 1999 Constitution contains a provision known as the Federal Character principle, under Section 14(3) which states:

"...to promote national unity and also to command national loyalty, thereby ensuring that there shall be no predominance of persons from few states or a few ethnic or other groups in government or in any of its agencies".

This simply means that he must appoint ministers from at least two-third of the 36 states of the federation. This is to ensure that all ethnic groups are fully represented in the administration. Apart from the constitutional provision, appointing people from different geopolitical zones of the country is just another vote-winning strategy the President may want to employ.

It cannot be assumed that the party or the President will not be interested in consolidating on covering more areas or zones in the next election. The administration must be able to at least have a fair representation across the country.

There are certain instances when the President appoints some cabinet members due to special needs. For example, the Ministry of Niger Delta, is to be headed by a person from the Niger Delta by the law that created that ministry. The office of the Attorney-General of the Federation must be occupied by a professional lawyer. The Minister of Women Affairs cannot be a female. The President must look for persons with these qualifications to occupy these positions. There is no gainsaying the fact that the choice of the President's cabinet will in no small ways make or mar the lives of Nigerians at least in the next four years. This is why the President must display deliberate wisdom in his choice of his cabinet as he promised some days ago in Ghana.

Immunity or Impunity Clause for National Assembly?

Some months ago, the Lekki home of Senator-elect Buruji Kashamu was barricaded by operatives of the National Drug Law Enforcement Agency (NDLEA) reportedly to arrest the "wanted drug baron" at the request of the United States Government. As soon as his house was barricaded by NDLEA men, the debate started about the "legality" of his impending arrest. Many of those in the senator's support cited his "immunity" being a senator, even though he was then yet to be sworn in. As usual, there were no shortages of emergency "public affairs analysts" speaking for or against the "arrest" of the senator. I simply avoided contributing to the matter at that period because all that mattered to me then was for the President-elect, General Muhammadu Buhari (as he was then known) to be sworn in. So, Kashamu's case was the least of my concerns!

Afterward, a certain Leo Ogor who is the Minority Leader in the House of Representatives came up with a shocker: there should be Immunity clause to cover the National Assembly too. I had to convince myself to be sure this man wasn't speaking from an excessive dosage of alcoholic beverage for him to ejaculate this (for want of more appropriate words to describe it) trash. One wonders; with clowns and drug barons like Kashamu in the Senate and other fraudsters who have numerous cases of corruption against them, including the principal officers, that Ogor specifically solicited immunity for; how the so-called immunity will not translate to impunity!

Still on Ogor, let me quote him (I am assuming *The Vanguard* reporter got him right): "If the head of the executive arm, the President and his vice should enjoy immunity, the heads of the other two arms of government, the legislature and the judiciary, should also benefit from the immunity" (*The Vanguard* 5 October, 2015). Let us agree with this man for a moment that the Principal Officers of the National Assembly, in fact, need not be distracted, hence deserve immunity. Let us equally accept without conceding that members of the National Assembly are, in fact, the "Honourables" they are taken to be, so should be excused from prosecution during their tenure in office. What baffles me then is how they will account for offenses committed before some of them fraudulently joined the House. What happens to persons with questionable integrity who find their way into the House hence bringing it to disrepute? Should they also be granted immunity? If these last classes of people have immunity, we can easily conclude that they will commit acts of impunity!

Was Ogor talking about "Parliamentary Immunity"? I have heard it said by one of the lawyers who as a guest panelist on a national television station during the Kashamu saga that after being sworn in, he is immune from arrest or prosecution because of "parliamentary immunity". Oh my God! I am not a lawyer but I know this man must have either been poorly educated or he is just doing his best to look stupid. If there is anything I know about Parliamentary Immunity, as the name connotes, it is that the immunity covers only "offenses" or speeches committed during parliamentary debates or committee meetings. This has little to do with criminal prosecutions!

The issue of parliamentary immunity started in England during the Glorious Revolution that led to the adoption of the English Bill of Rights in 1689. It sharply limited this practice by granting immunity to members against civil or criminal action stemming from the performance of their legislative duties. The Bill provided that "the Freedom of Speech, and Debates or Proceedings in Parliament, ought not to be impeached or questioned in any Court or Place out of Parliament." In the United States, parliamentary or immunity preserves the independence of the legislature by reinforcing the Baron de Montesquieu's principle of separation of powers, thereby, preventing intimidation of legislators by the executive, and protecting parliamentarians from unwarranted appearances before a possibly hostile judiciary. So much so for parliamentary immunity!

Ogor and people like him need to hear this. The most important thing in applying parliamentary immunity is whether the legislator's actions fall within the "sphere of legitimate legislative activity." There are actions a legislator may take, even when s/he is engaging in activities related to his/her legislative office, that does not fall within this sphere. If an action is not a legitimate legislative activity, the legislator is not protected by legislative immunity. Nothing in granting parliamentary immunity to National Assembly members prevents them from arrests save from, performing their legislative duties. When we say, "legislative duties" we mean: actions that a legislator takes during formal legislative proceedings, such as chairing a committee, debating, making motions, and voting; legislative committee investigations; impeachment proceedings; enacting and enforcing legislative rules and others.

Also, a legislator is "immune" from arrest on his way to, or from a parliamentary proceeding; committee meeting or any other official legislative function(s) or for whatever he said or has done on the floor of the parliament. This is how far the issue of parliamentary immunity goes. Any other thing which people like Ogor are asking for will only end in impunity! So, as to whether Kashamu can be arrested while serving his term in the Senate, I say "Yes" with all the emphasis I can muster because parliamentary immunity does not extend to activities or "crimes" committed outside legislative spheres. But my question is: Will they ever arrest him, even if he were not in the Senate covered by the so-called "parliamentary immunity" this "charge and bail" lawyer referred to? This is the kind of impunity Leo Ogor and his ilk are advocating for.

Ministerial Screening and the Dance of Shame

After all the drama characterizing the screening of those who are to work with President Muhammadu Buhari as ministers, the Nigerian Senate in performing its constitutionally assigned duty cleared all those nominated. Though, legally speaking, we might conclude the screening is a foregone conclusion, the dust raised by the exercise, especially with the screening and confirmation of the immediate past Rivers State Governor, Rotimi Amaechi, is still with us.

Before the ministerial list was officially announced, the social and traditional media were filled with rumours of Amaechi being "used and dumped" by the "Hausa/Fulani cabal" has worked tirelessly for the emergence of the present administration. In fact, the ethnic juggernauts and tribalistic harlots amongst us have done their utmost to, on the one hand, prevent Amaechi from becoming minister while, on the other hand, praying earnestly for his appointment so as to serve as a propaganda tool to blackmail Buhari's anti-corruption stance. Their scripts were soon to be revealed after Amaechi was confirmed by the Nigerian Senate with the senators elected on the platform of the opposition People's Democratic Party (PDP) reportedly staging a walkout.

My question then is: Can the PDP appoint ministers for President Buhari? Many sophisticated Nigerians appear to have seen through the PDP's antics. Most Nigerians probably know that their worst fear is that Amaechi, who is expected to hold a powerful position considering his role in the Titanic 2015 election, will further sink the party's ship in its comfort zones. If they could not control him while he was governor on the PDP platform, how then could they control him if given a powerful position in the APC government? It is on record that Amaechi's only offense against PDP was that he, against all odds, supported a Daura man from Katsina as President against their "son" from Otuoke. He is on record to have, as chairman of the Nigerian Governor's Forum (NGF), demanded that things be done properly and according to due process. The misappropriation of the Excess Crude Account (ECA) and other oil revenues under President Jonathan's administration which is still the subject of investigations, was a revelation of Amaechi's NGF. The high chance of Amaechi's protégé, Dr. Dakuku Peterside, carrying the day at the re-run election can at best compound the party's woes – hence he must be stopped whatever the cost.

The fact that Amaechi, a dogged fighter who solicits for votes- won the Rivers State Gubernatorial election in 2007 can be better described as the beginning of the end of impunity in our history which the forces of reactions will never like to hear.

Need we say that if the history of the 2015 presidential elections were to be written today, Amaechi will be described as the David who conquered the Goliath Jonathan, by effectively ending the 16-year old PDP Empire? Can all these be why they fear him so much to have engaged in such a dance of shame on the floor of the senate? Let me look at the issues a bit from PDP's lenses. Amaechi is corrupt; a Rivers State Government Panel has found him to have misappropriated some amount of money; the government's "White Paper" is before the Senate and on the basis of this, Amaechi cannot be a minister of the Federal Republic. One will only be left to wonder if the party suffers from amnesia. If not, how come they forget so soon? I will address the question raised above later. But let me still address, to the best of my ability, the question of whether Amaechi can be a minister with the "White Paper". As far as the laws of Nigeria are concerned, allegations remain allegations until proven otherwise. As far as the law is concerned, at the four corner of my room, I can say for as long as I like that my step-father stole public money, even going on the pages of newspapers to lay bare my allegations. Let us even say that I got my step-dad arrested on the basis of my allegations, then, he was interrogated and later released for want of evidence. Does that make my step-father guilty just because some unpatriotic elements in the police got him arrested for an offense they hastily investigated? Again, the PDP recites it like a nursery rhyme that none of its members is guilty of corruption until proven by a competent Court of Law.

When President Buhari's anti-corruption trail got to Diezani Alison-Madueke's doorstep, the party was quick to shout "witch-hunting" (even though the witches now walk in the day time), but heaven must fall because a doctored "White Paper" says Amaechi stole some money. If this is the case, my best guess is either that the PDP is confused or ridiculously ignorant of the provisions of the law.

Witches are only hunted when they are becoming a nuisance to the community, just as the farmer will not wait for the goat to finish *the yams* just because he thinks he will eat *the yams* as part of the goat's meat! Lest we forget, some months earlier, a certain Musiliu Obanikoro was to be screened and confirmed minister in the teeth of protests from all APC senators. He was confirmed not minding the fact that all the three senators from Lagos, the state he was appointed to represent, opposed his nomination as the Senate rules clearly state. The PDP-controlled Senate saw nothing wrong in appointing "Koro" as he is often called, screening and confirming him as a minister, even with a damning petition on his involvement in election rigging earlier in Ekiti. If there was nothing wrong in "Koro", then nothing is, with Amaechi's nomination.

Close observers will also see the fact that PDP appears not to know what it is afraid of. It, on one hand, insists on "Federal Character" with one of its senators saying that the Senate will not approve Buhari's ministers unless he appoints ministers from all the 36 states; on the other hand, it fears Amaechi's appearance in the cabinet could only spell doom for it. The walk out some of them staged could be best described as a dance of shame.

Rebranding the PDP: An Outsider's Advice

Things don't just happen; circumstances create events. When things happen to us mortals, it is not just our experiences that define us, but how we react or respond to them. After all, it is a common saying that whatever does not kill one can only make one stronger. This appears to be the situation with Nigeria's erstwhile ruling party, the PDP today. Since its shocking defeat in the presidential election in March, the party is still licking its wounds. Will the party ever be able to play the role of the opposition? Will it just self-destruct or seek a merger with other political parties to challenge its bitter rival, the All Progressives Congress (APC)? Should it change its name to a more acceptable name that Nigerians will easily identify with? All these are the questions bothering the post-Presidency PDP. The situation the party finds itself today is not new. The party will not be the first to lose its prized possession; neither will it be the last. So, no one should weep for, or lose sleep over that for the party. The party has to be able to weather the storms, so it must work extra hard, if not harder; fight tooth and nail; go the extra mile to maintain its only one thing left – its brand.

After the PDP's loss, APC spokesman, Alhaji Lai Muhammed gave the party an unusual advice – "rebrand or go into extinction". Call it coincidence or whatever you chose, the PDP set up what is now known as "Rebranding Committee" headed by a media mogul, High Chief Raymond Dokpesi. The second – to go into extinction – is not even an option at all. The question will then be whether the party has ever had a brand.

For the purpose of this piece, we will look at a brand as an image or feature that suddenly comes to mind when a product, service or idea is mentioned. We may also try to see it – in the traditional sense – as a name, design, symbol or distinguishing feature that sets a product or service apart. Giving these two definitions, can we say the PDP had or has a brand?

Let us be quick to admit that all political parties in Nigeria presently, without exceptions, suffer from "brandlessness", but the PDP's case is peculiar. When one talks about "small governments and big businesses", we are either thinking about the United States' Republicans or the British Conservatives. When the issue is about the "welfare state", we need not look further than the Democrats or the Fabians. In Nigeria, we remember great political parties like late Chief Obafemi Awolowo's Unity Party of Nigeria (UPN) for its popular Four Cardinal Programmes. We remember free education; rural integration; free health care and full employment. Even though the UPN was not given the opportunity to govern at the federal level, the five or so states it controlled in the Second Republic (1979-83) attests to its brand.

Now let us go back to the rebranding issue in PDP. Let us also not get it twisted, every political party wants power since there is no point in permanently being in the opposition. I am not sure even if the party will take all the advice given to it by the more "experienced" APC about how to play opposition politics, will it take Lai's advice on having to wait longer than four years? Being in opposition is like staying in the fire; you don't want to be there for too long! The Dokpesi Committee itself needs rebranding. We say this because of the ignoble roles some members of that committee played during the election. The presence of some people in that committee can at best create "brand crisis". It can also further create the impression that the party is yet to shed itself of what it truly represents – corruption, impunity and garrison politics. Jesus Christ's admonition, "Physician, heal thyself" appears to apply here. When the deliverer himself or herself needs deliverance, then the deliverance itself suffers. Are we really serious about rebranding the PDP? The PDP wants Nigerians to forget so soon that it once boasted that it would "rule" the country for 60 or more years. They want Nigerians to forget how they treated as "family affair" several monumental corruptions involving their members. The party wants us to forget how 16 became greater than 19 in the Nigerian Governors' Forum (NGF) leadership election. They still want us to forget how they did their very best to prove to us that STEALING is not CORRUPTION. They like us to forget how they told us that it is not the fault of the yam-eating goats but the presence of the tubers of yams in the same room with the goats.

There is no problem with forgiving, but forgetting is another matter altogether. The party is barely a year into its new role as the opposition, yet it is already feeling the heat. The party is not leaving any stone unturned in its ambition to "take over" from the APC in 2019. As ambitious as these sounds, the party must realize that taking a "great fall" is always easier than getting back to the top. The Mexican Institutional Revolutionary Party (PRI) held on to power for an uninterrupted 71 years since 1929, winning every presidential election.

Although some critics point out that it won the 1988 and 1994 elections through fraudulent ballots, the party, like the PDP, never lost a national election till 2000 when it relinquished power peacefully. It had to wait another twelve years to return to power at the national level in 2012. We are not sure our dear party has the pedigree or the brand that the PRI has or had! The PDP honestly has a lot to learn from the APC, especially while it is in the opposition. While the party held sway since 1999, the opposition changed its name severally. At one point it was the Alliance for Democracy (AD); later it was the Action Congress (AC); further on it was the Action Congress of Nigeria (ACN) and now the All Progressives Congress (APC). We must not forget that at some point we had the All Peoples Party (APP), which became All Nigerian Peoples Party (ANPP), which is now a legacy party, with the formation of the APC.

The name PDP, if they will take our advice, needs to change to reflect the current reality in Nigeria, if truly they want to wrestle power from the APC. The name PDP and its outdated slogan "power to the people" needs to be reconsidered. The "people" are no longer in power, and the days of grabbing power as its right is gone, and for good. Many people may not know this but the PRI is on record to have changed its name at least on three occasions in its history, just as many other great parties have done. The PDP can take a cue from this. As a matter of recommendation, if the party's strategists are working, they must look for ways to create a new image or brand for the party which will pave ways for a new orientation, new directions, and a more corporate culture. The party's "brand" which has been utterly battered for many years being associated with impunity, corruption and mediocrity must be re-created if they are really serious about rebranding. Do we need to be told they do not have a brand?

Sambo Dansuki and Steven Davies' Report

"Hide nothing from the masses of our people. Tell no lies. Expose lies whenever they are told. Mask no difficulties, mistakes, failures. Claim no easy victories. "- Amilcar Cabral

This drama series called Nigeria My Country is never in want of Acts and Scenes with its peculiar dramatis personae as professional politicians. When one is left to think that one event is at anti-climax, another event within the same plot is in 'rising action'. The question on the minds of the audience is: when will this film come to an end?

Sometime last year, while Nigerians were still doing their best to cope with how to live in the face of the dreaded Boko Haram, suddenly came the Ebola Virus Disease (EVD) with its dramatic entry into Nigeria through a Liberian Diplomat, Patrick Sawyer. Just as we were getting relief of the country's capacity to contain the world's deadliest virus, then came a damning report from an Australian hostage negotiator (for the release of over 200 abducted Chibok girls), Dr. Stephen Davies. For me, Mr. Davies has not said what is not in public knowledge about the Islamic sect, Boko Haram. The only intriguing aspect of his report is the inclusion of one name–the ex-Chief of Army Staff, Lt General Azubuike Ihejirika, in addition to ex-Governor of Borno State, Ali Modu Sheriff and a senior official (which Mr. Davis did not name) of the Central Bank of Nigeria(CBN). We also need to add that Dr. Davies' report came at the time when speculations about the sponsors almost about one's political affiliations; a period when the country's two leading political parties are in verbal warfare of who is the sponsor of the group; a period when the APC was under serious investigation for being the sponsor of the group and was busy defending itself in the United Kingdom's House of Commons; a period when the Government has always told us it "knows" the sponsors of the sect; a period when the Nigerian public, more than ever before, wants the sponsors of the sect unveiled!

Expectedly, the Federal Government responded, this time through the Department of State Services (DSS). The Department through its then spokesperson Ms Marilyn Ogar categorically denied the involvement of Lt General Ihiejirika or the Military High Command of complicity of several Boko Haram massacres but said ex-Borno Governor, Sheriff, is under investigation by the Department.

The Government went ahead to declare Mr. Davies as self-appointed, acting on his own and not on behalf of the Federal Government of Nigeria. The Government went on to query why he went with such information to foreign media without first reporting to the federal government. To this, it is only natural to get two replies.

First, the denial by the federal government that Mr. Davies is acting on its behalf is just normal. No government is known to directly negotiate with terrorists. They do use third-party negotiators like Mr. Davies. This is not the first time the renowned hostage negotiator is coming to Nigeria for this kind of mission.

Secondly, the government is querying his going to the media with such information. Wasn't Mr. Davies supposed to be an independent, self-appointed negotiator? Why should he report to a Government that didn't appoint him in the first instance? At this point, we need to flash back as a reminder to link some related events. Early 2012, former President Goodluck Jonathan came out publicly to say (except he said this under duress) that members of the dreaded Islamic sect, Boko Haram served in his own cabinet. After making this careless statement many thought it was one of those "unpresidential" remarks which the former President was known to make; he unconsciously gave a major clue to deciphering the real sponsors of insecurity in Nigeria. Later in 2012 when General Andrew Owoye Azazi (rtd) the then National Security Adviser (NSA) told us what some of us never wanted to hear: the People's Democratic Party (PDP) was behind the veil of Boko Haram. Had this statement come from a Northerner, some of our Southern friends would have publicly demanded his head. But, will they? Instead of doing this, the cabinet "branch" of Boko Haram put enormous pressure on President Jonathan to get him sacked from his position; afterwards, he died in a plane crash. Those who are familiar with these events know Azazi was actually living on borrowed time on that job since making the statement. At this point, let us bring in a latterly-appointed NSA, Colonel Sambo Dansuki (rtd).

Though he wasn't expressly indicted in the Davies' report, but with the revelations that he actually profited from the alleged stealing of more than $2 billion (£1.3bn) meant to buy weapons for the military to fight Islamic militants, Boko Haram, Sambo Dasuki is culpable. Mr Dasuki also allegedly got some compromised staff in the CBN to help him transfer $142.6 million to a company with accounts in the United States, the United Kingdom and in West Africa for unknown purposes and without contracts. Do we still doubt the authenticity of Mr Davies' report? Let us look at this whole issue from another angle, outside the negotiator's original report.

Now we are talking about the content of his revelations and not the procedural blah blah blah. Let us assume, in his report, he has fingered any or all the following people: General Muhammadu Buhari (RTD), Alhaji Atiku Abubakar, Dr Rabiu Musa Kwankwaso, Asiwaju Bola Tinubu, Ogbeni Rauf Aregbesola or Mallam Sanusi Lamido Sanusi. The news headline in, say, *The Vanguard*, the next day, would most likely have been:

"Foreign Negotiator Indicts Buhari, Tinubu, Others As Boko Haram Sponsors", or "APC Leaders Behind Boko Haram– Australian Negotiator." I am sure if this were to be the Australian's "revelations", the then loquacious DSS spokesperson, Ms Marilyn Ogar, will be in the high vindictive mood. She would have been on the pages of newspapers for days, even weeks, speaking on the top of her voice that her Department was aware all the while. She would have used the "revelations" to strengthen her earlier argument that APC was behind all the bomb blasts in the country. Maybe Mr Davies, by now, will be going about with the Grand Commander of the Order of the Niger (GCON) or a higher award conferred on him by President Jonathan for a "well deserved service to the nation".

At that point, there will be no question of Mr. Davies' "authority to negotiate with Boko Haram." Before we forget, at what point did Senator Ali Ndume Senator (Borno South) stop being the sponsor of Boko Haram? What has become of his case at the courts since he joined the PDP? Are the Boko Haram members who the former President said are in his Government responsible for the sacking of General Andrew Azazi as the National Security Adviser? What was Senator Ali Modu Sheriff doing on the former President's delegation to Chad after he has severally been linked to the sect and at a time when it was declared that he was under investigation by the DSS? Was he in another country to welcome the President as a diplomat or a staff of the Foreign Service? What was Sheriff's mission to the extent he was seen sitting in the company of our President and Idris Deby, the President of Chad, with no other member of the President's delegation named by the Government? Looking at the Davies report particularly his mention of the name of the ex-Chief of Army Staff – which is a remote possibility, but not an impossibility, convinces me that there is a direction we are not looking at in our resolve to fight and flush out the seeming ubiquitous sect.

Let us not forget, Sambo Dasuki the then NSA requested the Independent National Electoral Commission (INEC) to shift the February 14 elections by six weeks to enable the Army to confront the terrorists. A dramatic event happened in Gombe State during this period. Boko Haram allegedly attacked some parts of the state before an air raid of fliers warning the residents to stay away from the elections or they would be attacked (written in Hausa) became visible. The question is: Who was distributing these fliers? At what point did Boko Haram begin to concern itself with elections? Something tells me that the compromised Nigerian Army or Jonathan's cabinet faction of Boko Haram was at work to scare people away from voting. The recent trial of the ex-NSA convinces me now who was behind the flier distribution.

This writer is of the considered view that former President Jonathan, at this time, should take a hard look at his own administration, within his government, his advisors, the military, security agencies and other para-military institutions to smoke out sponsors of the group and those he worked with. This advice is particularly a harsh one. The enemy within was more dangerous than those without. They were the ones that praised him the most. They were the most active. They were the ones who licked his boots publicly. They were, still, the ones that desperately wanted him to fail.

Because he couldn't identify the enemies within, it was easy for those without to operate. As the Yoruba adage says: the thief outside cannot devour you unless with the permission of he who is inside. The owner of the house must identify the thief within to keep pilfers at bay. If they had looked well enough, they would have discovered that Mr Steven Davies' report contains that important clue. The quotation at the beginning of this piece is from Amílcar Cabral, the great African revolutionary who led Guinea-Bissau and Cape Verde's struggle against Portuguese colonialism before his cold-blooded assassination in January 1973, which effectively prevented him from leading the newly-liberated nation. When he urged his comrades to "Hide nothing from the masses... Tell no lies... Mask no difficulties, mistakes, failures. Claim no easy victories," he knew they will be saved a great deal, now or in the future, if they tell the truth.

This is where I sympathize with Dasuki, for doing a thankless job.

National Assembly "Crises": Searching Seriously

If you have been frantically looking out for my opinion on the National Assembly leadership election, you are probably searching too seriously. My only conclusion is that you must be an extremely interested party for pushing so hard to know my views on the matter. For those who know, I have never been interested in who occupies the positions of Senate President and the Speaker of the House of Representatives until the day of the inaugural sitting. My disinterestedness stems from the fact that the contestants are those who do not, in my estimation, have the ingredients for exciting leadership for that important arm of government, at least as their profiles show. As I said earlier, I became only interested when the drama started. I see nothing wrong in the June 9 election. I also do not share in the All Progressives Congress (APC) official position on the outcome. Quoting the party's spokesman, Lai Muhammed, he argued: "The party duly met and conducted a straw poll and clear candidates emerged for the posts of Senate President, Deputy Senate President and Speaker of the House of Representatives, supported by a majority of all Senators-elect and members-elect of the House of Representatives." The APC's thinking was on establishing party supremacy, but I am afraid, that is not a concept we are used to in Nigeria.

The meeting the party had to select its "candidates" for the positions is not in any way binding on all members of the National Assembly. A mistake like this is too important to be ignored! Quoting him further, he said: "All National Assembly members-elect who emerged on the platform of the party are bound by that decision. The party is supreme and its interest is superior to that of its individual members." It is at this point that I understood APC's frustration. A strategy is good when it works wonders, but it can hurt when one loses a game in one's own maneuvers. This appears to be the position of the party today. Four years ago, I watched members of the defunct Action Congress of Nigeria (ACN) in the National Assembly display victory signs at the announcement of Aminu Tambuwal as the new Speaker. Suffice to say, Tambuwal joined the newly registered APC to which ACN is a partner.

Again, let us look for the Constitutional requirements on the matter. To form a quorum of the Chambers of the National Assembly requires in attendance, one-third of its members. If that is correct, those who voted in both Chambers constituted more than half of its members in attendance. It is why I said I saw nothing wrong in any decision that might have been taken.

Those members-elect who decided to attend an event at the International Conference Centre (ICC) while such an important event was going on in the National Assembly could be classified as "boycotts". I am not in the position to know if the APC simply decided to boycott the event or if it was just a time-buying tactic. Whatever the case, nothing positive ever comes out of a boycott. It is only an early acceptance of defeat! In my article, *APC: The Question of Strategies*, I argued that the party's strategies are, in fact, dangerous. The party won the election, not as a result of a super-fantastic strategy, but thanks to an abysmally poor tactical approach from the People's Democratic Party (PDP).

The APC must be thankful to people like Femi Fani-Kayode and Adamu Muazu for poor handling of the PDP campaigns. I am sorry to say this, it appears to me that APC strategists largely went on a honeymoon after President Muhammadu Buhari was declared the winner on March 31. They largely assumed that with 64 party members in the Senate, all was well. It also appears they assumed the PDP was "dead" beyond resurrection as a result of its loss of power at the centre. President Buhari's indifference as to who leads the National Assembly only complicated matters. In general, APC post-election strategies are at best below average. Can this be a case of mental fatigue?

My unsolicited advice to the APC is that they should now live in the reality of having both houses of the National Assembly out of their control (except things change), at least for the next four years!

Buhari and the Nigerian Foreign Exchange

The naira is known to have dropped against major currencies in recent times. Perhaps, this was why, during the 2015 Nigerian presidential election, President Muhammadu Buhari made the point of "making the naira equal to the dollar." He was speaking against the backdrop of the depreciation of the value of the naira during the elections.

Is it just by mere announcements or campaign rhetoric that the naira will be made equal to the dollar? Let us concede that the fall in naira value during the elections can be due to the scramble for the dollar by politicians for the elections on the one hand and the panic buying of travelers moving out of the country for fear of violent reactions that might characterise the announcement of the result; we, therefore, cannot wave off Buhari's statement as a cheap attempt to score political points. As Nigerian Head of State (1983-1985), Buhari was known to have run his regime based on strong fiscal prudence and rigorous financial discipline, which at that period the naira was said to be stronger than the US dollar.

But is this just as simple as making the naira equal to the US dollar?

Since 1999, the inflation rate in the country has been on the high. The near-total dependence on oil (which is usually dictated by the international market) hasn't helped matters. The increase in the domestic price of oil has also taken its toll on the national price level. All these put the naira in a weaker position against major foreign currencies. Presently, Nigeria lacks the capacity to refine its own crude oil which makes her depend totally on importation. There is an argument that the presently devalued naira will only encourage exportation (of crude oil). In fact, this was exactly the same

Bretton Woods Institutions' arguments, and their Nigerian supporters, in defense of the Structural Adjustment Programme (SAP) in the 1980s. Lending credence to this argument was the International Monetary Fund (IMF) Czar, Christiane Lagarde, who in early 2012 justified her position on the devaluation of the naira with this argument. We were spoon-fed with this argument in elementary and intermediate Economics classes, yet it still appears to make a lot of sense. When will this child grow up?

If President Buhari is serious about strengthening the position of the naira against, say the dollar, his government must make deliberate policies to diversify the economy from oil dependence; increase its productive base through innovation and youth entrepreneurship, and stimulate demand for domestically-made goods.

PART 7
PREPARING FOR 2019

PDP: A Strategy for 2019

Those familiar with politics (and the game of power in general) know that there are no rules; and if there are, these are often flouted. It is a "win or be damned" situation.

The opposition is a camp some are just waiting in pending the time there will be "vacancies" in the ruling party. There are many things "winners" do that "losers" do not do: as a winner, you make important political appointments (and terminate them in some cases); you write a book, a likely bestseller; you have guaranteed news coverage on daily basis; you are made guest of (dis)honour at social functions; your community proudly associates with your ("our son's") accomplishments; somehow, everyone gets your number and the phones are always ringing.

These opportunities elude losers, not only in Nigeria but everywhere. In Nigeria, one is an unfortunate species if one is in the opposition. Tinubu and Awolowo can tell you their experiences of being in the opposition. Incumbent office-holders are in perpetual campaign mode. You will hear things like, we are holding a "Thank You Rally" organized by any willing group who can get the administration to provide the funds for this. After winning an election, the victorious party immediately starts planning and campaigning for its re-election bid. The opposition or the challengers make the error of waiting until the "traditional" election season comes to begin their campaign. This is a mistake the People's Democratic Party (PDP) does not want to make, as it has rolled out its plans not to stay in the opposition for more than four years! Since PDP does not want to leave anything to chance in challenging the incumbent APC, it has become imperative for it to define its opponent, in this case, President Muhammadu Buhari, before he gets a chance to define himself. The several appellations, "#TyrantBuhari", "#BudgetOfYams" and the likes are veiled PDP attempts to define the Buhari administration before it could define itself. A good political strategy the party can consider using is to be different. This means deliberately choosing a different set of activities, orientations or brand to deliver a unique mix of values, if it is serious about wrestling power from the hard-fighting APC. Is the PDP really ready for this? Let us look at some clues given by the party that is public knowledge.

This writer is not a member of the PDP neither does he flirt with the party.

In one of his interviews with an online news medium, Naij.com, PDP's (now embattled) spokesman, Chief Olisa Metuh, confirmed that at the next general elections, his party will be fielding a "Northern presidential candidate." While one fairly understands the logic behind the reported "zoning" of its 2019 presidency to the North as a vote-catching tactic, it looks like the party needs its strategists, if they have, to get to work. The fact that APC produced Buhari who won 12 million votes in the region, and ultimately won the election, does not automatically translate into "victory" for PDP if they present say, Sambo Dasuki.

In parenthesis, the same Metuh told the world that "The APC and its leaders fear that Dasuki, given his vast political and security network, may be harbouring a presidential ambition, more so that the PDP has zoned its presidential ticket to the North." Presenting the great grandson of Uthman Dan Fodio (Dasuki) to challenge Buhari or APC in 2019 may look like a good calculation to win (or divide northern votes), but how "safe" are southern votes for PDP? Need we remind the PDP that in 2011 Buhari contested on the platform of a largely new (unknown) platform, Congress for Progressive Change (CPC), and could still poll over 10 million votes? It takes only Buhari to defeat Muhammadu Buhari in that region with the cult-like following he enjoys in the region! With the reported zoning of its presidency to the North, the party is doing little to show its difference from APC. Nothing in adopting a "northern presidential candidate" shows that PDP is ready to draw a sharp contrast between itself and the ruling APC.

There's only one reason people vote an incumbent out of office: when they find someone better. You have to present the voters with a better alternative to your opponent. Show them why your candidate is clearly different, and why that difference makes him a superior choice. The party will have a difficult task convincing the typical Northern voter, considering the terrible reputation the PDP has with Northern politicians, especially the insults its members hurled at the APC on African Independent Television (AIT), during the 2015 electoral campaigns, making it look like being a Northerner was evil. We keep our fingers crossed to see how the party rebrands its image in the strategic Northern region. Let me say this for the purpose of analyses that of Nigeria's six geopolitical zones, the PDP can only boast of the South-East as being its stronghold for now. The party is fast growing a reputation of being an "Igbo party" (it was once regarded as an "Ijaw party" though). How long the party can hold on in the South-South is yet to be seen. I say this in the light of the region's historical romance with the centre. For instance, the region (now comprising Cross River, Akwa Ibom, Delta, Edo, Rivers and Bayelsa States) voted the Hausa-Fulani-dominated National Party of Nigeria (NPN) during the Second Republic (1979-83). Bendel, now Edo and Delta, is historically part of old Western Region, which was largely why they voted for Chief Obafemi Awolowo's Unity Party of Nigeria (UPN) then. If PDP strategists do a proper diagnosis of its post-presidency era, they should realise the fact that even with a block vote from the South-East, their ambition of staging a comeback into Aso Rock in 2019 remains a pipe dream. Let us engage in a little speculation about the possible options for the PDP.

Let us imagine that Metuh only made a big joke of the possibility of Dasuki emerging as the party's presidential candidate in 2019. If he were serious, I suspect an easy job in the works for APC strategists, as they will have no problem sleeping soundly through the election season and defeating the PDP at the same time. So, let us hope Olisa Metuh made a big joke! If the party's strategists are only interested in considerably reducing APC's and Buhari's strong showing in the North, it may consider drawing to its side the North-Central geopolitical zone where Buhari has not historically had it so good. In this case, maybe, the party could consider presenting Bukola Saraki, a party protégé in APC. But Saraki will need to first survive the onslaughts of the hard-fighting APC on his position as Senate President.

The South-West remains a battleground where the PDP needs to do more work if it must be taken seriously. The party cannot continue to rely on the votes from only Ekiti, arguably the smallest state in the region. Its leaders in the region are at best uninspiring. The party will need to do a serious rebranding in the zone because of its perceived terrible reputation among the Yorubas.

The monumental onslaught or "Tsunami" of 2003, and the bloody 2007 elections in the zone are still fresh in the minds of the region's voters. Somehow, people still associate the brutal murder of former Attorney-General and Minister of Justice, Chief Bola Ige, with the party.

Though the PDP has persistently denied this, the assassination of the "Cicero of Esa Oke" featured prominently during the 2014 Osun gubernatorial election, with the party doing very little to rub itself off the dirt! If the PDP is truly serious about getting back to Aso Rock in 2019, it must do some reality check. As things stand, should a presidential election hold today, other things being equal, it has less than 40 percent chance of winning. I say this because it is not always as easy as just "zone" its presidency to the North, or presenting "a northern presidential candidate". Had the APC presented any candidate other than General Buhari, even if this were Abubakar Atiku or Rabiu Kwankwaso, it would have been an easy ride for the PDP in the 2015 presidential election. Zoning its presidency to the North is a good move on the surface, but much work remains to be done for the party to recover lost grounds and reconstruct its battered image. There is still a long way to 2019!

PDP: Where Is Thy Thinking Cap?

When many thought the People's Democratic Party (PDP) is ticking the right boxes for 2019, the party leadership came up with something unique. There appears to be a drama series which is never in want of acts and scenes with its peculiar *dramatis personae* as professional politicians or "garrison commanders". When one is left to think that one event is at anti-climax, another event within the same plot is in "raising action". The question on the minds of the audience is: when will this film come to an end?

Since its shocking defeat in the presidential election in March 2015 the party is still licking its wounds. Will the party ever be able to play the role of the opposition? Will it self-destruct or seek a merger with other political parties to challenge its bitter rival, the All Progressives Congress (APC)? Should it change its name to a more acceptable name that Nigerians will easily identify with? All these are the questions bothering the post-Presidency PDP.

Sometimes in January, a former political adviser to President Goodluck Jonathan, Ali Gulak, stormed the Wadata Plaza (also known as PDP secretariat) and openly declared himself as the chairman of the party. Many thought things could only get messier as a court declared that any politician from the North East geo-political zone could take over the office of national chairman meaning that that Uche Secondus was occupying the position illegally. No one then needed to tell Mr. Secondus that his romance with the title "acting national chairman" was over and a substantive national chairman would soon be appointed.

On Tuesday February 17, we received the much-awaited news of whom to occupy the exalted position. It was not to be Mallam Nuhu Ribadu neither was it to be Gulak. But to our greatest surprise it was to be the ex-Borno Governor, Ali Modu Sheriff. I had to run multiple litmus tests just to be sure of the authenticity of the news.

On the same day, the blogosphere was filled with information of a man "accused of sponsoring Boko Haram" as being "unanimously nominated as the substantive national chairman" of Nigeria's largest opposition party. I came across a post on Twitter by a known PDP supporter who maintained that Modu's appointment is a "Good strategic decision". My first instinct on reading his tweet was to know if this man knows what constitutes a "Good strategic decision" at all in relation to Sheriff's appointment.

My best guess about the "Good strategic decision" PDP made about Modu Sheriff is probably based on the assumption of his political and financial prowess. Some of Modu's supporters recall his experience as two term Borno state Governor and his understanding of the politics of the North East as an important advantage the party may capitalise on in 2019. These people also maintain that considering the financial challenges the party may be facing, Modu appears to be the "game changer".

While on the surface, these two positions may look potent. Let us be quick to register our reservations. First, the PDP looks to be making the same mistake again. The case of Mallam Ibrahim Shekarau, a former Governor of Kano in 2014 should be instructive in this regard. With the way the party leadership celebrated (including President Jonathan's famous "*Azonto*" dance) when he defected from APC, one would think the state was already in the bag.

Second, one also recalls how the party overestimated the political prowess of people like Musiliu Obanikoro, who promised to "deliver Lagos" and groups like *Afenifere* which promised to deliver Yoruba votes to the party– in 2015. If the result of the Borno elections are anything to go by, we may not be too far from correct to think the party is still overrating some politicians. The rest, as they say, is history.

For the records, the situation the party finds itself today is not new. The party will not be the first to lose its "priced possession"; neither will it be the last. So, no one should continue weeping for, or lose sleep over that for the party. The party has to be able to weather the storms, so it must work extra hard, if not harder; fight tooth and nail; and go the extra mile to maintain its only one thing left – its brand.

For the purpose of this piece, we will look at a brand as an image or feature that suddenly comes to mind when a product, service or idea is mentioned. We may also try to see it – in the traditional sense – as a name, design, symbol or distinguishing feature that sets a product or service apart. Giving these two definitions, can we say the PDP needs a brand?

If the party's brand must be worked on, then whatever the party strategists were thinking about before appointing Modu Sheriff as national chairman needs some thorough analyses.

It was Mr. Olisa Metuh, incidentally the same man who accused the All Progressives Congress (APC) in 2014 of housing sponsors of Boko Haram, who reportedly made the much-awaited announcement. Metuh said: "However, the peculiar trend of the Nigerian version… summarises a well-considered agenda of national destabilisation for a purely selfish political cause. We pointedly finger the opposition." And the evidence for that pointed fingering is: "We recall statements by some politicians, vowing to make the country ungovernable for President Jonathan on the eve of the 2011 general election." Metuh added. Note that, at the time he made this statement, Modu Sheriff was still in the APC. The question Metuh will struggle hard to answer is, *"What suddenly changed?"*

For those who do not know, Modu Sheriff has, at several times, been linked with the notorious insurgent group in the North East – the Boko Haram. In fact, some sources claim he was the principal financier of the group since its inception before his fallout with Muhammed Yusuf, the group's leader who was murdered in 2009. Associating the party's brand with this man– bad enough as it is– cannot be regarded as a "Good strategic decision" as my friend will want us to believe.

Now, I will not like to act like a deaf man who only sang the last song he heard before turning deaf. Rather, I believe the politician should be made to come out and clear his own name. I ran into a transcript of his interview with BBC Hausa Service in a frantic attempt to clear his name. According to *Leadership,* he said: "Therefore, I am more concerned than anybody in this country, because what Borno State did for me has not been done to any other indigene. You know, in Borno State, a governor has never been re-elected apart from me; in Borno State, no senator has ever been elected thrice apart from me. So, Borno people have done everything for me, and there is no one in this world that I know other than Chad, which I think could help Borno." The truth is that Modu may be innocent of all the allegations about his sponsoring book Haram, but another thing is whether anyone believes him.

Let us be quick to admit that all political parties in Nigeria presently, without exceptions, suffer from *brandlessness*, but the PDP's case looks peculiar. When one talks about "small governments and big businesses", we are either thinking about the United States' Republicans or the British Conservatives. What image does the party portray to Nigerians and the world with the face of Sheriff as its national chair?

Let us equally think with the PDP's think-tank in assuming Modu Sheriff knows and can "deliver" the votes come 2019. Since every serious political party has the primary objective of winning elections, the party's strategists may be right in this regard. (I do not know of any party, if not properly so-called that is formed for the purpose of being in opposition.) Having said that it is my considered opinion that Sheriff as national chairman may not achieve optimal results for the party in the next election. This is because, the fact that APC presented a certain General Buhari who won 12 million votes in the North, and ultimately won the presidential election, does not automatically translate into "victory" for PDP if they present say, a Sambo Dasuki even though he is a Sokoto prince or make billionaire Sheriff party chairman!

There's only one reason people vote an incumbent out of office: when they find someone better. You have to present the voters with a better alternative to your opponent. Show them why your candidate is clearly different, and why that difference makes him a superior choice.

We keep our fingers crossed to see how the party rebrands its image in the strategic Northern region, the worst hit since the inception of Boko Haram insurgency. Let us keep our fingers crossed to see how Modu salvages this situation for the party.

If PDP strategists do a proper diagnosis of its post-presidency era, they should realise that even with a block vote from the South East, their ambition of staging a comeback into Aso Rock in 2019 remains a pipe dream. This is because the only base the party can boast of having real political presence is in that zone. This is why there is a school of thought that the party, the action(s) of Gulak and his supporters, the other time in the party's secretariat is to prevent the party from degenerating into a south east party. Justifying this position will be that the, perhaps, most visible leaders in the party (Secondus, Metuh and Ekweremadu) are Igbos. Though many party supporters may not like to admit this, most PDP supporters I know today, on social media, appear to come from that region.

If, by chance, (I am just engaging in speculation) the party's strategists are only interested in considerably reducing APC's and Buhari's strong showing in the North East by Modu's appointment, it may consider drawing to its side the North-Central geopolitical zone where Buhari has not historically had it so good. In this case, maybe, the party could consider presenting Bukola Saraki, a party protégé in APC. But Saraki will need to first survive the onslaughts of the hard-fighting APC on his position as Senate President.

Whatever the PDP strategists were thinking before appointing Sheriff, I may not know, since I am not a member of the party. But this is sure – the party will do a hard job reconciling their earlier views that the APC sponsors Boko Haram.

Another job will be how they can explain to us who stole their thinking cap when taking the "Good Strategic Decision."

References

Adeniran, T. *An Introduction to International Relations,* (Lagos: Macmillian Publishers, 1983).

Adisa, T. "Buhari in the North Myth or reality?" *Nigerian Tribune* 13 March 2011.

African Elections Database, *Elections in Nigeria,* 2003, http://africanelections.tripod.com/ng.html Accessed on 24 April, 2016.

Akhaine, S and Abuh, A. 'ANPP chiefs are against my ambition, says Buhari.' *The Guardian,* July 30, 2002

Albashir, A. 'CPC: The meteoric rise of a phenomenon.' *Vanguard* 1 April, 2011.

AllAfrica.'Presidential Primaries - APC's Moment of Decision.' *AllAfrica.*9 December, 2014 http://allafrica.com/stories/201412101193.html Accessed on 30 April, 2016.

Austin, S. O. 20 Reasons Why Nigerians Have Rejected Buhari Since 2003 *Point Blank News,* October 31, 2014 http://pointblanknews.com/pbn/exclusive/20-reasons-nigerians-rejected-buhari-since-2003/ accessed on 20 April, 2016

Aziken, E. 'APC presidential ticket: The power of money.' *Vanguard* 10 December, 2014 http://www.vanguardngr.com/2014/12/apc-presidential-ticket-power-money/#sthash.zU2HYUgy.dpuf Accessed on 30 April, 2016

Babara, F. *Roosevelt and the Munich Crisis: A Study of Political Decision-Making.* Princeton: Macmillan Publishers, 1997.

Balogun, I. 'Buhari's assassination attempt intended to destabilise Nigeria – Ekhomu.' *Vanguard,* 26 July, 2014 http://www.vanguardngr.com/2014/07/buharis-assassination-attempt-intended-destabilise-nigeria-ekhomu/ Accessed on 28 April, 2016.

Boettcher, W.A. 'The Prospects for Prospect Theory: An Empirical Evaluation of International Relations Applications of Framing and Loss Aversion.' *Political Psychology,* 25(3), 331-62, 2004.

Bolashodun, O. 'Buhari Takes 2015 Elections To Facebook.' *Naij* https://www.naij.com/346307-buhari-takes-2015-elections-to-facebook.html Accessed on 28 April, 2016

Brunell, T. 'The presidential and congressional elections in the USA.' November 2008. *Electoral Studies,* Volume 28, Issue 2, June 2009, Pages 322-325, ISSN 0261-3794.

Cable, The. 'I'm not opposed to Muslim-Muslim ticket, says Buhari.' *The Cable* 25 October, 2014. https://www.thecable.ng/exclusive-interview-im-opposed-muslim-muslim-ticket-says-buhari Accessed on 1 May, 2016.

Collier, P. *Wars, Guns and Votes: Democracy in Dangerous Places.* London: Vintage Books. 2010.

Conn, P. *Conflict and Decision Making: An Introduction to Political Science.* New York: Harper and Row, 1971.

Dare, L and Oyewole, A. *A Textbook of Government*. Ibadan: Onibonoje Press, 2000.

Elens-Eigbokhan, E and Oluwatola, T. 'Election Analysis: Why a Buhari Victory is Probable.' *Premium Times*. February 5, 2015. http://blogs.premiumtimesng.com/2015/02/05/election-analysis-buhari-victory-probable-eronmonsele-elens-eigbokhan-tobi-oluwatola/ Accessed on 4 May, 2016.

Gossett, C.W "Politics in Tanzania", in Almond, G. A & Powell Jr, G.B, (Eds) *Comparative Politics Today: A World View* Second Edition, (Boston: Little, Brown & Company, 1980).

Grandy, G. "Intrinsic case study" in A. Mills, G. Durepos, & E. Wiebe (Eds.), *Encyclopaedia of case study research*. (pp. 500-502). Thousand Oaks, CA: SAGE Publications, Inc, 2010.

Greene, R. *The 33 Strategies of War*. London: Viking Penguin. 2006.

Hamburg, M., *Statistical Analysis for Decision Making*. Second Edition, New York: Harcourt Brace Jovannovich. 1977.

Human Rights Watch. 'Presidential Election Marred by Fraud, Violence' *Election Report*, 25 April, 2007

Iduh, S. 'Nigeria's Post 2007 Elections: A Time For Healing Process And National Reconciliation', *NigeriaWorld* http://nigeriaworld.com/articles/2007/may/121.html Accessed on 25 April, 2016.

Israel, O. 'APC Presidential Ticket: Can Buhari make it?' *Desert Herald*, 14 October, 2014.

Johns, R & Shephard, M. 'Gender, Candidate Image and Electoral Preference.' *The British Journal of Politics & International Relations*.9 (3), 434-460, 2007.

Mamah, E. "Buhari Joins Congress for Progressive Change". *Vanguard*. 18 March 2010.

Mazen, M. 'Nigeria's Four Biggest Opposition Parties Agree to Merge.' *Bloomberg* 7 February, 2013. http://www.bloomberg.com/news/articles/2016-04-26/1mdb-says-it-s-in-default-after-missing-interest-payment Accessed on 25 April, 2016.

Naij.'Sammie Okposo Blasts Buhari, 2015.'*Naij* https://www.naij.com/369994-sammie-okposo-blasts-buhari.html (Accessed on August 30, 2016).

Naij. 'GMB's Handshakes With Women Irk Muslim Fundamentalists.' *Naij*. March, 2015. https://www.naij.com/440686-gmbs-handshakes-with-women-irks-muslim-fundamentalists.html Accessed on April 30, 2016.

Naij. 'Army Find Buhari's Missing Certificate After Election.' *Naij* https://www.naij.com/415257-army-find-buharis-missing-certificate-after-election.html Accessed on 5 May, 2016.

Naij. 'PDP in Panic Over Osinbajo's Emergence As APC VP.' https://www.naij.com/346131-pdp-in-panic-over-osinbajos-emergence-as-apc-vp.html Accessed on May 4, 2016.

Naij. '5 Factors that Robbed Jonathan of His Goodluck.' Naij https://www.naij.com/413564-opinion-5-factors-robbed-jonathan-goodluck.html Accessed on May 10, 2016.

Nation, The. 'Buhari: ANPP, petitions and a divided house.' *The Nation* 15th September, 2007   http://www.thenationonlineng.net/archive2/tblnews_Detail.php?id=31246 Accessed on 25 April, 2015.

Net Naija. 'Sammy Okposo Apologizes To Buhari Over Forged Result.' *Net Naija* https://www.netnaija.com/forum/entertainment/celebrities/8181-sammy-okposo-apologises-buhari (accessed on August 30, 2016).

Nigerian Eye. '(Opinion Poll) APC Presidential Primaries: Buhari beats Atiku, Okorocha, others.' *Nigerian Eye.* http://www.nigerianeye.com/2014/12/opinion-poll-apc-presidential-primaries.html Accessed on 28 April, 2016.

Nwanegbo, C. J and Alumona, I. M. 'Incumbency Factor and Democratic Consolidation in Nigeria's Fourth Republic.'*Medwell Journals.*Volume: 6 | Issue: 2 | Page No.: 125-130, 2011. http://www.medwelljournals.com/fulltext/?doi=sscience.2011.125.130 Accessed on May 7, 2016.

Olaitain, K. 'Buhari never lost any election -David West.' in *The National Mirror* 3 November, 2014   http://nationalmirroronline.net/new/buhari-never-lost-any-election-david-west/ Accessed on 25 April, 2016.

Olokojobi, S. 'Ume-Ezeoke's action, a betrayal, says Buhari.' *The Nation,* http://www.thenationonlineng.net/archive2/tblnews_Detail.php?id=28513 Accessed on 25 April, 2015.

Otorofani, F. "Buhari's Victory: Product of Geo-Ethnic Cleavages, Conspiracies and Betrayals". *African Herald Express* April 27, 2015 http://africanheraldexpress.com/blog8/2015/04/27/buharis-victory-product-of-geo-ethnic-cleavages-conspiracies-and-betrayals/ Accessed on 20 April, 2016

Owete, F. "Congress for Progressive Change considers going to court". *Next* 21 April 2011.

Owete, F. 'ANALYSIS: APC Presidential Primary: How the candidates stand.' *Premium Times* 10 December, 2014. http://www.premiumtimesng.com/news/172848-apc-presidential-primary-how-the-candidates-stand.html   Accessed on 30 December, 2014.

P i t n e y, Jr., J o h n J . *The Art of Political Warfare* Norman: University of Oklahoma Press, 2000.

Point Blank News. '2015: APC Plot to Dump Buhari for Tambuwal Thickens.' *Point Blank News* November 10, 2014 http://pointblanknews.com/pbn/exclusive/2015-apc-plot-dump-buhari-tambuwal-thickens/ Accessed on 6 September, 2015

Premium Times.' We will expose the real Buhari — Femi Fani-Kayode.' 7 January, 2015 http://www.premiumtimesng.com/news/top-news/174455-will-expose-real-buhari-femi-fani-kayode.html Accessed on 30 August, 2016.

Premium Times. 'Cambridge University provides more details on Buhari's WASC results.' *Premium Times* http://www.premiumtimesng.com/news/headlines/175777-cambridge-university-provides-details-buharis-wasc-results.html   Accessed on August 30, 2016.

Premium Times. "2015: Buhari's loyalists pledge to buy APC nomination form for him" *Premium Times* 11 October, 2014.

Premium Times. 'ANALYSIS: Research group, Eurasia, predicts big win for Buhari.' *Premium Times* March 15, 2015.

Premium Times. 'Finally, Buhari settles for Tinubu ally, Yemi Osinbajo, as running mate.' *Premium Times* 17 December, 2014. http://www.premiumtimesng.com/news/headlines/173401-finally-buhari-settles-for-tinubu-ally-yemi-osibajo-as-running-mate.html Accessed on 10 May, 2016.

Premium Times. "Buhari, Jonathan meet, sign another peace accord." Accessed on http://www.premiumtimesng.com/regional/north-central/179153-buhari-jonathan-meets-sign-another-peace-accord.html (16 January, 2017).March 26, 2015.

Reef, M. S. 'Elections: The controversial Supreme Court Verdict.' *Daily Trust* 14 December, 2008.

Scan News. 'Why APC appointed Amaechi as campaign manager by Wike.' *Scan News* http://scannewsnigeria.com/featured-post/why-apc-appointed-amaechi-as-campaign-manager-by-wike/ Accessed on 30 April, 2016.

SaharaReporters. 'If APC Survives One Year, Don't Call Me Okupe, Presidential Aide Boasts.' *SaharaReporters,* 24 April, 2013. http://saharareporters.com/2013/04/24/if-apc-survives-one-year-don%E2%80%99t-call-me-okupe-presidential-aide-boasts Accessed on 26 April, 2016

Stupak, R., Gilman S. & Hartzer, C. *Understanding Political Science — The Arena of Power* New York: Alfred Knopf, 1977.

Udo, B. "There will be bloodshed if Jonathan loses in 2015, says Asari-Dokubo" *Premium Times.* http://www.premiumtimesng.com/news/144368-there-will-be-bloodshed-if-jonathan-loses-in-2015-says-asari-dokubo.html (Accessed on 16 January, 2017). September 9, 2013.

Udo, B. "America, Britain warn Nigerian officials against manipulating presidential, national assembly elections results." Premium Times. Accessed on http://www.premiumtimesng.com/news/headlines/180193-america-britain-warn-nigerian-officials-against-manipulating-presidential-national-assembly-elections-results.html (Accessed on 16 January, 2017). March 30, 2015.

Ukaibe, C and Nwaogu, C. 'Orubebe Disrupts Collation Of Results In Abuja.' *Leadership* April 1, 2015. http://leadership.ng/news/422249/orubebe-disrupts-collation-of-results-in-abuja Accessed on August 29, 2016.

Ukwu, J. 'Muslim-Muslim Ticket Is Dropped, Now it's GMB Vs GEJ.' Naij https://www.naij.com/346221-gmb-vs-gej.html Accessed on April, 28, 2016.

Umoru, H. Buhari. 'Certificate Saga: Jonathan accuses INEC of cover-up.' *Vanguard* 13 January, 2015. http://www.vanguardngr.com/2015/01/buhari-certificate-saga-jonathan-accuses-inec-of-cover-up/ Accessed on 5 May, 2016.

Vanguard, The. 'Buhari wins APC presidential primaries.'11 December, 2014 http://www.vanguardngr.com/2014/12/buhari-wins-apc-presidential-primaries/ Accessed on 30 April, 2016.

Weick, K.E. and Sutcliffe, K. M. *Managing the Unexpected: Resilient Performance in an Age of Uncertainty*. Second Edition. San Francisco: John Wiley & Sons, Inc. 2007.

White, L. G. *Political Analysis: Technique and Practice*, California: Wadsworth Publishing Company, 1994.

Will, The. 'Certificate Saga: Buhari Sinks Deeper With Lies, Says Fani-Kayode.' *The Will*.29 January, 2015. http://thewillnigeria.com/news/certificate-saga-buhari-sinks-deeper-with-lies-says-fani-kayode/ Accessed on 5 May, 2016.

About the Author

Olalekan Waheed ADIGUN is an award-winning writer and researcher. He is a campaign consultant cum political analyst.

His acclaimed (intriguing, incisive and highly analytical) articles have appeared on reputable media like *Premium Times, SaharaReporters, The Guardian, The Punch* and others of suck ilk. In December, 2015 he won the Ships and Ports National Essay Competition "Outstanding Essay Award" category.

Olalekan obtained his BSc (Politics, Philosophy & Economics) from Obafemi Awolowo University, Ile-Ife. He recently submitted his MSc (Political Science) thesis titled *Social Protests and Political Outcomes: Analysing the Political Outcomes of the Protests Against Neo-Liberal Policies in Nigeria (2012-2016)* at the University of Lagos.

His passion for politics began as an undergraduate at Ile-Ife where he served the Students' Union in several capacities including his election on two consecutive occasions as member of the influential Students' Representatives Council. In 2014, he served as volunteer for several organisations supporting General Muhammadu Buhari (GMB), including #iHaveDecided, #GoOutToVote, Coalition for Change and others. He wrote several articles and gave series of interviews on the 2015 presidential elections.

His write-ups can be viewed on his website: OlalekanAdigun.com

End Notes

---

[i] The Cuban Missile Crisis was one of the events that nearly resulted to Mutual Assured Destruction (MAD) during the Cold War between the US and Soviet Union in 1962. The handling of the complicated issue resulted in Washington deciding on a blockade and the Soviets voluntarily withdrawing the facilities.

[ii] #Youth4Change is one of the social media initiatives by some passionate youths to encourage young people to turn out to vote. It wasn't endorsed by the Buhari campaign even though it went with the inscription "Change". Those interested in my interview can access it by typing my name into Google.

www.ingramcontent.com/pod-product-compliance
Lightning Source LLC
Chambersburg PA
CBHW081146280526
45787CB00008B/3247